MEMBERS OF PARLIAMENT I.

THE LIBRARY OF LEGISLATIVE STUDIES

ISSN 1357-2334

General Editor: Philip Norton

A series of new and recent books exploring the role of legislatures in contemporary political systems. The volumes typically draw together a team of country specialists to provide in-depth analysis.

# MEMBERS OF PARLIAMENT IN WESTERN EUROPE: ROLES AND BEHAVIOUR

*edited by*

WOLFGANG C. MÜLLER
and
THOMAS SAALFELD

FRANK CASS
LONDON • PORTLAND, OR

*First published in 1997 in Great Britain by*
FRANK CASS AND COMPANY LIMITED
Newbury House, 900 Eastern Avenue, London IG2 7HH, England

*and in the United States of America by*
FRANK CASS
c/o ISBS
5804 N.E. Hassalo Street, PortlAnd, Oregon 97213-3644

British Library Cataloguing in Publication Data

Members of parliament in Western Europe: roles and
behaviour
1.Legislators - Europe, Western
I.Müller, Wolfgang C. 1957-  II. Saalfeld, Thomas,
328.4'0922

ISBN,0 7146 4821 3 (hbk)
ISBN 0 7146 4369 6 (pbk)

Library of Congress Cataloging-in-Publication Data

Members of parliament in Western Europe: roles and behaviour
edited by Wolfgang Müller and Thomas Saalfeld
    p.    cm.
"This group of studies first appeared in a special issue of the
Journal of legislative studies, vol.3, no.1 (spring 1997)" – T.p.
verso
ISBN 0-7146-4369-6. — ISBN 0-7146-4821-3
1. Legislators – Europe, Western. I. Müller, Wolfgang C., 1957–
II. Saalfeld, Thomas, 1960–
JN94.A71M45  1997                      97-764
328'.092.24—DC21                       CIP

This group of studies first appeared in a Special Issue of
*The Journal of Legislative Studies*, Vol.3, No.1 (Spring 1997),
[Members of Parliament in Western Europe: Roles and Behaviour].

Printed in Great Britain by
Antony Rowe Ltd., Chippenham, Wilts.

# Contents

# Roles in Legislative Studies:
# A Theoretical Introduction

## THOMAS SAALFELD and
## WOLFGANG C. MÜLLER

The terminology of role theory is borrowed from the stage. Superficially, similarities between stage and parliaments may have encouraged scholars to apply it to legislatures. Indeed, everyone who has an opportunity to watch the spectacle of Speaker's Procession in the British House of Commons, or the highly ritualised conduct of Prime Minister's Question Time, will find the analogy intuitively plausible. The adoption of ancient and ultimately aristocratic forms of behaviour even by early twentieth-century Labour Members of Parliament with a classical working-class background seems to testify to the validity of one of role theory's central claims, namely that role structures, once stabilised, tend to persist, regardless of changes in the actors. Yet, the importance of role theory in legislative studies goes far beyond analogies of this type. In its various guises, it has constituted one of the most influential traditions in social theory and research[1] and has had a significant impact on empirical legislative research. This volume will provide a survey of empirical work on legislative roles in some western European parliaments: Belgium, Denmark, Germany, the Netherlands, Norway and the United Kingdom.

The empirical evidence presented aims to broaden the debate and provide both empirical material and theoretical stimuli to use, test and further develop role theories of legislative behaviour. Kaare Strøm's contribution to this volume and Donald Searing's works (see below) show that role theory can and does provide useful theoretical elements, even if its structural-functionalist premises are no longer the predominant paradigm in the social sciences. The individual contributions have not been based on a tightly formulated, common theoretical framework. They originated from papers presented to the Vienna Conference on the Political Roles of MPs in West European Countries (April 1995). Nevertheless, all contributions have been theoretically informed by two classical works in the field which will be referred to below and by a number of 'guiding' questions set out later in this introduction.

Thomas Saalfeld is Lecturer in Politics at the University of Kent at Canterbury. Wolfgang C. Müller is Reader in Politics at the University of Vienna.

The volume's primary aim is to take stock of our empirical knowledge on legislative roles in different western European parliaments and explore possibilities to integrate some of the fundamental findings of traditional role theory and more recent approaches to the study of parliamentary behaviour. Some authors (Philip Norton, Thomas Saalfeld) attempt to explore how roles help us to understand the impact of changes at the macro- and meso-levels on parliamentary behaviour. Most contributions to this volume (Rudy B. Andeweg, Erik Damgaard, Lieven De Winter, Knut Heidar and Werner J. Patzelt), however, focus upon individual-level data. They present a wealth of empirical findings that are not easily accessible outside the respective countries. These data should help assess the interaction of roles and varying institutional constraints – the importance of which becomes particularly evident in Werner Patzelt's study of roles in the 'quasi-experimental' context of Germany after unification. Instead of a conclusion, Kaare Strøm presents a theoretical chapter which explores the meaning and usefulness of the concept of role for scholars who do not necessarily share the 'holistic' assumptions of early role theories.

## THE CONCEPT OF ROLE IN THE SOCIAL SCIENCES

The concept of role concerns 'the tendency of human behaviors to form characteristic patterns that may be predicted if one knows the social context in which those behaviors appear'.[2] Role theorists have never been particularly modest in their claims. Robert E. Park, for example, maintained that 'everyone is always and everywhere, more or less consciously, playing a role. ... It is in these roles that we know each other; it is in these roles that we know ourselves'.[3] According to another definition,

> role provides a comprehensive *pattern* for behavior and attitudes; it constitutes a *strategy* for coping with a recurrent type of situation; it is *socially identified*, more or less clearly, as an entity; it is subject to being played recognizably by *different individuals*; and it supplies a major basis for *identifying* and *placing* persons in society.[4]

With respect to legislatures, Wahlke *et al.* have defined 'role' as

> a coherent set of "norms" of behavior which are thought by those involved in the interactions being viewed, to apply to all persons who occupy the position of legislator. It is important to emphasize the normative aspect of the concept in order that the role of legislator not be confused with the office, or position, of legislator. ... the concept postulates that legislators are aware of the norms constituting the role and consciously adapt their behavior to them in some fashion.[5]

Role theory evolved in various traditions with contrasting definitions of concepts and frequent disagreement about substantive issues. It is beyond the scope of this introduction to provide an exhaustive survey of these different traditions. It seems to be appropriate, however, to draw attention to two traditions that have had a fundamental impact on some of the early classical studies on legislative roles, namely the functionalist tradition and symbolic interactionism. The functionalist perspective was strongly influenced by the contributions of Talcott Parsons to social theory. It was concerned with the problem of explaining social order. Functionalists in the Parsonian tradition hold, in essence, that the stability of social systems arises from consensual expectations, or roles. Roles provided norms for conduct. Compliance with norms was induced either because the social system imposed sanctions on actors or because actors had internalised them. Internalisation of norms was a result of socialisation processes: those in the system were thought to be aware of the norms they held and taught them to novices.[6] Symbolic interactionists think of a role as a line of action that is pursued by individuals within a given context of pre-existing norms, beliefs, attitudes, the actors' conception of self and the 'definition of the situation' that evolves as the actors and others interact. This perspective can be applied to describe the complex network of relationships amongst Members of Parliament and between Members and other actors in the political system.

Both the functionalist and interactionist perspectives have been subject to criticism. Critics of functionalism have pointed out that individual behaviour cannot be explained as a result of its function for a social system. According to Jon Elster, 'explanations' of this sort are necessarily flawed. He argues that there is a host of norms 'that make everybody worse off, or they shift the balance of benefits to favour some people at the expense of others'.[7] Furthermore, '[m]any norms that would be socially useful are in fact not found to exist'.[8] It can be argued

> that persisting behaviors may or may not be functional for social systems, that norms for conformity are often in conflict, that actor conformity need not be generated by norms alone but can also reflect other modes of thought (such as beliefs or preferences), that norms might or might not be supported by explicit sanctions, that norms internalized by the actor may be at odds with those that are supported by external forces, and that processes of socialization are problematic.[9]

Symbolic interactionism has been criticised for its 'tendency to use fuzzy definitions, recite cant, and to ignore structural constraints that affect behaviors'.[10]

Nevertheless, role theory in both traditions has had a profound, and fruitful, influence on the empirical study of parliaments and parliamentarians. In 1962, John C. Wahlke, Heinz Eulau, William Buchanan and LeRoy C. Ferguson published their seminal study on *The Legislative System*[11] which is based on role theory. More than 30 years on, Donald Searing published his work on legislative roles in the British House of Commons.[12] These two studies have stimulated research not only in the United States and Britain but also in a large number of other parliaments.

## THE LEGISLATIVE SYSTEM – A PIONEERING STUDY

*The Legislative System* by Wahlke and his associates is an exploratory study of four United States state legislatures (California, New Jersey, Ohio and Tennessee) in 1957. The study's authors think of a legislature as 'a network of relationships among legislators and others, all taking roles in certain ways'.[13] They consider role theory as a useful theoretical device to link distinct but interdependent traditions in legislative studies: institutional, behavioural and – especially relevant at the time of the study – functionalist approaches.[14] Wahlke and his associates postulate

> that the office of legislator is a clearly recognizable position in the four states studied, that legislators and many other persons in those societies associate certain norms of behavior with those positions, i.e., expect certain types of behavior from occupants of the position of legislator simply because they occupy that position, and that a significant portion of the behavior of legislators is role behavior consistent with legislators' role concepts. To study the role of legislators, then, is to study particular sets of norms which underlie relevant legislative behavior.[15]

Wahlke and his associates believe that their essentially normativist approach is better suited to explain the interaction between individuals and institutions than do individualistic rational-actor or psycho-analytic models: They argue that 'the behavior of legislators is clearly "institutional behavior," not merely aggregated or symbiotic behavior of individuals'.[16] One important characteristic of role is that it assumes interpersonal relations. 'The set of norms which make up a person's role can be divided into subsets of norms according to the position, status, or character of the other person (the alter) with whom the role player in question (ego) is called upon to deal.'[17] Therefore, Wahlke and his associates divide roles into different sectors, each of which comprises those norms 'appropriate to some particular "counter-role," that is, to encounters with persons occupying some particular counterposition'.[18] The fundamental legislative system of roles, which Wahlke and his associates develop, is depicted in Figure 1.

FIGURE 1

THE ROLE OF LEGISLATOR

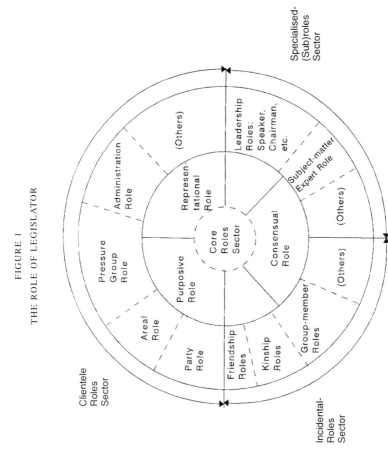

*Source:* John C. Wahlke et al., *The Legislative System* (New York: Wiley, 1962), p.14.

The sector of *'core roles'* includes 'all the norms guiding the legislator's behavior with reference to other legislators'.[19] Core roles are defined by three fundamental types of norms: consensual roles, purposive roles and representational roles: *'Consensual roles'* include written prescriptions such as constitutions, statutes or rules of procedure, as well as unwritten but informally understood norms and rules of the game. *'Purposive roles'* refer to the parliamentarians' purposive or functional conception of the ultimate aim of their activities, to behaviour appropriate to the substantive goals or purposes of legislation and other parliamentary activity. *'Representational roles'* are a set of norms referring to the method or process of individual decision making deemed appropriate to pursuit of the substantive goals.[20]

Elements of the core-roles sector influence the parliamentarians' behaviour in encounters with other parliamentarians 'inside' the parliamentary chamber. The sector of *'clientele roles'*, by contrast, refers to norms for behaviour in encounters with occupants of counterpositions in political party organisations, constituencies and constituency organisations, organised interest groups as well as administrative agencies. Therefore, Wahlke and his associates subdivide the clientele-role sector into a *party role*, an *areal* (or *constituency*) *role*, a *pressure-group role* and an *administrative role*.[21]

Wahlke *et al.* also maintain that the role of legislator included a *'specialized-subrole sector'* comprising norms of behaviour for occupants of various specialised positions within the legislature. Amongst the most important roles in this sector are *'formal-leadership roles'* such as speaker, committee chairman or party leader as well as *'subject-matter-expert roles'*.[22] Finally, the model distinguishes an *'incidental-role sector'* comprising role relationships between individual members and political 'outsiders', referring to phenomena such as kinship, friendship or other associations and extraparliamentary group memberships.[23]

One of the main difficulties of role theory is that 'it does not follow from role theory that all behavior in the legislature is appropriate role behavior, and that legislative role concepts, therefore, strictly determine the course of events'.[24] Wahlke and his associates point out, however, that the legislature would cease to exist as an institution without a *minimum of consensus about norms*. They distinguish between two fundamental kinds of role consensus: *inter*personal and *intra*personal consensus. Interpersonal consensus refers to the role consensus between each member of a role relationship (for example, parliamentarian and lobbyist). Intrapersonal consensus refers to the agreement between a number of egos about what they should all do in relation to a common alter.[25] Nevertheless, complete agreement is hardly to be expected. The emergence of deviant behaviour is explained as a result of role conflicts. Wahlke *et al.* distinguish between *intra*-role conflict and

## WESTMINSTER'S WORLD – RESTORING THE CONCEPT OF 'ROLE' IN POLITICAL ANALYSIS

In the late 1980s and 1990s Donald D. Searing started to restore the concept of roles which had gradually disappeared from the core of political science since the 1960s. According to Searing this could be accounted for by changes in intellectual fashion – the march from *homo sociologicus* to *homo oeconomicus* – the weariness with conceptual confusion which accompanied the early stage of role 'theories' (which were no theories and were over-burdened with neologisms) and the fact that roles were apparently unable to explain behaviour.[35]

Searing starts from the conviction that 'the roles of politicians are much too important to be overlooked. They are central concepts in the symbolic worlds of the people we study'.[36] He rejects the three considerations which contributed to the removal of roles as a central political science concept. First, Searing argues that intellectual fashion has again changed. Whilst the individual preferences and choices emphasised by the first generation of rational choice models were articulated in the context of an overstylised world, the relevance of actual formal rules such as constitutions, laws, contracts, and other institutional arrangements for the behaviour of politicans was acknowledged when these models were employed in a real-world context. Moreover the 'new institutionalism' of the March and Olsen type,[37] but also some rational-choice authors, have acknowledged that informal norms shape the behaviour of politicians. Searing corroborates this claim by empirical evidence from his own study. Second, Searing tries to clarify the conceptual confusion, *inter alia*, by 'sending most of the neologisms down the memory holes of history'. Finally, he takes issue with the methods employed by previous research on political roles. Searing points to the fact that the political roles which constitute the typology of Wahlke *et al.* were *not* 'roles that exist in the minds of politicians'.[38] Rather, academics in survey questions had imposed their essentially normative concepts upon politicians. This explains the lack of correspondence between political roles – which were the roles perceived by academics rather than politicians – and political behaviour.

Searing calls his approach 'motivational'. It conceives of political roles as resulting from the interplay between institutional frameworks and individual preferences, the balance of which varies greatly from one role to another. He distinguishes position roles and preference roles. Position roles are 'closely tied to, and highly defined by, prominent positions in the institutional structure'.[39] Examples of such roles are Cabinet Minister or Chief Whip. In contrast, preference roles 'allow considerable scope for individual preferences to shape role interpretations'.[40] Searing considers backbench MPs as falling into the latter category. Although backbenchers have the opportunity to shape their roles to a large extent, this always occurs within a given institutional structure, which constrains role interpretation.

The chief methodological recommendation of the motivational approach is 'the reconstruction of political roles as they are understood by their players'.[41] According to Searing, 'position roles are comparatively easy to see'.[42] In contrast, 'preference roles are more difficult to extract and are best discovered through interviews that probe the topic with a number of open-ended questions'.[43] This is exactly the methodological approach used by Searing in *Westminister's World*. In the course of his research project 521 of 630 British MPs were interviewed, the interviews tape-recorded, transcribed, and coded. The study resulted in typologies of MPs which are reproduced in Figures 2 and 3.

According to Searing, the roles of backbenchers 'have nearly as much to do with their preferences as they have to do with the established rules of their institution'.[44] Backbenchers can decide upon which of the principal tasks of parliament they wish to concentrate: checking the executive (policy advocates), institutional maintenance (parliament men), becoming ministers (ministerial aspirants), and redressing grievances (constituency members).[45] Each of these choices allows for further specialisation.

*Policy advocates* try to influence government policy. Searing identifies three sub-types. While the *ideologues* try to promote abstract and often radical political ideas, *generalists* are concerned with concrete issues, but do not specialise too much. Coming to grips with the details of policy is left to the *specialists*, who aim to influence policy 'in very small, localised, specialised fields'.

*Ministerial aspirants* see parliament mainly as the recruiting ground for government and concentrate on strategies which might lead to promotion. *Constituency members*, in contrast, do not look up but down. Their priority is to provide services to their constituencies, either of a collective or individual kind. *Parliament men* are absorbed by the conduct of business in Westminster, though they have varying degrees of involvement, ranging from the *spectator*, who watches the political drama from where it unfolds, to the *good House of Commons men*, the service of whom is essential for maintaining the conduct of parliamentary business.

As mentioned before, leadership roles are far better defined than these backbench roles. However, from a comparative point of view, *junior minister* and *minister* roles hardly constitute typical parliamentary roles. Likewise, the role of *parliamentary private secretary* is genuinely British and deserves less attention in comparative perspective. In contrast, all parliaments and parliamentary parties have leadership positions which may be modelled after the *whip* role in the House of Commons. Searing

FIGURE 2

BACKBENCH ROLES IN THE BRITISH HOUSE OF COMMONS

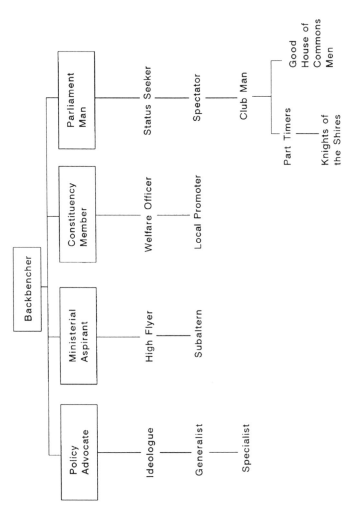

Source: Donald D. Searing, *Westminster's World* (Cambridge, Mass.: Harvard University Press, 1994), p.32.

FIGURE 3

LEADERSHIP ROLES IN THE BRITISH HOUSE OF COMMONS

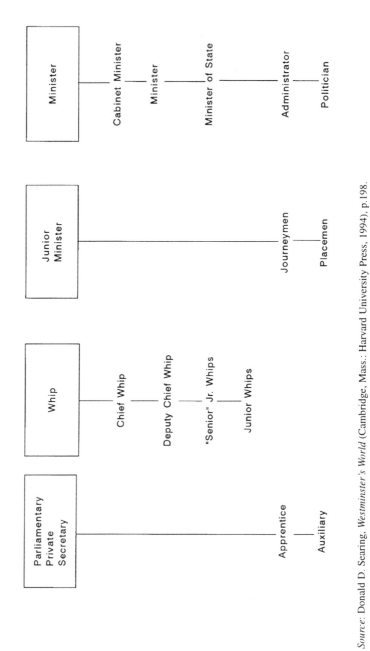

*Source:* Donald D. Searing, *Westminster's World* (Cambridge, Mass.: Harvard University Press, 1994), p.198.

characterises this role by three principal goals: liaison, management and discipline.

## PLAN OF THE VOLUME

Most country chapters will provide a brief outline of theoretical and empirical work on roles in the respective legislature. This section on the 'state of the art' will serve to take stock of the empirical and conceptual work that has been carried out in the respective countries. It is hoped it will serve to encourage more comparative work on legislative roles. The latter is particularly important in order to assess the crucial impact of institutional contexts on role orientations and behaviour. Some authors (Rudy B. Andeweg, Erik Damgaard, Lieven De Winter, Knut Heidar and Werner J. Patzelt) will present results from their own empirical work in the field. These works are (with the exception of Andeweg) predominantly 'snapshots' of parliamentarians' attitudes at a particular point in time. Other authors (Philip Norton and Thomas Saalfeld) will largely use aggregate data and try to relate roles and role behaviour to longer term developments in the respective parliaments. Finally, Kaare Strøm will attempt to assess legislative role theory from an institutional rational-choice perspective. All authors will address, explicitly or implicitly, the following research questions:

- What roles can be identified in the respective parliamentary chamber? Are there data suggesting changes in MPs' role perceptions over time?

- What are the most important counter-roles?

- Are MPs subject to conflicting role expectations? Are there discrepancies between MPs' intra-parliamentary role perceptions and the role expectations of extra-parliamentary actors and the general public? How are MPs shielded from cross-pressures of this nature? Does the parliament, or do the parliamentary parties, provide organisational means of resolving role conflicts?

- Some authors argue that there is a 'tendency for stabilised roles to be assigned the character of legitimate expectations, implying the deviation from expectation is a breach of rules or violation of trust'.[46] Is there evidence of tensions between 'legitimate expectations' and role behaviour?

- Which actors in the system have the power of role allocation? Are there legitimate role definers? How centralised or decentralised is the system of role allocation in the respective parliament?

- 'Role behavior tends to be judged as "adequate" or "inadequate" by comparison with some definite conception of the role in question.'[47] Is there empirical information on role evaluation in the general public and amongst parliamentary peers?

- How closely do roles and actual behaviour correspond? Are role perceptions good predictors of behaviour?

- To what extent is there consensus regarding the content of legislative roles?

- How formalised are legislative roles, that is, to what extent are roles incorporated into a parliament's organisational setting, either through tradition or through formal rules?

- Is there evidence on how individual MPs cope with role strain arising from role contradiction, role conflict and role inadequacy?

- Are there data on the process of socialisation through which norms are internalised?

- Is there information on individual role conceptions and 'role distance', that is, the extent to which MPs must play roles that contradict their self-conceptions?

- Is there evidence for a gradual decline of coherently defined parliamentary roles and a tendency towards 'individualisation' (Mezey)?[48]

This volume would not have been possible without the support of several institutions and individuals. The Austrian Parliamentary Society (*Öster-reichische Parlamentarische Gesellschaft*) supported the conference, on which this volume is based, through their generous sponsorship. We wish to thank the Austrian Parliamentary Society and its Chairman and President of the *Nationalrat*, Dr Heinz Fischer, its former Vice-Chairman and former President of the *Bundesrat*, Mr Jürgen Weis and its Secretary General, Dr Walter Labuda, for their hospitality. We would also like to thank the staff of the Austrian Parliament, who helped prepare and organise the conference. Last but not least Sally Clark at the Centre of Legislative Studies of the University of Hull and Joan Dale Lace of Frank Cass have – as usual – been more than patient, efficient and helpful in the process of copy editing and organising the publication.

## NOTES

1. Cf., *inter alia*, G.H. Mead, *Mind, Self and Society* (Chicago: University of Chicago Press, 1934); R. Linton, *The Cultural Background of Personality* (New York: Appleton-Century-Crofts, 1945), especially pp.76–7; S.F. Nadel, *The Theory of Social Structure* (Glencoe, IL: The Free Press, 1957); T. Parsons, *The Social System* (Glencoe, IL: The Free Press, 1951), especially pp.25–26, 39–40, 236–42; T. Parsons and E. Shils, *Toward a General Theory of Action* (Cambridge, MA: Harvard University Press, 1951), especially pp.19–20, 208–18; R.K. Merton, *Social Theory and Social Structure* (Glencoe, IL: The Free Press, 1957), chs. 8 and 9.

2. B.J. Biddle, 'Role Theory', in E.F. Borgatta and M.L. Borgatta (eds.), *Encyclopedia of Sociology*. Vol.3 (New York: Macmillan, 1992), p.1681.

3. R.E. Park, 'Behind Our Masks', *Survey*, 56 (1926), p.137.

4. R.H. Turner, 'Role: Sociological Aspects', in D.L. Sills (ed.), *International Encyclopedia of the Social Sciences*, Vol.13 (New York: Macmillan & Free Press, 1968), p.552.

5. J.C. Wahlke, H. Eulau, W. Buchanan and L.C. Ferguson, *The Legislative System. Explorations in Legislative Behavior* (New York: Wiley, 1962), pp.8–9.

6. Cf. Wahlke *et al.*, *The Legislative System*, p.1682. For an application see B. Badura and J. Reese, *Jungparlamentarier in Bonn – ihre Sozialisation im Deutschen Bundestag* (Stuttgart: Frommann-Holzboog, 1976).

7. J. Elster, *The Cement of Society: A Study of Social Order* (Cambridge: Cambridge University Press 1989), p.147.

8. Elster, *The Cement of Society*.

9. Biddle, 'Role Theory', p.1683.

10. Biddle, 'Role Theory', p.1684.

11. (New York: John Wiley, 1962).

12. D.H. Searing, *Westminster's World. Understanding Political Roles* (Cambridge, MA: Harvard University Press, 1994).

13. Wahlke *et al.*, *The Legislative System*, pp.17–18.

14. Cf. Wahlke *et al.*, *The Legislative System*, pp.4–7.

15. Wahlke *et al.*, *The Legislative System*, p.9.

16. Wahlke *et al.*, *The Legislative System*, pp.9–10, quotation p.10.

17. Wahlke *et al.*, *The Legislative System*, p.10.

18. Wahlke *et al.*, *The Legislative System*, pp.10–11.

19. Wahlke *et al.*, *The Legislative System*, p.11.

20. Wahlke *et al.*, *The Legislative System*, pp.11–12.

21. Wahlke *et al.*, *The Legislative System*, pp.12–13.

22. Wahlke *et al.*, *The Legislative System*, p.13.

23. Wahlke *et al.*, *The Legislative System*, pp.13–14.

24. Wahlke *et al.*, *The Legislative System*, pp.14–15.

25. Wahlke *et al.*, *The Legislative System*, p.15.

26. Wahlke *et al.*, *The Legislative System*, p.15.

27. Wahlke *et al.*, *The Legislative System*, p.16.

28. Wahlke *et al.*, *The Legislative System*, p.16.

29. Wahlke *et al.*, *The Legislative System*.

30. Wahlke *et al.*, *The Legislative System*, p.17.

31. Wahlke *et al.*, *The Legislative System*, pp.19–23.

32. H.P. Frisema and R.D. Hedlund, 'The Reality of Representational Roles', in N.R. Luttberg (ed.), *Public Opinion and Public Policy* (Itasca, IL: F.E. Peacock), pp.316–20.

33. Wahlke *et al.*, *The Legislative System*, pp.18–19.

34. Wahlke *et al.*, *The Legislative System*, p.19.

35. D.D. Searing, 'Roles, Rules, and Rationality in the New Institutionalism', *American Political Science Review* 85 (1991), pp.1239–60; Searing, *Westminster's World*, ch.1.

36. Searing, 'Roles', p.1240.

37. See J.G. March and J.P. Olsen, *Rediscovering Institutions. The Organizational Basis of Politics* (New York: Free Press, 1989).

38. Searing, 'Roles', p.1250.
39. Searing, 'Roles', p.1255.
40. Searing, 'Roles', p.1253.
41. Searing, 'Roles', p.1252.
42. Searing, 'Roles', p.1255.
43. Searing, 'Roles', p.1255.
44. D.D. Searing, 'Backbench and Leadership Roles in The House of Commons', *Parliamentary Affairs* 48 (1995), p.419.
45. Searing, 'Roles', p.1253.
46. Turner, 'Role', p.554.
47. Turner, 'Role', p.555.
48. See M.L. Mezey, 'New Perspectives on Parliamentary Systems: A Review Article', *Legislative Studies Quarterly*, 19 (1994), pp.429–41.

# Roles and Behaviour of British MPs

## PHILIP NORTON

The work of Donald Searing provides a snapshot of the motivational roles of British Members of Parliament in the early 1970s. Drawing on Searing's work, this paper considers the emergence of the Policy Advocate, identifying the likely reasons for the decline of more traditional roles, the unexpectedly large number of Policy Advocates in the 1970s, and the presumed increase in the number of Policy Advocates in later parliaments. Cognitive mobilisation has generated a new breed of MP and changes in parliamentary behaviour and structures have consolidated the position of the Policy Advocate. The rise of the Policy Advocate has important implications for the House of Commons and, given increasing demands made of MPs, the number of Policy Advocates is anticipated to increase in the future.

Once elected, Members of Parliament (MPs) in Britain serve in an institution that has a history spanning more than seven centuries. It is an institution that is remarkably well known. However, the study of it has not been as extensive as might have been expected given its longevity and reputation. And, until recently, the study of Parliament has been noted more for focusing on the institution than on its members.

The dearth of material, certainly before the 1970s, reflected the nature of political science in Britain.[1] It also reflected a perception that there was little point in engaging in analysis of the House of Commons or its members. The focus of enquiry was elsewhere. The behaviour of MPs was viewed as predictable and of little relevance. Cohesion was a marked feature of parliamentary voting behaviour, so much so that by the end of the 1960s the distinguished American political scientist, Samuel H. Beer, was able to declare that cohesion had increased 'until in recent decades it was so close to 100 per cent that there was no longer any point in measuring it'.[2] Parliament was viewed as peripheral in the policy cycle, party cohesion ensuring that the government got its way in any parliamentary vote.

This view of Parliament also affected the perception of MPs' roles. The principal role of MPs was recognised as being allocated by external actors. The role was essentially representational. The constitution generated a constituency sub-role for the MP. Each MP is elected for a defined

Philip Norton is Professor of Government and Director of the Centre for Legislative Studies at the University of Hull geographical area and is expected to defend and pursue the interests of citizens within that area. Political reality, however, determined that the dominant sub-role was that of the party MP. Since the nineteenth century and the advent of mass politics, party has been the dominant force in British politics. Electors cast their ballots on the basis of party labels. Candidate selection is in the hands of the local party associations. The local parties also raise money for the election campaign and then run that campaign. Most parliamentary seats in the UK are 'safe' seats, the winning candidate achieving a majority that represents ten per cent or more of the total poll. Selection as candidate in a safe seat is tantamount to being chosen as the MP. The local party retains the power to deny re-selection to the candidate at the next election. Loyalty to the party is expected by party supporters and so, once elected, the MP follows the party line.

The externally imposed roles were also not incompatible with the principal role that MPs were believed to allocate to themselves, that of a ministerial role. Many, indeed most, MPs were believed to have ministerial aspirations, indeed to aspire to being Prime Minister. This ministerial role was certainly compatible with the party role, loyalty to the party leadership being considered helpful in achieving promotion to leadership positions. The constitution gives the Prime Minister freedom in the selection of ministers, so ministerial office is determined, when the party wins power, by the party leader. The constituency role was deemed by many ministerial aspirants as a chore and a role taken up more enthusiastically by those MPs whose ministerial careers were over or who were at such an age that they were never likely to have one. The roles, though, were not seen as conflicting with one another. Not all MPs were ministerial aspirants. Some were believed to be content simply to serve, in essence to be spectators.

These perceptions derived from and reinforced the view of a marginal institution. MPs did as they were told by the party. Their own role orientations reinforced that loyalty. There appeared little point in taking the analysis further. There certainly appeared little point in investigating how MPs saw their own role.

Recent years, however, have seen a notable change in the extent and quality of systematic analysis of the House of Commons.[3] As a result of the pioneering research of Donald Searing, this change now includes role analysis.[4] This paper takes Searing's work as its starting point. Searing, as explained in the introduction to this volume, provides a snapshot of the roles of MPs at the beginning of the 1970s. The principal purpose of the paper is to consider changes in parliamentary composition, behaviour and structures since the 1970s and their relationship to the contemporary roles of Members of Parliament. What we find is that MPs are not as monolithic in their roles and behaviour as was previously thought and that the trend is toward greater independence of the executive.

## Searing's Role Analysis

Searing and his associates interviewed 521 Members of Parliament (83 per cent of the membership of the House) in a 21-month period from January 1972 to September 1973. The interviews were then transcribed and have been used for various published works by Searing and others. The principal work arising from the study is Searing's *Westminster's World* which provides a detailed analysis of MPs' roles. As explained in the introduction, Searing adopts a motivational approach that defines roles as patterns of goals, attitudes and behaviour and he constructs a typology of roles for both backbenchers and those occupying leadership positions. The motivational approach is especially important in that it moves us away from a concentration on an externally imposed role (the party role) to the impulses that determine what MPs do within or even beyond the political context set by the party.

Searing identified predominant roles. Given that our concern is with MPs *qua* MPs, our interest lies principally with backbench roles. The most interesting finding of Searing's work was the number of MPs who were predominantly Policy Advocates, that is, wanting to have some influence on public policy. Of the 334 MPs who fell into the backbench category, the largest single number – 136 (40.5 per cent) – fell into the category of policy advocates. Of these, 81 were classed as specialists, 48 as generalists and seven as ideologues.

Given the popular assumption that most MPs aspire to ministerial office, the number of backbenchers found to be Ministerial Aspirants was surprisingly small – only 82 MPs (24.5 per cent), of whom Searing classified 45 as high flyers and 19 as subalterns (those expecting junior rather than senior ministerial office); the remaining seven were classed as a 'mixed' sub-group. Eighty five MPs (25 per cent) were classified as Constituency Members, the predominant predisposition being to serve the constituency, either in the role of a welfare officer (pursuing the grievances of individual constituents; a sub-group comprising 64 MPs) or as a promoter of local interests (a sub-group comprising 13 Members, the remaining eight constituting a 'mixed' sub-group). Only 31 MPs fell into the group designated as 'Parliament Man', with the predominant orientation being to the institution itself. These 31 were spread over three sub-groups: status seekers (three Members), spectators (content to watch the exercise of power from the parliamentary wings, a sub-group comprising 14 Members) and club men (content to enjoy the House as the best club in town, a category also comprising 14 MPs). The 31 were also divided between part-timers and those who devoted themselves to the House.

Searing's work provides a fascinating snapshot of the role orientation of MPs at the beginning of the 1970s. Given the absence of any previous such comprehensive survey, and the virtual impossibility of achieving such a high response rate in any future survey of Members of Parliament (many now suffering from survey fatigue), there is no comparable data that would allow us to undertake a reliable analysis of historical trends. However, there is some material that will allow us to make some informed assumptions as to changes up to the 1970s and a greater body of material, including hard data, that will allow us to identify changes in behaviour and structures since the early 1970s. From that, we will be able to draw some plausible, if not provable, conclusions as to changes in the role orientations of Members of Parliament.

*The House of Commons 1900–1970*

From the material that is available to us, it would appear that Parliament Men were far more prominent in the House of Commons in the early decades of the twentieth century than was to be the case when Searing conducted his study. Conversely, there would appear to have been fewer MPs who saw their roles as Policy Advocates or Constituency Members.

Nineteenth-century perceptions of a 'good' House of Commons lingered well into the twentieth century. The emphasis was on the chamber, where MPs of independent means were able to deliberate on the great affairs of the nation. Membership of the House was seen variously as a public service or a means of social – and political – advancement. The domain of public affairs was limited and MPs had other interests to pursue. Until 1912, no salary was paid to Members. Though party came to achieve a stranglehold in the House in the latter half of the nineteenth century, the role orientation of Members did not appear to change greatly.

There appeared to be a body of Ministerial Aspirants, often the offspring of well-established families who viewed their role as offering leadership to the nation. This tradition was maintained by members of less grand families as the decades progressed, from those who entered politics before the Second World War – such as R.A. Butler, who held every important office other than Prime Minister – to those who entered immediately after the war, such as Iain Macleod, later Chancellor of the Exchequer. During war service, Macleod was asked what would be his aim in politics. 'To be Prime Minister' he replied.[5]

Such aspirants, though, would appear to have constituted a minority of the House. As Anthony King observed, 'most of the rich and aristocratic members of the Conservative party in the House of Commons before 1939 – the "knights of the shires" – probably regarded politics as something of a sideline'.[6] This is not to say they they would not like, or accept, ministerial office if offered it, but they had other interests to pursue and were frequently content to serve and, in the words of one of them, watch politics 'from the wings'.[7] Many occupied the category of part-timer.

The nature of parliamentary activity, and the stranglehold of party, meant that the Parliament Man need only attend as directed by the whips and otherwise spend time in the smoking room or library of the House or attend to business outside the House. On the Conservative side, most Members had business connections or – more often – were drawn from the professions.[8] It was not uncommon for many of them to spend their weekend – even some weekdays – hunting. Most MPs elected under the banner of the Labour Party – the official opposition party from 1922 onwards – had only an elementary education and were drawn from the ranks of skilled and semi-skilled workers.[9] Having been immersed in the trade union movement, they were attached to the principle of solidarity. The emphasis within the party was on intra-party democracy, with decisions being taken in party meetings and then supported publicly by all party members.

The demands made on Members at Westminster were not great. Nor were the demands made on them by constituents. Some constituency activity was expected, but it was as a local dignitary and sometimes, especially on the Conservative side, as local benefactor.[10] There were demands made for the redress of specific grievances – notably so during the Second World War – but they were not extensive in number, and could be accommodated – or, in some cases, ignored – by Parliament Men at Westminster. Stories of Members who ignored constituency mail, or were little bothered by it, were still current into the 1970s. Searing's work found that not all the stories were apocryphal. During his survey in 1972–73, Searing was told by one MP: 'I hunt three days a week, always. Probably hunt four days a week. I don't get any letters anyhow. I only have a secretary part-time. I have one woman, at home, who deals with Parliamentary letters on a Monday and that's it'.[11]

The material so far presented is suggestive of the importance of Parliament Man and of the existence of this type of MP on a scale greater than that detected by Searing. Though we have no means of identifying the precise number of Parliament Men in the first half of the century, we can make some assumptions about the preponderance of this category from the nature and activity of parliamentary life. We would expect a Parliament Man to emphasise the importance of *being* an MP, of giving time to watching the political fight in the chamber, voting loyally with the party, making little use of the procedures available to pursue particular issues, and spending little time in the constituency or devoting himself to pursuing the mundane grievances of constituents. Conversely, we would expect Policy

Advocates to emphasise *doing* the job of a Member and to use and develop parliamentary means, other than the chamber, for influencing public policy – especially the detail of policy. Following Searing, it would also seem plausible to hypothesise that Policy Advocates would be more likely than Parliament Men to pursue an independent line in voice and vote. Both Policy Advocates and Ministerial Aspirants we would expect to pay attention to constituency needs in order to ensure their re-election. Constituency Men we would expect to devote not only more time to constituency activity but to seek out actively constituency problems and promote the interests of the constituency as a whole.

From the aggregate data available to us, we can conclude that Parliament Men predominated in the parliaments of the first half of this century. The emphasis was very much on the floor of the House. Little use was made of committees, and what use was made of committees was for the benefit of government (standing committees, allowing government to get more bills considered simultaneously) rather than for the benefit of MPs wanting to influence public policy. Cohesion remained a marked feature of parliamentary life.[12] Parliamentary questions were used sparingly by Members. There are no residence requirements for British MPs.[13] Even in the early 1960s, only a minority of MPs listed home addresses in or near their constituencies.[14] In combination, these data would suggest that Parliament Man held sway in the House of Commons. Examination of the data on a decade by decade basis would also suggest that he (rarely she) held sway until the 1950s and even in to the 1960s.[15] Only in the 1960s and 1970s is there a paradigmatic change in role orientation.

However, to assert that there was no paradigmatic change in the first half of the century is not to claim that there was no change. There were some changes that may be taken to suggest that Parliament Men were becoming less predominant as the century progressed. The 1920s and 1930s saw the development of party committees within the parliamentary Conservative party. The committees provided a means by which backbench MPs could discuss issues in particular sectors (such as foreign affairs, finance and agriculture), listen to outside experts, and question and put pressure on frontbenchers. The committees were especially active in the 1930s and were often well attended.[16] These, we would hypothesise, were more likely to be the favoured territory of the Policy Advocate and the Ministerial Aspirant (a means of getting noticed) than the Parliament Man, especially the part-time Parliament Man.

The change would appear to reflect a slight change in the nature of the social composition of the parliamentary party, with an emphasis on the MP drawn from a professional rather than a business background. An increase in numbers and in the middle-class composition of the party also facilitated the growth of party committees in the parliamentary Labour party in the years after 1945.[17] The war years and immediate post-war years also saw some MPs demanding the greater use of committees for scrutiny of executive actions. The MPs had limited success -- a statutory instruments committee established in 1944 and a committee on nationalised industries created in 1955 – but the significant point for our purposes is that there was pressure from some Members who appeared keen to have a greater impact on the actions of the executive. Parliaments in which governments had a large overall majority also saw some occasions of substantial cross-voting by government backbenchers, though never on a scale that robbed the government of its majority.[18]

These sometimes modest changes do not suggest that Parliament Man ceased to be the predominant figure for much of this century, but do suggest that Parliament Man was becoming less predominant as the years progressed. The century appears to have witnessed the decline of Parliament Man in favour of the Policy Advocate. The extent to which that decline had taken place by the 1970s was tapped by Searing's survey. What was surprising was the extent to which the Policy Advocate had come to the fore.

## THE RISE OF THE POLICY ADVOCATE

The explanation for the number of Policy Advocates found by Searing is, I would hypothesise, to be found in the social background of new Members of Parliament. The rise of the Policy Advocate was facilitated by developments internal to the House and had as one of its consequences a major change in the structures and working practices of the House. These structures and practices served to encourage and consolidate the predominance of the Policy Advocate in the House.

The period since the 1960s has also seen other changes that have forced a greater emphasis on the constituency activity of MPs. This is a consequence of events external to the House but has forced a response from Policy Advocates – and Ministerial Aspirants – who see re-election as a necessary but not sufficient condition for them to fulfil their political roles.

### The New Breed of MP

There were significant changes in the social composition of the House in post-war decades. There was a large intake of Labour MPs in the general election of 1945, a significant number from middle-class backgrounds. However, the most dramatic change was to take place in the 1960s. There was a large turnover in Members in the general elections of 1964 and 1966. Following the general election of 1966, there were 112 fewer Conservative

MPs in the House than there were following the 1959 general election and 105 more Labour MPs. These figures do not do full justice to the turnover in membership, given that many long-serving MPs retired, to be replaced by new members of the same party. (At the end of the 1959–64 Parliament, for example, 60 MPs retired from the House, including Winston Churchill.) Not only were there more Labour MPs, those MPs were different in social background to Labour MPs elected in earlier parliaments. The new Labour Members were more likely to have a secondary and university education. Before 1966, less than one in three of new Labour MPs in each parliament had been to secondary school and university. In 1966, the proportion shot up to almost 50 per cent and stayed at more than 40 per cent in subsequent parliaments.[19] Less dramatic changes were taking place on the Conservative side of the House and were to be more apparent in later parliaments, perhaps not surprisingly given Labour ascendancy in the 1966–70 Parliament.

The explanation for this change – and for changes that were to be more apparent on the Conservative side in subsequent decades – was to be found in what Inglehart has termed 'cognitive mobilisation'.[20] The late 1940s and the 1950s saw the expansion of educational opportunities, with secondary education for all children, and the growth of radio and television as media of mass communication. There was a greater awareness of politics and political issues. This generated a new political generation, or rather succeeding generations of politically aware citizens. There was a consequent increase in political activity. This was manifested most notably in membership of pressure groups. One directory of pressure groups published in 1979 revealed that, of the groups listed, more than 40 per cent had come into existence since 1960. Established groups witnessed a growth in membership. (By the early 1990s, for example, the Royal Society for the Protection of Birds had a membership far in excess of that of the Labour Party.) Greater awareness and opportunities appear also to explain the rise in the emergence of a new breed of MP – drawn from modest social backgrounds and achieving success through a grammar school and then university education. A grammar school education became available on grounds of merit as a consequence of the 1944 Education Act. The 1950s and more especially the 1960s saw a growth in the number of universities, though the more able grammar school pupils still went to Oxford or Cambridge.

A change in the rules governing the selection of candidates also facilitated the selection of Conservative candidates from more modest backgrounds. From the end of the 1940s, Conservative candidates were limited in the amount that they could contribute to the local party. The effect was to prevent the purchase of candidatures by wealthy individuals. Even so, for some years local parties still tended to select candidates from privileged backgrounds. The practice declined only in the 1960s and, on a more notable scale, in later decades. In any event, there was a natural time lag, since many candidates elected in 1945 or selected before 1949 stayed in the House of Commons until the 1960s or even 1970s. The new MPs were, or certainly appeared to be, more committed to politics than their predecessors who saw their roles more as Parliament Men. The result was an influx of Policy Advocates, dedicated to a life in politics[21] and seeking to have some impact on public policy.

If this is a valid hypothesis, then we have the basis for assuming a continuing increase in the number of Policy Advocates in the House of Commons. The period since the early 1970s has seen a further growth in the number of MPs drawn from the middle classes. The rise of the 'grammar school boy' (rarely girl) became more apparent on the Conservative side of the House in the 1970s and since. Up to and including the two general elections of 1974, half or almost half of all Conservative MPs went to private schools and then to Oxford or Cambridge University. In 1979 the proportion dipped a few percentage points to 43 per cent and following the 1992 general election stood at only 32 per cent. The proportion of MPs educated at private schools dropped especially after 1979. Whereas one in four Conservative MPs were Old Etonians in 1945, only one in ten (34 out of 336 MPs) were by 1992.[22]

There has also been a notable shift in the occupational background of MPs. In the Parliament elected in 1992, the proportion of Labour MPs drawn from manual occupations was at its lowest level ever, with even lower proportions of the new intake coming from such occupations.[23] On the Conservative side, there has been a decline in the number of farmers, military officers and those holding senior positions in companies. There has been a notable increase in the number drawn from what King has termed 'the business of self-expression': journalists, authors, public relations personnel and teachers.[24] Of Labour MPs elected in 1992, 28 per cent had previously been lecturers or teachers. A significant proportion of new MPs are elected having spent some time previously in a post in the domain of politics, such as serving as a political consultant or a minister's special adviser. There were estimated to be 105 MPs falling in this category following the 1992 election.[25] The proportion drawn from what Peter Riddell has termed 'proper jobs' – occupations wholly independent of political activity – has fallen.[26]

The commitment of the new breed of MPs to a life in politics is reflected in the fact that they enter the House of Commons earlier than their predecessors and stay longer.[27] It would also seem reasonable to hypothesise that career politicians are more likely than the status seekers, spectators or club men – that is, Parliament Men – to engage in a greater degree of parliamentary activity. Two obvious indicators are the number of parliamentary questions put down and the number of early day motions (EDMs) tabled. Until the 1960s, there had been little change in the number of questions tabled for oral and written answer. In the 1958–59 session, 3,369 questions were tabled for written answer. In 1989–90, the figure was 41,358.[28] An increase in the number of EDMs tabled is of more recent origin. In the 1970s and early 1980s, it was not unusual for between 300 and 400 such motions to be tabled. By the mid-1990s, it was common for well in excess of 1,000 to be tabled each session.

*Behavioural Changes*

The rise of the Policy Advocate was also facilitated by important behavioural changes in the House. Until the 1970s, cohesion was – as we have noted – a marked feature of parliamentary life. This feature was to change in the period after 1970.

In the Parliament of 1970–74, Conservative backbenchers voted against their own government on more occasions, in greater numbers, and with more effect than before. Almost one in five of all votes saw one or more Conservative MPs voting against their own side. No previous Parliament had witnessed anything approaching this proportion.[30] Indeed, with one exception (the 1959–64 Parliament), the proportion of votes in any post-war Parliament witnessing a Conservative MP cross-voting was less than one in 20.

The size of the dissenting lobbies was also markedly larger in the 1970–74 Parliament. Before 1970, it was common for intra-party dissent to constitute no more than a lone dissenter and in most cases it did not amount to more than five MPs. In the 1970–74 Parliament, most incidents of cross-voting involved six or more Conservatives; on 64 occasions, the number of cross-voters was ten or more.[31] On six occasions, the extent of cross-voting by Conservative MPs denied the government a majority. Of these six defeats, three took place on three-line whips.

This level of intra-party dissent was thus significant relative to previous parliaments. Cohesion remained – and remains – a feature of parliamentary voting.[32] However, government was no longer able to take its majority for granted in the way that it had before 1970. The increase in intra-party dissent also proved more than a temporary phenomenon. Given the low or non-existent overall majorities of the Labour government from 1974 to 1979, it had a particular effect in the latter half of the 1970s.[33] Labour backbenchers proved willing to vote against their own government, sometimes in sizeable numbers. In 44 votes, 50 or more Labour MPs voted against the government.[34] The result was a string of defeats on important issues, including the government's major measure of constitutional reform – the Scotland and Wales Bill, designed to provide elected assemblies in

Scotland and Wales. The Labour government elected in October 1974 suffered 23 defeats as a result of its own supporters entering the Opposition lobby. It suffered a further 19 defeats after it lost its overall majority in the House and the opposition parties combined against it.

This increase in voting independence by backbench MPs in the 1970s consolidated the position of the Policy Advocate. Once backbenchers realised what they were able to achieve, they made greater use of the facility, producing what Samuel Beer has termed a more participant attitude on the part of Members, displacing their previously deferential attitude.[35] They wanted to be more involved in influencing public policy. The change thus consolidated the position of Policy Advocates and may also have served to enlarge their ranks, given that the change in attitude was, as Beer noted, pervasive.[36]

The behavioural change that precipitated this was not itself the result of the new breed of Member entering the House, the change taking place on the Conservative benches prior to the notable change in the entry of Conservative MPs from more middle-class backgrounds. Empirical analyses have failed to establish a clear correlation between the increase in cross-voting and the new breed of MP, with other theses being offered to explain the change in voting behaviour.[37] Policy Advocates benefited from what happened in the lobbies in the early 1970s but were not themselves solely or disproportionately responsible for it.

Government backbenchers continued to vote against their own side in parliaments after 1979, both in terms of breadth (the number of votes in which cross-voting took place) and depth (the number of MPs voting against the whip on each occasion).[38] However, the cross-voting had less effect, simply because of the size of the government's overall majority.[39] Cross-voting could be more easily absorbed by a large majority than a small one. Even so, the government was not immune to defeat. In each succeeding parliament, it suffered at least one parliamentary defeat. In 1986, despite the largest overall Conservative majority since 1935, the Conservative government of Margaret Thatcher saw a bill thrown out by the House when 72 Conservatives voted with the Labour Opposition to defeat it.[40]

Such defeats, however, were rare and MPs were increasingly reported as being exasperated at their failure to influence policy. Indeed, in addressing journalists, the Speaker in the 1983–87 Parliament described it as the 'frustration Parliament'.[41] Such characterisation, though, highlights the significance of the Policy Advocate in Parliament. Parliament Men or Ministerial Aspirants would be less concerned by the consequences of large government majorities. Furthermore, backbench frustration was not without its effects. The threat of defeat or of some embarrassment in the division lobbies variously induced government to listen to backbench disquiet and respond to it. The Government Chief Whip for part of the 1980s, John Wakeham, saw his role explicitly as one of a 'fixer', acting as a go-between for backbenchers and ministers and brokering deals between them. As significant, though, was the fact that Policy Advocates found more structured, institutional means for influencing policy.

## Structural Changes

In the 1950s and 1960s, there were few parliamentary means available to MPs to influence public policy. The government controlled most of the timetable on the floor of the House. Cross-voting gave MPs the opportunity to defeat the government, but the exercise of that power was reactive and negative (and not employed). Standing committees were appointed on an *ad hoc* basis and were characterised by partisan conflict. There was little opportunity for MPs to specialise in particular sectors and to influence government at a formative stage of deliberation.

During the 1970s, there were calls for select committees of the House to be used for scrutinising and influencing government in particular sectors and to be used on a more extensive basis than before. In 1976, the Select Committee on Procedure began an extensive inquiry and in 1978 issued a report advocating the creation of a series of select committees to cover the various government departments. After the 1979 general election, a combination of a new Leader of the House, Norman St John-Stevas, with backbenchers intent on achieving change resulted in the introduction and acceptance of motions to set up the proposed committees. Though most members of the Cabinet opposed the proposal (a category that included the Prime Minister, Margaret Thatcher) or were agnostic on the issue, they were not prepared to stand up to an assertive House of Commons.[42] The House voted to establish 12 committees, soon increased to 14, 'to examine the expenditure, administration and policy in the principal government departments ... and associated public bodies'. Their creation constituted the most important parliamentary reform for more than 70 years. Unlike previous committees, these were almost comprehensive in scope and they were as much the creatures of the House as they were of the government.

The committees have proved important means of specialisation by MPs and for scrutinising and influencing government, allowing scrutiny of a particular sector on a continuous basis not achievable on the floor of the House. The committees have attracted commitment from MPs and have been prolific in their output, producing in total more than 900 reports between 1979 and 1992.[43] The reports usually embody recommendations for government action. The committees have no formal sanctions to ensure that government acts on the recommendations, but a proportion of recommendations emanating from the committees are accepted by government.[44] The committees also serve to influence government indirectly through providing information – information that otherwise would not be available – to the House and to attentive publics.

The creation of committees constituted the most important of several reforms that took place within the House of Commons[45] and the committees are now an important and central part of parliamentary life. Though the subject of calls for strengthening, their work to date has demonstrated a capacity to influence government that otherwise would be denied to MPs.[46] Furthermore, they have been built upon in recent years. The number of committees has increased since 1979, essentially reflecting changes in the structure of government departments and a desire on the part of many MPs that the committees should be comprehensive in their coverage of departments. With the appointment of a Select Committee on Northern Ireland in 1994, comprehensive coverage was achieved. There are now 17 committees covering all government departments. Other committees have also been created, independent of the departments. These include a Committee on Standards and Privileges and a Deregulation Committee. The Scottish Grand Committee, which considers Scottish measures, has been given additional powers and a statutory committee has been created for the security services. At the same time, the sitting times of the House have been rationalised.

There has, in short, been a shift of emphasis from the chamber (the domain of Parliament Man) to committee (the domain of the Policy Advocate). The committees provide a structured means by which Policy Advocates can have some influence on public policy and by their existence serve to consolidate the position of Policy Advocates in the House and to influence other Members, or prospective Members, in terms of their perception of the role of the Member of Parliament.

CONCLUSION

Searing's invaluable study provided a snapshot of the role orientation of Members of Parliament at the beginning of the 1970s. By drawing on other evidence, we are able to suggest – plausibly if not definitively – that he identified a large body of Policy Advocates at a point when their number had grown significantly compared with preceding decades and that their number has increased since, their activity facilitated – and their role perception reinforced – by behavioural and structural changes that have taken place independent of their entry into the House.

There is thus the basis for asserting that Policy Advocates are more numerous on the backbenches of the House of Commons than previously assumed, and more than was found by Searing at the beginning of the 1970s.

Their number we would expect to increase as the demands made on MPs – from the ever-growing number of pressure groups and from constituents, as well as from the growing volume of public business[47] – squeeze out those MPs who are oriented to the role of Parliament Men. Policy Advocates and Ministerial Aspirants are prepared to do the constituency work necessary to satisfy local party demands and constituents' expectations; Parliament Men are not. We would thus expect the trend we have identified to continue.

## NOTES

1. S.C. Patterson, 'The British House of Commons as a Focus for Political Research', *British Journal of Political Science*, Vol.3, No.3 (1973), pp.363–81. See also P. Norton, 'Parliament Redivivus?', in J. Hayward and P. Norton (eds.), *The Political Science of British Politics* (Brighton: Wheatsheaf Books, 1986), pp.130–21; and P. Norton and J. Hayward, 'Retrospective Reflections', in the same volume, pp.204–6
2. S.H. Beer, *Modern British Politics* (London: Faber, 1969 edn.), p.350.
3. See S.C. Patterson, 'Understanding the British Parliament', *Political Studies*, Vol.37, No.3 (1989), pp.449–62.
4. D.D. Searing, *Westminster's World* (Cambridge, MA: Harvard University Press, 1994).
5. N. Fisher, *Iain Macleod* (London: Andre Deutsch, 1973), p.54.
6. A. King, 'The Rise of the Career Politician in Britain – and its Consequences', *British Journal of Political Science*, Vol.11 (1981), p.260.
7. T. Cazalet-Keir, *From the Wings* (London: The Bodley Head, 1967).
8. M. Rush, 'The Member of Parliament', in S.A. Walkland (ed.), *The House of Commons in the Twentieth Century* (Oxford: Oxford University Press, 1979), p.101.
9. Rush, 'The Member of Parliament', pp.113–14.
10. See P. Norton, 'The Growth of the Constituency Role of the MP', *Parliamentary Affairs*, Vol.47, No.4 (1994), pp.708–9.
11. Searing, *Westminster's World*, p.181.
12. See A.L. Lowell, *The Government of England, Vol. II* (New York: Macmillan, 1924); and P. Norton, *Dissension in the House of Commons 1945–74* (London: Macmillan, 1975).
13. D.N. Chester and N. Bowring, *Questions in Parliament* (Oxford: Oxford University Press, 1962).
14. P. Norton and D.M. Wood, *Back from Westminster* (Lexington, KY: University Press of Kentucky, 1993), Ch.3.
15. See P. Norton, 'Parliament Since 1945: A More Open Institution?', *Contemporary Record*, Vol.5, No.2 (1991), pp.217–34.
16. P. Norton, 'The Organisation of Parliamentary Parties', in Walkland, *The House of Commons in the Twentieth Century*; and P. Norton, 'The Parliamentary Party and Party Committees', in A. Seldon and S. Ball (eds.), *Conservative Century* (Oxford: Oxford University Press, 1994).
17. Norton, 'The Organisation of Parliamentary Parties'.
18. Norton, *Dissension in the House of Commons 1945-74*.
19. C. Mellors, *The British MP* (Farnborough: Saxon House, 1978), p.50.
20. R. Inglehart, *The Silent Revolution* (Princeton NJ: Princeton University Press, 1977). See also R. Dalton, *Citizen Politics in Western Democracies* (Chatham, NJ: Chatham House, 1988).
21. See King, 'The Rise of the Career Politician'.
22. B. Criddle, 'Members of Parliament', in Seldon and Ball, *Conservative Century*, p.161.
23. B. Criddle, 'MPs and Candidates', in D. Butler and D. Kavanagh (eds.), *The British General Election of 1992* (London: Macmillan, 1992), pp.224–5.
24. King, 'The Rise of the Career Politician', p.262.

25. P. Norton, 'A "New Breed" of MP?', *Politics Review*, Vol.3, No.3 (1994).

26. P. Riddell, *Honest Opportunism* (London: Hamish Hamilton, 1993), p.22.

27. King, 'The Rise of the Career Politician'.

28. H. Irwin, A. Kennon, D. Natzler and R. Rogers, 'Evolving Rules', in M. Franklin and P. Norton (eds.), *Parliamentary Questions* (Oxford: Oxford University Press, 1993), p.26.

29. Norton, *Dissension in the House of Commons 1945–74*.

30. P. Norton, *Conservative Dissidents* (London: Temple Smith, 1978), p.208.

31. Norton, *Conservative Dissidents*, p.212

32. R. Rose, 'Still the Era of Party Government', *Parliamentary Affairs*, Vol.36 (1983), pp.282–99.

33. P. Norton, *Dissension in the House of Commons 1974–1979* (Oxford: Oxford University Press, 1980).

34. Norton, *Dissension in the House of Commons 1974–1979*, p.439.

35. S.H. Beer, *Britain Against Itself* (London: Faber, 1982), pp.184–92.

36. Beer, *Britain Against Itself*, p.190.

37. See especially Norton, *Conservative Dissidents*, Ch.9; M. Franklin, A. Baxter and M. Jordan, 'Who Were the Rebels?', *Legislative Studies Quarterly*, 11 (1986), pp.143–59; and P. Norton, 'Dissent in the House of Commons: Rejoinder to Franklin, Baxter and Jordan', *Legislative Studies Quarterly*, 12 (1987), pp.143–52.

38. See P. Norton, 'Parliamentary Behaviour Since 1945', *Talking Politics*, 8 (Winter 1995–96), pp.107–14; and P. Norton, 'Are MPs Revolting? Dissension in the British House of Commons 1979–92', Paper presented to the Second Workshop of Parliamentary Scholars and Parliamentarians, Wroxton College, UK, 3–4 August 1996.

39. See Norton, 'Parliamentary Behaviour Since 1945'; and D. Melhuish and P. Cowley, 'Whither the New Role in Policy Making? Conservative MPs in Standing Committees 1979 to 1992', *The Journal of Legislative Studies*, Vol.1, No.3 (1995).

40. P. Regan, 'The 1986 Shops Bill', *Parliamentary Affairs*, 41 (1988), pp.218–45; and F.A.C.S. Bown, 'The Shops Bill', in M. Rush (ed.), *Parliament and Pressure Politics* (Oxford: Oxford University Press, 1990).

41. P. Norton, 'The House of Commons: Behavioural Changes', in P. Norton (ed.), *Parliament in the 1980s* (Oxford: Basil Blackwell, 1985), p.32.

42. P. Norton, *The Commons in Perspective* (Oxford: Martin Robertson, 1981), p.232.

43. Norton, *Does Parliament Matter?*, p.100.

44. See G. Drewry (ed.), *The New Select Committees* (Oxford: Oxford University Press, 1989 edn.); and D. Hawes, *Power on the Back Benches?* (Bristol: SAUS Publications, 1993).

45. See P. Norton, 'Independence, Scrutiny and Rationalisation: A Decade of Changes in the House of Commons', *Teaching Politics*, Vol.15, No.1 (1986), pp.69–98.

46. See *The Working of the Select Committee System: Second Report from the Select Committee on Procedure, Session 1989–90*, HC 19, 1990; P. Norton, 'Select Committees in the House of Commons: Watchdogs or Poodles?' *Politics Review*, Vol.4, No.2 (1995), pp.29–33.

47. See P. Norton, 'The House of Commons: From Overlooked to Overworked', in B. Jones and L. Robins (eds.), *Two Decades in British Politics* (Manchester: Manchester University Press, 1992); and Norton and Wood, *Back from Westminster*.

# Professionalisation of Parliamentary Roles in Germany: An Aggregate-Level Analysis, 1949–94

## THOMAS SAALFELD

The professionalisation of parliamentary politics and the rise of the career politician is one of the most important changes in post-war German parliamentarism. In the first part of this article, aggregate data are used to describe the nature and extent of this trend over time (1949–94). In the second part, Robert K. Merton's concept of 'role-set' is used to examine how professionalisation affects the strategies to reduce disturbances within role-sets. First results, which are only tentative at this stage, suggest that the great emphasis on committee work in the Bundestag is consistent with Merton's strategy of 'abridging role-sets' and 'insulating role activities from observability', while the high degree of voting cohesion and party solidarity could be explained with Merton's strategies of mutual 'social support' and 'differences in power'.

## INTRODUCTION

In recent years, students of the Bundestag have made major advances in the empirical analysis of German parliamentarians' attitudes and role orientations.[1] I will not deal with these studies in great detail as Werner J. Patzelt, one of the most accomplished researchers in the field, summarises some important results of his work in this volume. Important as these works are, they are necessarily 'snapshots' of a moving target. They provide indispensable micro-level information on parliamentarians' role orientations and behaviour at particular points in time. However, the very depth of such intensive interviews comes at a price (even in a literal sense). In-depth interviews, therefore, have remained sporadic. Follow-up studies have been rare (one of the few exceptions is Rudy Andeweg's work on the Dutch Parliament; see his contribution to this volume). It is thus difficult to capture longer term attitudinal and behavioural changes and relate them to variations in societal and political developments at the macro- and meso-levels. The nature, extent, causes and consequences of long-term changes such as the professionalisation of parliamentary roles are difficult to trace

Thomas Saalfeld is Lecturer in Politics at the University of Kent at Canterbury.

with 'one-off' interviews. Other sources are required to complement crucial individual-level analyses. In this article, an attempt is made to shed some light on the extent of the professionalisation of parliamentary roles in postwar Germany and its behavioural implications.

Since the early 1980s, the data basis for systematic studies of long-term trends and changes at the *aggregate level* has vastly improved through the publication of several excellent data handbooks on the Bundestag. Under the editorship of Peter Schindler, the Bundestag's Research Division has compiled and published an impressive amount of time-series data on legislative behaviour.[2] These data are usually aggregated; that is, they mostly provide information on the Bundestag as a whole or certain parliamentary parties rather than individual Members of Parliament. They are by and large very reliable, easily accessible and allow researchers to analyse long-term fluctuations and trends in parliamentary behaviour. Although most of these data do not tell us much about *individual* attitudes, they are indispensable to validate individual-level interview data and to make diachronic as well as cross-national comparisons. Such comparisons are important to describe and explain variations across time and space (for example, to assess the impact of variations in institutional contexts).

The *professionalisation of parliamentary roles* is frequently believed to have caused significant changes in parliamentarians' behaviour.[3] In the following sections, we shall first attempt to establish empirically to what extent there has been such a professionalisation over the last decades using aggregate data (Section 2). In a second step (Section 3), we shall look at Robert Merton's notion of 'role-set' and sketch some of the possible implications of professionalisation for parliamentarians' 'role-sets'. Subsequently, it will be investigated to what extent professionalisation has, in conjunction with strategies to reduce disturbances in role-sets, influenced parliamentary behaviour (Section 4). Finally, there will be a summary of some of the main findings (Section 5).

## IS THERE EVIDENCE OF PROFESSIONALISATION?

There is little doubt in the literature that politics in Germany has increasingly become a professional career. In this respect, the developments in Germany are similar to the experience of other Western democracies. This is not to say that the occurrence of professional career parliamentarians is entirely a recent *phenomenon*. There have been career politicians since the late nineteenth century. The epitomy of early professionals were the Social Democratic functionaries of the Weimar Republic and the early 1950s, the *'Hauptamtliche Mitarbeiter'*. Nevertheless, part-time *'Honoratiorenpolitiker'*, local dignitaries who owed their mandate to their elevated professional position and social status outside politics rather than *vice versa*, remained the predominant type of parliamentarian, especially in the conservative and liberal parties. After 1945, the experience of war, defeat and reconstruction brought a relatively large share of 'outsiders', who had not previously pursued a political career, into politics and the Bundestag. Today, by contrast, most politicians' careers are said to follow typical, predictable patterns. Before entering Parliament, most deputies have followed a typical career path. A majority of them have obtained a university degree and some professional experience in 'politics-facilitating occupations'[4] (for example, solicitors, civil servants [including, in Germany, university professors and school teachers], journalists, authors, publishers, public-relations personnel and other 'communicators') – either in terms of certain professional skills or in terms of potential politicians' 'availability' for a political career (especially in the initial stages when professional career and political career are pursued simultaneously). Politicians usually require and acquire specific professional skills and resources, such as communicative skills, knowledge of the workings of relevant organisations, access to political networks, familiarity with relevant political issues and general political 'knowhow'. Political parties serve as the major gatekeepers in a political career – much like professional associations. The parties' size, organisational structure, electoral success and internal norms determine an individual's chances of achieving political office. The path to parliamentary or ministerial office usually begins with extra-parliamentary party leadership positions at the local level and electoral office in local government. Political leadership positions at the local level are usually a springboard to mid-level elite positions and eventually to a career either in the federal-state parliament (*Landtag*) or the Bundestag. In order to maintain a local power base, Members of Parliament frequently retain their local leadership positions even after their election to the Bundestag ('vertical cumulation' of leadership positions). As a result of their relatively similar backgrounds and career patterns, German parliamentarians have been found to share, at least to some extent, certain 'professional' norms.[5]

There are no satisfactory *direct* quantitative indicators of the growing tendency of politics to be pursued as a professional career. Indirect measures include the average age at which MPs are first elected to Parliament, the average number of years they spend as deputies in Parliament, the extent to which they employ specialised staff and the degree to which politics becomes their predominant professional occupation.

The longer parliamentarians remain Members, the less likely they are to have a significant pre- or post-parliamentary career outside politics. At the beginning of the respective Bundestag terms between 1961 and 1994, the average Member had between 5.56 (1972) and 8.17 (1987) years'

TABLE 1

AVERAGE DURATION OF MEMBERSHIP OF MEMBERS OF THE
GERMAN BUNDESTAG AT THE BEGINNING AND END OF A
PARLIAMENTARY SESSION (1949–94)

| Bundestag term | Average duration of membership at the beginning of a legislative term | Average duration of membership at the end of a legislative term |
|---|---|---|
| 1949-1953 (1st) | 0.00 | 3.70 |
| 1953-1957 (2nd) | 1.94 | 5.59 |
| 1957-1961 (3rd) | 4.03 | 7.66 |
| 1961-1965 (4th) | 5.73 | 8.89 |
| 1965-1969 (5th) | 6.60 | 10.01 |
| 1969-1972 (6th) | 6.41 | 8.84 |
| 1972-1976 (7th) | 5.56 | 9.08 |
| 1976-1980 (8th) | 6.70 | 9.95 |
| 1980-1983 (9th) | 6.76 | 8.70 |
| 1983-1987 (10th) | 7.17 | 10.52 |
| 1987-1990 (11th) | 8.17 | 9.05 |
| 1990-1994 (12th) | 6.19 | n.d. |

*Sources*: Peter Schindler, *Datenhandbuch zur Geschichte des Deutschen Bundestages 1949 bis 1982*. 2nd edition (Bonn: Presse- und Informationszentrum des Deutschen Bundestages, 1983), p.176; Peter Schindler, 'Deutscher Bundestag 1976–1994: Parlaments- und Wahlstatistik.' *Zeitschrift für Parlamentsfragen*, Vol.26, No.4 (1995), p.556.

experience of *previous* service in the House. At the end of the respective Bundestag terms, the average member had between 8.70 (1983) and 10.52 (1987) years' experience of Bundestag service (Table 1). The figures prior to 1961 are low because the first Bundestag was only elected in 1949 (although there were numerous Members of the first Bundestag who had had parliamentary experience prior to 1933). Between 1972 and 1990, the average duration of MP's membership of the Bundestag increased steadily from just over five and a half years to more than eight years (measured at the beginning of the respective legislative term). The drop in the 1990–94 Parliament is largely due to the large intake of new Eastern German Members (with no prior Bundestag experience) after unification. Thus, the data provide some support for the assertion that there has been a gradual process of parliamentary professionalisation. Although there has been an increase in the length of parliamentary service, the data do not seem to suggest that German parliamentarians devote even the largest share of their professional lives to service in the Bundestag. Yet, as we shall see below, these data underestimate the extent to which German deputies are professional politicians because professional political careers in Germany frequently begin at the local level.

TABLE 2

SHARE OF MEMBERS OF THE BUNDESTAG IN THREE AGE COHORTS
AFTER THE RESPECTIVE ELECTION (1949–94)

| | 1949–53 | 1953–57 | 1957–61 | 1961–65 | 1965–69 | 1969–72 |
|---|---|---|---|---|---|---|
| % < 40 | 13.9 | 11.6 | 12.1 | 11.9 | 15.1 | 15.3 |
| % 40–59 | 69.3 | 70.5 | 65.9 | 62.8 | 64.1 | 71.0 |
| % ≥ 60 | 16.8 | 17.9 | 22.0 | 25.3 | 20.8 | 13.7 |

| | 1972–76 | 1976–80 | 1980–83 | 1983–87 | 1987–90 | 1990–94 |
|---|---|---|---|---|---|---|
| % < 40 | 22.6 | 20.5 | 21.0 | 14.7 | 11.4 | 13.1 |
| % 40–59 | 70.1 | 72.0 | 74.2 | 77.1 | 77.6 | 76.3 |
| % ≥ 60 | 7.3 | 7.5 | 4.8 | 8.2 | 11.0 | 10.6 |

*Sources*: Peter Schindler, *Datenhandbuch zur Geschichte des Deutschen Bundestages 1949 bis 1982.* 2nd edition (Bonn: Presse- und Informationszentrum des Deutschen Bundestages, 1983), p.165; *Datenhandbuch zur Geschichte des Deutschen Bundestages 1983 bis 1991* (Baden-Baden: Nomos, 1994), p.236.

Given the fact that parliamentary politics has increasingly become a professional career, the share of Members under the age of 40 (between 11.4 in 1987 and 22.6 in 1972, see Table 2) has been surprisingly low. This can be explained by the fact that the average Member's political career begins with a political 'apprenticeship' of between two and six years as a local councillor.[6] Thirty one per cent of the 194 Members of the Bundestag interviewed by Dietrich Herzog in 1988/89 had held local electoral office as councillors *prior* to their election to the Bundestag, 38 per cent had held such a mandate and *continued* to hold it even after their election to the Bundestag and only 31 per cent had never held elected office at local level. These results are similar to those found in earlier elite studies during the late 1960s.[7] The long local apprenticeship of a majority of Bundestag deputies also explains why the average duration of membership of the Bundestag (Table 1) has remained surprisingly low – despite the professionalisation of the career of parliamentarian since the 1960s.

Membership of federal state parliaments (Landtage) is not usually a preparatory step towards a Bundestag mandate. Membership of a Landtag and the Bundestag are parallel careers of almost equal 'value'. 'Cross-over' is minimal for backbench Members of the larger federal states. Exceptions are federal-state prime ministers and ministers, who frequently continue their careers as parliamentary leaders or federal ministers in the federal capital, and deputies of the small city-states (Berlin, Hamburg, Bremen), where local and federal-state mandates are intertwined.[8]

Nevertheless, the Bundestag's composition in terms of age cohorts (Table 2) indicates that the share of Members in the age bracket of 40–59 has steadily increased since 1961. If we assume that this is exactly the age when professionals are at the height of their careers, it is plausible to assume that the share of professional career politicians has increased.

TABLE 3

STAFF EMPLOYED BY MEMBERS OF THE BUNDESTAG, 1969–91

| Year | Number of MPs[c] | Total number of full- and part-time staff | | employed in | | | |
|---|---|---|---|---|---|---|---|
| | | | | Bonn | | constituency | |
| | | N total | N per MP | N total | N per MP | N total | N per MP |
| 1969 | 518 | 398 | 0.77 | 270 | 0.52 | 128 | 0.25 |
| 1970 | 518 | 663 | 1.28 | 444 | 0.86 | 219 | 0.42 |
| 1971 | 518 | 705 | 1.36 | 452 | 0.87 | 253 | 0.49 |
| 1972 | 518 | 688 | 1.33 | 460 | 0.89 | 228 | 0.44 |
| 1973 | 518 | 781 | 1.51 | 515 | 0.99 | 266 | 0.51 |
| 1974 | 518 | 841 | 1.62 | 546 | 1.05 | 295 | 0.57 |
| 1975 | 518 | 860 | 1.66 | 558 | 1.08 | 302 | 0.58 |
| 1976 | 518 | 889 | 1.72 | 568 | 1.10 | 321 | 0.62 |
| 1977 | 518 | 1013 | 1.96 | 648 | 1.25 | 365 | 0.70 |
| 1978 | 518 | 1200 | 2.32 | 617 | 1.19 | 583 | 1.13 |
| 1979 | 518 | 1396 | 2.69 | 639 | 1.23 | 757 | 1.46 |
| 1980 | 519 | 1323 | 2.55 | 616 | 1.19 | 707 | 1.36 |
| 1981 | 519 | 1239 | 2.39 | 585 | 1.13 | 654 | 1.26 |
| 1982 | 519 | 1378 | 2.66 | 651 | 1.25 | 727 | 1.40 |
| 1983 | 520 | 1401 | 2.69 | 662 | 1.27 | 739 | 1.42 |
| 1984[a] | 520 | 1425 | 2.74 | 673 | 1.29 | 752 | 1.45 |
| 1985 | 520 | 1995 | 3.84 | 837 | 1.61 | 1158 | 2.23 |
| 1986 | 520 | 2223 | 4.28 | 932 | 1.79 | 1291 | 2.48 |
| 1987 | 519 | 2308 | 4.45 | 969 | 1.87 | 1339 | 2.58 |
| 1988 | 519 | 2674 | 5.15 | 1161 | 2.24 | 1513 | 2.92 |
| 1989 | 519 | 2682 | 5.17 | 1172 | 2.26 | 1510 | 2.91 |
| 1990[b] | 662 | 3682 | 5.56 | 1308 | 1.98 | 2374 | 3.59 |
| 1991 | 662 | 4008 | 6.05 | 1546 | 2.34 | 2462 | 3.72 |

Sources: Peter Schindler, Datenhandbuch zur Geschichte des Deutschen Bundestages 1949 bis 1982. 2nd edition (Bonn: Presse- und Informationszentrum des Deutschen Bundestages, 1983), pp.113 and 987; Datenhandbuch zur Geschichte des Deutschen Bundestages 1980 bis 1987 (Baden-Baden: Nomos, 1988), p.863; Datenhandbuch zur Geschichte des Deutschen Bundestages 1983 bis 1991 (Baden-Baden: Nomos, 1994), p.173 and 1282.

Notes: a  For 1969–1984, the figures represent annual averages, from 1985 data refer to 31 December.

   b  The increase is in part a result of unification. The data for 1990 include 144 members of staff of the delegates of the People's Chamber.

   c  In election years, the number of MPs has frequently changed. For each election year, the number of MPs after the election was used.

Table 3 presents data on the number of the full-time and part-time staff employed by Members of the Bundestag in Bonn and in their constituencies. These data include all members of staff, from secretarial staff to research assistants with a university degree, as well as part-time and full-time employees. They do not allow very detailed analyses. Nevertheless, certain trends are discernible corroborating the impression that parliamentary politics has become more professional as more and more resources have been made available to, and used by, Members to carry out their professional duties as politicians. Between 1969 and 1991 the number of full- and part-time staff employed by individual Members of the Bundestag has increased almost by a factor of eight from 0.77 to 6.05 per Member.

Between 1969 and 1975, two-thirds of the average Member's staff were employed in the federal capital while one-third was allocated to the constituency. In the second half of the 1970s, this relationship was inversed. From 1979 onwards, the average Member has allocated more staff to the constituency than to his or her Bonn office. Indeed, in 1991, the staff resources employed by the average MP were divided 3:2 in favour of the constituency. This development indicates that constituency work has become more important. Interview data corroborate this impression. Members of the Bundestag devote a considerable amount of time and other resources to their general representation in the constituency, to constituency service and to the collection of information at this level.[9] Together with the frequent practice of retaining local mandates, this demonstrates that German MPs try to secure their parliamentary careers by establishing and/or maintaining a strong local power base.

Infrequent surveys of Members' time budgets show that a Bundestag mandate is a full-time job. Although evidence is patchy (there have been only two major surveys in 1972[10] and 1988/89[11]) and it is not always easy to distinguish between a Member's political and 'non-political' activities, the available data confirm that being a parliamentarian is a full-time job with little time to spare for a non-parliamentary career. In 1988/89, the average Member of the Bundestag worked 77.9 hours per week when the Bundestag was in session (1972: 86.6 hours) and 78.1 hours per week when it was not (1972: 78.3 hours). Out of approximately 78 working hours per week, the average MP devoted approximately 1.0 hours per week to a non-political profession when the Bundestag was in session (1972: 2.0 hours), and about 7.9 hours per week when it was not (1972: 7.9).[12]

## ROLES, ROLE-SETS AND PROFESSIONAL PARLIAMENTARIANS

Role theory makes ambitious claims. Its intellectual 'ancestors' from Emile Durkheim to Talcott Parsons have not been content with classifications of persons according to certain attitudinal patterns. The role approach claims to bridge the theoretical gap between political and social macro-structures on the one hand and individual behaviour on the other.[13] Individual behaviour is to be explained as a result of institutional constraints such as norms, roles, values, ideological orientations or systems of symbols (language). Roles are believed to be shaped and reproduced in the process of socialisation (see Introduction). Thus, role theory should be able to relate parliamentary behaviour in a theoretically meaningful way to broader institutional developments.

Roles are often highly complex and multi-dimensional. According to Robert K. Merton, each position in a social structure is associated not with a single role but with a specific 'role-set'. In his view, a role is the 'behavioral enacting of the patterned expectations attributed to that position'.[14] Parliamentarians, for example, interact with a host of individuals and groups whose 'patterned expectations' of a deputy's role behaviour may vary. They may even be contradictory. For example, the role expectations held by a parliamentarian's peers in the chamber, by party activists, by constituents or by interest-group representatives, may differ from each other. Finally, they may also differ from the deputy's own definition of his role. For example, party activists may see him as a 'delegate' faithfully representing party conference resolutions, constituents may expect him to be a 'local promoter' or 'welfare officer' (Searing) and the Member himself may define his own role as that of a Burkean 'trustee'.

The concept of 'role-set' is to be distinguished from the concept of 'multiple roles', which are associated not with a single social status, but with the various statuses in which individuals operate. Not only is a specific role-set associated with the status of Member of Parliament. The Member usually holds multiple roles in different institutional contexts: as a politician, spouse, parent, Christian, Conservative and so on.

Tensions, contradictions and changes in a Member's role-set make it difficult for academic observers to predict behaviour from any one particular role. They also pose problems for parliamentarians themselves as they may cause 'disturbance or disruption of the role-set, creating conditions for structural instability'.[15]

> These disparate and inconsistent evaluations complicate the task of coming to terms with them all. ... As things now stand, this appears to be the major structural basis for potential disturbance of a stable role-set. The question does not arise, of course, in those special circumstances in which all those in the role-set have the same values and same role-expectations. But this is a special and, perhaps historically rare, situation. More often, it would seem, and particularly

in highly differentiated societies, the role-partners are drawn from diverse social statuses with, to some degree, correspondingly different social values. To the extent that this obtains, the characteristic situation should be one of disorder, rather than of relative order.[16]

Therefore, the fact that most modern societies are in reality characterised by 'a substantial degree of order rather than of acute disorder' cannot be taken for granted, but requires explanation.[17] Empirical evidence suggests that the problem of disturbances in role-sets is a very real one for modern Members of Parliament – stress, family and health problems are a frequent consequence of a heavy work load, contradictory multiple roles and substantial disturbances in the Members' role-sets.[18] The more politics has become a professional career and the more dependent Members have become on their continued career in politics, the more pressing has been the need for mechanisms to reduce such disturbances. Role theorists identify characteristic mechanisms that help to avoid disturbances and instability. Although not incompatible, explanations of such mechanisms differ from the (usually) contract-based solutions offered by rational-choice theorists. Some of the mechanisms identified by Merton are highly relevant for students of parliaments. Four of Merton's mechanisms could be particularly important for the study of parliaments: abridging the role-set, insulating role-activities from observability, social support by others in similar social statuses and differences in the power of those involved in a role-set.

## HOW ARE CAREER POLITICIANS COPING WITH ROLE-SET DISTURBANCES?

### Abridging Role-Sets

In extreme cases of role-set conflicts, role-sets can be abridged and disturbances thereby reduced:

> Certain relationships are broken off, leaving a consensus of role-expectations among those that remain. But this mode of adaptation is possible only under special and limited conditions. It can be effectively utilized only in those circumstances where it is still possible for the status-occupant to perform his other roles, without the support of those with whom he has discontinued relations. Otherwise put, this requires that the remaining relationships in the role-set are not substantially damaged by this device.[19]

Members of Parliament, who feel they are exposed to a number of contradictory role expectations, could withdraw from politics and return to a non-political profession. This would be the most radical strategy of abridgement. Alternatively, they could break off relationships with occupants of certain 'counter-roles' whose role expectations are creating disturbances in their role-sets.

This strategy would mainly seem to be a possibility for 'Club Men' in Searing's terminology, that is, in essence, amateurs who may be 'Knights of the Shires', part-time parliamentarians continuing their professional career outside politics or classical German *'Honoratiorenpolitiker'* of the nineteenth century. Professional parliamentarians should be less likely to be able to abridge their role-sets in such a radical way. They have invested heavily in their political careers and incurred considerable 'sunk costs' in this process. The opportunity cost of changing careers would be exceedingly high. Breaking off contacts with certain groups (that is, 'counter-roles' with expectations creating disturbances with other components of the role-set) would also be difficult as successful parliamentarians tend to secure their re-election chances by maintaining extensive networks with a great many organisations. As Merton emphasises, the abridgement of role-sets 'requires that the remaining relationships in the role-set are not substantially damaged by this device'.[20] Therefore, one could hypothesise (on the aggregate level) that the higher the degree of professionalisation in a parliament, the lower the average number of Members reducing disturbances in their role-sets by leaving parliament or using other methods of radical role-set abridgement.

Table 4 provides moderate evidence that the use of radical abridgement 'exit option' has decreased in importance since the mid-1960s. The number of newly elected Members securing re-election in the following Bundestag has steadily increased between 1961 and 1980. Nine-tenths of the 117 newly elected Members of the 1976–80 Bundestag were re-elected at least once, more than three-quarters of them (78.6 per cent) were re-elected at least twice and about two-thirds (64.9 per cent) were re-elected at least three times afterwards. In the first four Bundestag terms (1949–65), only about one-third of the newly elected MPs secured re-election at least three times after their initial election to the Bundestag. Thus, there is evidence that MPs are increasingly looking to Parliament as a *long-term career*, which they are reluctant to give up early. Nevertheless, the data also suggest that it would not be justified to speak about a linear trend towards ever more frequent re-elections. Since 1980 the share of newly elected MPs who won re-election at least once has, in fact, decreased from 86.9 (1980) to 66.4 per cent (1987).

Data on MPs' time budgets show that, despite the stress caused by contradictory role-sets, parliamentarians devote a considerable share of their time to communication with the press, interest groups, party activists, parliamentary peers and citizens. In 1988/89, nearly one-quarter (19.1 out of 77.9 hours per week) of an average Member's time was spent on 'outside activities' of this type when the Bundestag was in session. When it was not

TABLE 4

RE-ELECTION OF NEWLY ELECTED MEMBERS TO THE BUNDESTAG, 1949–90

| | 1949-53 | 1953-57 | 1957-61 | 1961-65 | 1965-69 | 1969-72 | 1972-76 | 1976-80 | 1980-83 | 1983-87 | 1987-90 |
|---|---|---|---|---|---|---|---|---|---|---|---|
| Number of newly elected Members | 410 | 245 | 159 | 131 | 132 | 156 | 145 | 117 | 130 | 91 | 110 |
| Reelected (in %): at least ... | | | | | | | | | | | |
| ... once | 59.9 | 65.3 | 81.1 | 77.1 | 82.5 | 82.7 | 90.3 | 90.6 | 86.9 | 73.6 | 66.4 |
| ... twice | 42.6 | 50.6 | 54.7 | 53.4 | 63.6 | 68.0 | 73.8 | 78.6 | 76.9 | 53.8 | — |
| ... three times | 29.7 | 33.9 | 35.8 | 32.0 | 47.7 | 46.9 | 60.7 | 64.9 | 55.4 | — | — |
| ... four times | 16.8 | 16.7 | 21.3 | 20.6 | 31.8 | 33.4 | 45.5 | 46.1 | — | — | — |
| ... five times | 7.5 | 7.3 | 11.2 | 8.4 | 20.4 | 25.7 | 30.3 | — | — | — | — |
| ... six times | 2.6 | 3.6 | 5.6 | 5.4 | 10.6 | 15.4 | — | — | — | — | — |
| ... seven times | 2.4 | 1.6 | 4.4 | 0.8 | 3.0 | — | — | — | — | — | — |
| ... eight times | 1.2 | 1.6 | 2.5 | 0.0 | — | — | — | — | — | — | — |
| ... nine times | 0.7 | 1.2 | 0.6 | — | — | — | — | — | — | — | — |
| ... ten times | 0.2 | 0.0 | — | — | — | — | — | — | — | — | — |

*Source:* Peter Schindler, *Datenhandbuch zur Geschichte des Deutschen Bundestages 1983 bis 1991* (Baden-Baden: Nomos, 1994), p.243.

in session, this share increased to over two-fifths (33.2 out of 78.1 hours).

A more likely form of role-set abridgement (which overlaps with the strategy of 'insulating role activities from observability', see below) is legislative specialisation, segmentation and 'issue-decomposition'. Professional parliamentarians often become experts in specific policy areas. In their capacity as experts in a particular policy area, they are likely to be confronted with reduced sets of 'counter-roles'. For example, social or agricultural policies are prepared in the parties' respective specialised working groups and departmental Bundestag committees, mainly consisting of expert MPs with a relatively coherent 'definition of the situation', cultivating links with a relatively narrow range of interest groups and few government departments. By contrast, experts on, for example, economic policy – whose policies may be contradictory to the ones suggested by their colleagues specialising in the areas of, say, agricultural or social policy – prepare their decisions in different working groups and in co-operation with different role partners. The strategy of role-set abridgement through issue decomposition would seem to work as long as policy areas do not overlap. However, the formation of coherent policies becomes difficult if co-ordination across more than one policy area is required. The result may be lengthy bargaining processes and log-rolling with high decision-making costs, non-decisions, 'sitting problems out' or symbolic measures. None of these strategies will increase the chance of speedy and efficient decision making. Parliament's ability to produce innovative policies may be severely constrained.[21]

### Insulating Role-Activities from Observability

A second, closely related mechanism to reduce disturbances in a person's role-set is based on the fact that '[t]he occupant of a status does not engage in continuous interaction with all those in his role-set. ... To the extent that the role-structure insulates the status-occupant from direct observation by some of his role-set, he is not uniformly subject to competing pressures.'[22] The Bundestag is characterised by a considerable degree of division of labour. Members of Parliament spend a large share of their time in party working groups and parliamentary committees. As Werner J. Patzelt (drawing on Max Weber's ideal-typical terminology) has pointed out in this volume, a majority of German MPs define themselves as policy makers in a 'working parliament' ('arbeitendes Parlament') as opposed to members of a 'debating parliament' of the Westminster variety with an emphasis on plenary debates ('redendes Parlament'). Under these conditions, 'insulating role-activities from observability' by specialisation and committee work may appear to be an attractive strategy to reduce disturbances in one's role-set. (In addition, the expertise acquired through specialised committee work may increase an MP's influence in a particular policy area.) Unlike decision making in the plenary, which is dominated by majoritarian principles,[23] decision making in committees is often characterised by consensual 'sounding-out processes': 'The sounding-out process produces a low visibility for those not participating, and reduces their chances for raising criticism. Since the responsibility for the end-result is diffused among all participants, the level of internal criticism is also reduced.'[24] One disadvantage of such a strategy is that the function of Parliament as the 'great inquest of the nation' may suffer from the tendency of specialised committee members to use information strategically. As one observer remarked with regard to the US Congress, committee members may be tempted 'to squirrel away information' and may not 'even want some of the committee members to be well informed, much less the average member of Congress'.[25]

If insulating role-activities from observation is a significant strategy in the Bundestag, committee work should be expected to increase at the expense of plenary debates as parliamentary politics becomes more professional. This could be a theoretically grounded alternative to the explanation one journalistic commentator provides for the alleged decline in plenary debate in the British House of Commons: 'MPs today make up for their lack of power by being congenitally busy, meeting delegations, attending committees, dealing with their post, and generally using hyperactivity to cope with existential angst. Fewer and fewer have the patience to sit round the chamber simply to listen.'[26] Thus, one could hypothesise that professionalisation leads to an increase in committee work at the expense of plenary debates.

Table 5 does not fully corroborate this hypothesis. It confirms it in the sense that committee work has continued to be the dominant form of parliamentary activity in the German Bundestag. Between 1949 and 1994, there have been a total of 2,687 plenary sessions as compared to 28,368 regular committee meetings. In a typical *annual* session, the British House of Commons spends almost as many hours in session as does the Bundestag in a whole electoral term (*Legislaturperiode*) of usually four years.[27] However, there is no clear trend in the Bundestag and no inverse relationship between the number of plenary debates and committee meetings. On the contrary, there is a moderately positive correlation of 0.46 (Pearson's r) between the number of plenary sessions and committee meetings. Indeed, since 1983 the average number of hours per year spent in the plenary has been higher than at any time between 1949 and 1982. Thus, committees are the main 'work place' of professional parliamentarians. Reduced 'visibility' may help reduce disturbances in role-sets. Yet, this has not diminished the role of the plenary, at least in quantitative terms.

TABLE 5

PLENARY SESSIONS AND COMMITTEE SESSIONS IN THE BUNDESTAG, 1949-94

| Bundestag session (*Legislaturperiode*) | Number of plenary sessions (in brackets: average length in hours per year) | Number of committee sessions |
|---|---|---|
| 1949-53 | 282 (428) | 5,111 |
| 1953-57 | 227 (360) | 4,083 |
| 1957-61 | 168 (262) | 2,435 |
| 1961-65 | 198 (246) | 2,863 |
| 1965-69 | 247 (313) | 2,500 |
| 1969-72 | 199 (329) | 1,312 |
| 1972-76 | 259 (371) | 1,973 |
| 1976-80 | 230 (326) | 1,586 |
| 1980-83 | 142 (324) | 916 |
| 1983-87 | 256 (430) | 1,724 |
| 1987-90 | 236 (429) | 1,780 |
| 1990-94 | 243 (460) | 2,085 |
| Total | 2,687 (—) | 28,368 |

*Sources*: Peter Schindler, *Datenhandbuch zur Geschichte des Deutschen Bundestages 1949 bis 1982*. Second edition (Bonn: Presse- und Informationszentrum des Deutschen Bundestages, 1983), p.525; Peter Schindler, 'Deutscher Bundestag 1976–1994: Parlaments- und Wahlstatistik.' *Zeitschrift für Parlamentsfragen*, Vol.26, No.4 (1995), pp.558 and 560.

## Social Support by Others in Similar Social Statuses

Mutual social support is a further typical strategy to reduce disturbances in a person's role-set. Other actors occupying the same social status may 'have much the same problems of dealing with their role-sets'.[28] Such circumstances have encouraged the emergence of organisations and normative systems amongst those occupying the same social status. Organisations 'constitute social formations designed to counter the power of the role-sets; of being, not merely amenable to these demands, but of helping to shape them. ... They provide social support for the individual status-occupant. They minimize the need for his improvising private adjustments to conflict situations'.[29] German career politicians are often believed to have developed a certain *esprit de corps*.[30] There is some evidence of professional norms that transcend party lines (at least between the two main parties). If professional Members of Parliament share certain professional norms the following hypothesis should hold: an increasing share of professional parliamentarians leads to an increase in consensual legislation and a decrease in party-based opposition activity in the plenary.

Table 6 does not confirm this hypothesis. Since 1972 the share of bills passed unanimously by the Bundestag has declined, even if one controls for a bill's importance. This reflects an increased level of political polarisation between the governing coalition and the opposition parties, especially since the advent of the Green Party in 1983. It has to be pointed out, however, that 'a complete picture requires us to take into due account the legislative vote in the Bundesrat, the upper House, and in the Joint Mediation Committee of the Bundestag and the Bundesrat. It is in these latter institutions that co-operative strategies have often prevailed'.[31] Manfred G. Schmidt therefore observes a 'tension between co-operation in legislation and policy-making and the confrontational rhetoric and behaviour of the political parties'. He argues that this tension 'does not necessarily obstruct the one or the other, although it is likely that the political-electoral cost of co-operative strategies for the parties participating in the co-operation-and-confrontation game is increasing'.[32] This points to a conclusion similar to the one drawn by Rudy B. Andeweg in his contribution to this volume: there may be a coexistence of several role orientations or even 'role switching'.

The growing importance of an adversarial rhetoric between government and opposition suggests that if there has been solidarisation at all it is likely to be within parties rather than across party lines. In the 1960s and 1970s, observers have rightly emphasised that relationships between government and the major opposition parties have been 'preponderantly co-operative'.[33] The traditional hostility towards party conflict among both German elites and voters,[34] the logic of 'co-operative federalism' and the comprehensive nature of the Basic Law in combination with the system of judicial review have served 'to narrow the scope for political conflict in the Federal Republic' and created incentives which favour consensual policy-making.[35]

A look at the percentages in Table 7 confirms that two of the most important forms of questioning and short debate in the Bundestag (*Große Anfragen* and *Aktuelle Stunden*) have predominantly been a 'weapon' of the opposition parties. With a few exceptions, more than 50 per cent were initiated by the minority. *Große Anfragen* are one of the most important instruments for the opposition to force a debate on the floor of the House. They are 'the heaviest gun in the arsenal of parliamentary questions'.[36] They cannot be initiated by individual members but only by a parliamentary party or the equivalent number of MPs (five per cent of the total number of Members of the Bundestag) from several parties. They are essentially written questions followed by a short debate. The government is expected to answer the questions within a period of three weeks. The opposition's primary objective, however, is not the government's response but the possibility to discuss the matter itself and the government's answer in a

TABLE 6

VOLUME OF LEGISLATION AND CONSENSUAL LEGISLATION IN THE BUNDESTAG (1949–90)

| Bundestag Session | Total N of Acts Passed | Unanimous Bills (Total) | | Important Policy Bills | | | | Bills of Minor Importance and Administrative Bills | | | |
|---|---|---|---|---|---|---|---|---|---|---|---|
| | | N | % | Total N | Unanimous N | % | | Total N | Unanimous N | % | |
| 1949-53 | 545 | 105 | 19.3 | n.a. | n.a. | n.a. | | n.a. | n.a. | n.a. | |
| 1953-57 | 507 | 296 | 58.4 | n.a. | n.a. | n.a. | | n.a. | n.a. | n.a. | |
| 1957-61 | 424 | 270 | 63.7 | n.a. | n.a. | n.a. | | n.a. | n.a. | n.a. | |
| 1961-65 | 427 | 303 | 71.0 | n.a. | n.a. | n.a. | | n.a. | n.a. | n.a. | |
| 1965-69 | 453 | 322 | 71.1 | n.a. | n.a. | n.a. | | n.a. | n.a. | n.a. | |
| 1969-72 | 335 | 235 | 70.2 | n.a. | n.a. | n.a. | | n.a. | n.a. | n.a. | |
| 1972-76 | 516 | 364 | 70.5 | 72 | 32 | 44.4 | | 444 | 332 | 74.8 | |
| 1976-80 | 354 | 219 | 61.9 | 46 | 18 | 39.1 | | 308 | 201 | 65.3 | |
| 1980-83 | 139 | 71 | 51.1 | 35 | 9 | 25.7 | | 104 | 62 | 59.6 | |
| 1983-87 | 320 | 50 | 15.6 | 39 | 4 | 10.3 | | 281 | 46 | 16.4 | |
| 1987-90 | 369 | 64 | 17.3 | 45 | 0 | 0.0 | | 324 | 64 | 19.8 | |

*Sources:* Calculated from Peter Schindler, *Datenhandbuch zur Geschichte des Deutschen Bundestages 1980 bis 1987* (Baden-Baden: Nomos, 1988), p.571; *Datenhandbuch zur Geschichte des Deutschen Bundestages 1983 bis 1991* (Baden-Baden: Nomos, 1994), pp.845–46.

*Notes:* Schindler's categories 'essential' (*wesentliche*) and 'important' (*wichtige*) bills were fused into one: 'important policy bills'.

TABLE 7

SHORT DEBATES AND QUESTIONS IN THE BUNDESTAG (1949–94)

| Period | Große Anfragen | | Aktuelle Stunden | |
|---|---|---|---|---|
| | N | % tabled by opposition | N | % tabled by opposition |
| 1949-53 | 160 | 38.1 | — | — |
| 1953-57 | 97 | 52.6 | — | — |
| 1957-61 | 49 | 87.7 | — | — |
| 1961-65 | 35 | 68.6 | 2 | 50.0 |
| 1965-66 | 11 | 36.4 | 5 | 40.0 |
| 1966-69 | 34 | 35.3 | 12 | 58.3 |
| 1969-72 | 31 | 80.6 | 8 | 100.0 |
| 1972-76 | 24 | 75.0 | 20 | 90.0 |
| 1976-80 | 47 | 70.2 | 9 | 100.0 |
| 1980-82 | 32 | 75.0 | 6 | 66.7 |
| 1982-83 | 0 | — | 6 | 100.0 |
| 1983-87 | 175 | 84.6 | 117 | 76.9 |
| 1987-90 | 145 | 86.2 | 126 | 78.6 |
| 1990-94 | 98 | n.d. | 103 | n.d. |

*Sources*: Peter Schindler, *Datenhandbuch zur Geschichte des Deutschen Bundestages 1949 bis 1982*. (Bonn: Deutscher Bundestag, 1983), pp.762–63; *Datenhandbuch zur Geschichte des Deutschen Bundestages 1980 bis 1987* (Baden-Baden: Nomos, 1988), p.677; *Datenhandbuch zur Geschichte des Deutschen Bundestages 1983 bis 1991* (Baden-Baden: Nomos 1994), p.993; Peter Schindler, 'Deutscher Bundestag 1976–1994: Parlaments- und Wahlstatistik.' *Zeitschrift für Parlamentsfragen*, Vol.26, No.4 (1995), p.563.

major debate.[37] According to Table 7, the use of this instrument declined after the first Bundestag (1949–53). The 1983–87 Bundestag, however, seems to mark a turning point. Although the number of *Große Anfragen* dropped in the 1990–94 Bundestag, opposition activity on the floor of the House remains stronger than in the 1960s and 1970s. To a large extent, the increase between 1983 and 1990 has been caused by the competitive style of the Green Party, whose members initiated nearly half (155) of the total 320 *Große Anfragen* in the two Bundestag terms between 1983 and 1990. In the same period, the Social Democrats also tabled 118 *Große Anfragen* (1983–87: 61; 1987–90: 57) which is also a considerable increase if compared to the parliaments between 1957 and 1983.[38]

Since the 1983–87 Bundestag terms, the use of *Aktuelle Stunden* has also increased considerably. Again, the vast majority of these short, topical debates on current issues has been initiated by the opposition parties. The striking growth in number can largely be explained by the reform of the Bundestag's standing orders in 1980, by which the initiation of this form of debate was facilitated. Since 1980 it can be demanded by any parliamentary party or the equivalent number of members from several parties, independent of question time.

The decrease of consensual legislation since 1972 and the increasing use of short debates and questions by the opposition parties from 1983 onwards confirm the hypothesis, that – at least in terms of parliamentary style on its floor – the Bundestag has moved more closely towards the competitive and adversarial model of executive-legislative relations in the 'debating' parliament of Westminster.[39] On a purely rhetorical level, there is little evidence of a 'vanishing opposition' (Kirchheimer) or a significant decline in plenary activity. The high degree of consensual legislation appears to be a result of the institutional constraints of 'co-operative federalism' rather than of Members' role orientations and strategies to reduce disturbances in their role-sets.

### Differences in the Power of Those Involved in a Role-Set

Hierarchical co-ordination is the last of Merton's mechanisms of tension reduction (although he does not use this term). Hierarchical co-ordination is based on differences in power. Merton defines power (in a Weberian fashion) as 'nothing more than the observed and predictable capacity for imposing one's own will in a social action, even against the resistance of others taking part in that action'.[40] Individuals or coalitions of individuals can impose their expectations upon status-occupants. Confronted with contradictory behavioural expectations, a Member of Parliament may choose to follow the expectations of the most powerful actor in the role-set. Thus, hierarchical co-ordination in parliamentary parties may help to reduce disturbances in role-sets. Members of Parliament follow the authoritative decisions of their parliamentary caucuses and party leaders. (This may also be seen as setting up an organisation with norms protecting deputies in the sense of Merton's strategy of social support, see above.) The individual is not necessarily powerless in this context. Coalitions or competing powerful actors in a Member's role-set may give the parliamentarian relative freedom to proceed as he intended in the first place. Nevertheless, professionalisation would seem to lead to the following predictions: parties have a monopoly as quasi-professional associations. They control the career prospects and re-election chances of parliamentarians. Parliamentarians are highly dependent on their parties for reselection as parliamentary candidates, re-election and career advancement. Dependence is the most important cause of party solidarity.[41] Professional politicians, therefore, should be more likely to toe the party line in parliamentary votes. One could hypothesise, therefore that professionalisation provides incentives for an increasing degree of party cohesion in parliamentary votes. Since professionalisation has affected all

TABLE 8

PARTY COHESION IN RECORDED VOTES (RICE INDEX OF COHESION):
CDU/CSU, SPD, FDP (1949–90)

| Bundestag | Number of recorded votes | CDU/CSU | SPD | FDP |
|---|---|---|---|---|
| 1949–1953 (1st) | 133 | 86.29 | 99.67 | 83.98 |
| 1953–1957 (2nd) | 169 | 89.95 | 99.34 | 80.48 |
| 1957–1961 (3rd) | 46 | 93.63 | 99.66 | 95.11 |
| 1961–1965 (4th) | 37 | 89.55 | 98.49 | 84.88 |
| 1965–1969 (5th) | 24 | 87.26 | 93.05 | 97.37 |
| 1969–1972 (6th) | 38 | 98.79 | 99.92 | 97.92 |
| 1972–1976 (7th) | 51 | 93.67 | 98.28 | 98.86 |
| 1976–1980 (8th) | 59 | 97.44 | 98.40 | 94.86 |
| 1980–1983 (9th) | 26 | 99.26 | 99.26 | 95.85 |
| 1983–1987 (10th) | 343 | 99.77 | 96.03 | 97.72 |
| 1987–1990 (11th) | 216 | 98.90 | 95.69 | 95.88 |
| 1949–1990 | 1142 | 94.31 | 97.79 | 91.41 |

*Source:*  Thomas Saalfeld, *Parteisoldaten und Rebellen: Eine Untersuchung zur Geschlossenheit der Fraktionen im Deutschen Bundestag (1949–1990)* (Opladen: Leske+Budrich, 1995), pp.109–10.

parties, there should be a uniform trend towards increased voting cohesion in all parties.

Table 8 reveals more variation between the parties than the hypothesis would suggest. One of the most commonly used indexes measuring the voting cohesion of parliamentary parties is the Rice Index of Cohesion. It ranges from 0 (completely divided) to 100 (perfectly cohesive). Table 8 lists the average Rice Index of Cohesion for the three major Bundestag parties (CDU/CSU, SPD and FDP) in each Bundestag between 1949 and 1990. All recorded votes are included, that is, the data are not restricted to legislation. They include votes on all types of motions. The figures refer to recorded votes which constitute only a minority of all votes taken in the Bundestag but allow precise measurement of individual voting behaviour. Recorded votes are usually taken when an issue is highly contentious, when at least one party wants to signal its position to the public, or when the party whips need to assure Members' attendance. Pressure on individual Members is particularly high. Thus data on recorded votes tend to overestimate the general cohesion of the parliamentary parties.

Despite the generally high level of voting cohesion, there has been some interesting variation across time and parties. During the first four legislative terms of the Bundestag (1949–65), the SPD was the most cohesive party in the House. The period between 1965 and 1972 was a phase of transition, the period between 1972 and 1983 was a phase of growing similarity. The 1965–69 Bundestag witnessed a major drop in the SPD's Rice index reflecting the strong intra-party tensions during the time of the Grand Coalition between Social Democrats and Christian Democrats. The same phenomenon can be observed for the CDU/CSU whose cohesion also dropped. The FDP stabilised its voting cohesion on a high level, which it has maintained since. In the 1969–82 period, there were SPD–FDP coalitions under Chancellors Brandt and Schmidt. The slim majorities these coalitions usually had and the competitive attitude of the CDU/CSU opposition especially in the early 1970s, favoured a high degree of voting cohesion on both sides of the House. The CDU/CSU achieved much higher levels of cohesion than during the 1950s and 1960s. Since 1983, the SPD's voting cohesion has dropped slightly. While the SPD had been by far the most cohesive party in the first four legislative terms of the Bundestag, it was the least cohesive between 1983 and 1990, when a new generation of relatively 'unruly' MPs entered the Bundestag as SPD deputies.

Although, overall, German parliamentary parties have been extremely cohesive, there has not been a uniform trend towards increasing voting cohesion as parliamentary politics has become more professional. Party-specific (group effects), cohort-specific and period-specific developments seem to explain a significant part of the variation observed.

CONCLUSIONS

Parliamentary politics in Germany has become more 'professional' since 1949. Indirect quantitative indicators such as the number of years an average Member serves in the Bundestag, the chamber's composition according to age cohorts, the number of full- and part-time staff Members employed or their time budgets confirm the findings of interview-based studies. The aggregate data used in this study suggest, in addition, that the trend towards professionalisation has not been a linear one. There have been discernible group effects, cohort effects and period effects. The data discussed in this contribution reveal the significance of variations between parties, different periods (for example, immediately after 1949 and unification in 1990) and 'generational breaks' (such as the one following the 'watershed elections' of 1969 and 1972). Overall, however, there is little doubt that being a parliamentarian is no longer a 'retirement job' for accomplished trade-union officials or local dignitaries. It is a full-time profession which displays many general properties of a profession. A parliamentarian's career usually begins in his or her late thirties after several years of 'apprenticeship' in local politics. Very frequently, these local links are maintained even after a politician's election to parliament. Most parliamentarians spend their 'best years', that is, the years in which careers are made, in the Bundestag.

What consequences has professionalisation had for parliamentarians' role behaviour? Above all, in what way has it influenced their attempts at controlling conflicts inherent in their role-sets? Robert K. Merton's social theory offers general answers as to how persons can try to reduce disturbances in their role-sets. Some of these strategies are intuitively applicable to parliamentarians. For example, deputies can abridge role-sets by withdrawing from parliamentary politics, reducing the number of outside contacts or specialising and thereby withdrawing from certain policy areas. They can reduce the 'observability' of their activities by emphasising committee work. They can develop organisations and norms which protect them from the effects of conflicting pressures. Finally, they can reduce disturbances in their role-sets by accepting the policies suggested by powerful parliamentary leaders.

In this article, an attempt has been made to operationalise these strategies and test at least their plausibility. Abridging role-sets by withdrawing from parliamentary politics is an option that professional career politicians will tend to avoid. The evidence corroborates this relatively trivial assumption. More importantly, however, parliamentary specialisation and 'issue decomposition', mainly through committee work, could be seen as an attempt to abridge role-sets or at least reduce disturbances in role-sets by decreasing the observability of role-activities. This may explain why there is so much emphasis on committee work and so little plenary debate in the Bundestag. However, the quantitative indicators used here do not suggest that the strong emphasis on committee work has led to a decline in plenary activity. On the contrary, plenary activities have increased in the last two decades. This indicates a certain amount of 'role switching', where Members of Parliament combine consensual policy making (based on the role orientation of a law maker) in committees with ostentatiously adversarial elements (emphasising party roles or government-versus-opposition roles) in the plenary. It could also be explained by the fact that new opposition parties (the Greens and later the 'Party of Democratic Socialism' [PDS]) have not been fully integrated in the consensual negotiations between the three 'established' parties (CDU/CSU, SPD and FDP). Therefore, some of the strategies have not been available to them. Although parliamentarians have developed a certain *esprit de corps*, which transcends to some extent party lines, the data suggest that the main source of social solidarity (if it exists) are the individual parties rather than non-partisan organisations. The high degree of voting cohesion in all main parties suggests partly a high degree of internal solidarity, partly a high degree of hierarchichal co-ordination and integration. Thus, overall, Merton's theorising on the impact of disturbances in role-sets does provide interesting and theoretically grounded explanations of certain behavioural patterns typical for professional parliamentarians.

## NOTES

1. Cf., above all, Werner J. Patzelt, *Abgeordnete und Repräsentation: Amtsverständnis und Wahlkreisarbeit* (Passau: Wissenschaftsverlag Richard Rothe, 1993); Werner J. Patzelt, *Abgeordnete und ihr Beruf: Interviews – Umfragen – Analysen* (Berlin: Akademie Verlag, 1995); Dietrich Herzog, Hilke Rebenstorf, Camilla Werner and Bernhard Weßels, *Abgeordnete und Bürger: Ergebnisse einer Befragung der Mitglieder des 11. Deutschen Bundestages und der Bevölkerung* (Opladen: Westdeutscher Verlag, 1990). Further references can be found in Werner Patzelt's contribution to this volume.
2. Peter Schindler, *Datenhandbuch zur Geschichte des Deutschen Bundestages 1949 bis 1982*, 2nd edition (Bonn: Presse- und Informationszentrum des Deutschen Bundestages, 1983); *Datenhandbuch zur Geschichte des Deutschen Bundestages 1980 bis 1984* (Baden-Baden: Nomos, 1986); *Datenhandbuch zur Geschichte des Deutschen Bundestages 1980 bis 1987* (Baden-Baden: Nomos, 1988); *Datenhandbuch zur Geschichte des Deutschen Bundestages 1983 bis 1991* (Baden-Baden: Nomos, 1994).
3. Cf., for example, Philip Norton's contribution to this volume; see also Anthony King, 'The Rise of the Career Politician in Britain – And its Consequences', *British Journal of Political Science*, Vol.11 (1981), pp.249–85; Richard Rose, 'British MPs: More Bark than Bite?', in Ezra N. Suleiman (ed.), *Parliaments and Parliamentarians in Democratic Politics* (New York: Holmes & Meier, 1986), pp.8–40, esp. pp.22–31.
4. King, 'The Rise of the Career Politician in Britain', p.261.
5. Cf. Dietrich Herzog, 'Der moderne Berufspolitiker: Karrierebedingungen und Funktion in westlichen Demokratien', in Hans-George Wehling (ed.), *Eliten in der Bundesrepublik Deutschland* (Stuttgart: Kohlhammer, 1990), pp.34–5. Cf. also Ursula Hoffmann-Lange, *Eliten, Macht und Konflikt in der Bundesrepublik* (Opladen: Leske+Budrich, 1992), pp.402–3 *et passim*.
6. Dietrich Herzog, *Politische Karrieren: Selektion und Professionalisierung politischer Führungsgruppen* (Opladen: Westdeutscher Verlag, 1975), p.87. The data are from 1968. There is no evidence suggesting that they have changed significantly.
7. Dietrich Herzog, 'Der moderne Berufspolitiker', p.37; for 1968 see Herzog, *Politische Karrieren*, p.87.
8. Stefan Holl, 'Landespolitiker: eine weitgehend unbeachtete Elite. Sozialstruktur, Karrieremuster, Tätigkeitsprofile', in Hans-Georg Wehling (ed.), *Eliten in der Bundesrepublik Deutschland* (Stuttgart: Kohlhammer, 1990), pp.90–95.
9. Patzelt, *Abgeordnete und Repräsentation*, pp.403–10.
10. Paul Kevenhörster and Wulf Schönbohm, 'Zur Arbeits- und Zeitökonomie von Bundestagsabgeordneten', *Zeitschrift für Parlamentsfragen*, Vol.4, No.1 (1973), pp.18–37.
11. Dietrich Herzog *et al.*, *Abgeordnete und Bürger*, pp.83–100.
12. Kevenhörster and Schönbohm, 'Zur Arbeits- und Zeitökonomie von Bundestagsabgeordneten'; Herzog *et al.*, *Abgeordnete und Bürger*, pp.83–100.
13. Patzelt, *Abgeordnete und Repräsentation*, p.57; John C. Wahlke, 'The Problem of a Legislative Model', in Heinz Eulau and John C. Wahlke (eds.), *The Politics of Representation: Continuities in Theory and Research* (Beverly Hills and London: SAGE

Publications, 1978), p.30.

14. Robert K. Merton, *Social Theory and Social Structure*. Revised and enlarged edition (New York: Free Press, 1957), p.368 (Merton refers to Ralph Linton's definition).
15. Merton, *Social Theory and Social Structure*, p.370. Merton does not specifically refer to parliamentarians.
16. Merton, *Social Theory and Social Structure*, pp.370–71.
17. Merton, *Social Theory and Social Structure*, p.371.
18. Cf. Patzelt, *Abgeordnete und Repräsentation*, pp.403–14.
19. Merton, *Social Theory and Social Structure*, p.379.
20. Merton, *Social Theory and Social Structure*, p.379.
21. Cf. with regard to intra-party decision making Josef Schmid, *Die CDU: Organisationsstrukturen, Politiken und Funktionsweisen einer Partei im Föderalismus* (Opladen: Leske+Budrich, 1990), pp.273–5.
22. Merton, *Social Theory and Social Structure*, p.374.
23. Giovanni Sartori, *The Theory of Democracy Revisited. Part One: The Contemporary Debate* (Chatham, New Jersey: Chatham House, 1987), pp.225–7.
24. Johan P. Olsen, 'Voting, "Sounding Out" and the Governance of Modern Organizations', *Acta Sociologica*, Vol.15, No.3 (1972), p.274.
25. Quoted in Keith Krehbiel, *Information and Legislative Organization* (Ann Arbor: University of Michigan Press, 1991), p.69.
26. *The Economist*, 2 Nov. 1996, p.44.
27. Schindler, *Datenhandbuch 1983 bis 1991*, p.556; Robert Borthwick: 'The Floor of the House', in Michael Ryle and Peter G. Richards (eds.), *The Commons Under Scrutiny* (London: Routledge, 1988), p.57.
28. Merton, *Social Theory and Social Structure*, p.378.
29. Merton, *Social Theory and Social Structure*, p.378.
30. See, for example, Herzog, 'Der moderne Berufspolitiker', p.34.
31. Manfred G. Schmidt, 'Germany: The Grand Coalition State', in Joseph M. Colomer (ed.), *Political Institutions in Europe* (London: Routledge, 1996), p.77.
32. Schmidt, 'Germany', p.77.
33. William E. Paterson and Douglas Webber, 'The Federal Republic of Germany: The Re-Emergent Opposition?', in Eva Kolinsky (ed.), *Opposition in Western Europe* (London: Croom Helm, 1987), p.163. For a typology of oppositional behaviour see Robert A. Dahl, 'Patterns of Opposition', in Robert A. Dahl (ed.), *Political Oppositions in Western Democracies* (New Haven and London: Yale University Press, 1967), pp.332–47.
34. Dieter Grosser, 'Die Sehnsucht nach Harmonie: Historische und verfassungsstrukturelle Vorbelastungen der Opposition in Deutschland', in Heinrich Oberreuter (ed.), *Parlamentarische Opposition: Ein internationaler Vergleich* (Hamburg: Hoffmann und Campe, 1975), pp.206–21.
35. Paterson and Webber, 'The Federal Republic of Germany', p.145.
36. Eckart Busch, 'Parlamentarische Kontrolle', in Helmut Schellknecht (ed.), *Wegweiser Parlament* (Heidelberg: R. v. Decker & C.F. Müller, 1988), p.515 (my translation).
37. Busch, 'Parlamentarische Kontrolle', pp.515–20.
38. Schindler, *Datenhandbuch 1980 bis 1987*, p.677.
39. Heinrich Oberreuter, 'Der Deutsche Bundestag vor neuen Herausforderungen – Eine kritische Bilanz im Spannungsfeld von Westminster-Modell und deutschem Parlamentsverständnis', in Herbert Döring and Dieter Grosser (eds.), *Großbritannien. Ein Regierungssystem in der Belastungsprobe* (Opladen: Leske und Budrich, 1987), pp.89–90; Herbert Döring, 'Parteienstaat and "Party Government": Politische Verhaltensweisen und Entscheidungsstrukturen', in *Großbritannien und Deutschland: Nachbarn in Europa* (Hannover: Niedersächsische Landeszentrale für politische Bildung, 1988), pp.91–3.
40. Merton, *Social Theory and Social Structure*, p.372.
41. Michael Hechter, *Principles of Group Solidarity* (Berkeley: University of California Press, 1987), pp.78–103.

# German MPs and Their Roles

## WERNER J. PATZELT

Parliamentary role structures do not come into being as a consequence of the MPs' behavioural preferences alone. In the German case, five constructive features constitute the casting mould within which the roles of MPs are formed: 'team formation effects' of the parliamentary system of government; professionalisation and division of labour within a 'work parliament'; the fact that German MPs are, and hence behave as, party leaders; and role-shaping effects both of interest groups and of constituency work. Based on a survey conducted in 1994 among all 2,800 German MPs, and on a return rate of about a third, the effects thereof are described. Subsequently, the 'role partners' or 'counter roles' of German parliamentarians are presented, and data on role orientations, role behaviour, role conflicts and parliamentary socialisation are discussed. Role orientations and role behaviour of German representatives are clearly correlated, and both match quite well the functional logic of representative democracy. On balance it may be stated that the average German MP is doing a good job.

## ROLE-SHAPING EFFECTS OF THE POLITICAL SYSTEM'S STRUCTURE

Parliamentary role structures[1] do not come into being as a consequence of the MPs' behavioural preferences alone. Rather, the overall structure of the political system and the functional cohesion of its individual parts constitute the casting mould within which the roles of the MPs are formed. In the German case,[2] six constructive features of the governmental system bear important role-shaping effects on representatives.

### 'Team Formation Effects' of the Parliamentary System of Government

The greatest impact on the role of German representatives is that the governmental system is parliamentary. On both the national and the state level, the executive branch of government emerges from parliament and remains closely connected with the parliamentary majority group or a governing coalition of parliamentary groups. The 'old dualism' between parliament and the executive branch is, thus, replaced by a 'new dualism'

Werner J. Patzelt holds the Chair of Comparative Government in the Institute of Political Science at the Technical University of Dresden, Germany. He would like to acknowledge the help of Dipl.-Kauffrau Dirscherl and Dr Roland Schirmer for data analysis and comments on an earlier draft of this paper.

between the executive branch and its supportive parliamentary majority on the one hand, and the parliamentary opposition on the other.[3] For the MPs of the majority parliamentary group or of a faction participating in a governing coalition, the consequence of this 'new dualism' is that they behave in such a way as not to jeopardise the stability of 'their' government. That calls for consideration in dealing with each other so as to not call into question the internal cohesion of the governing parliamentary majority. The same applies to the parliamentary opposition parties. They increase their chances over the current majority parties in the next elections if they manage to portray themselves as strong teams with commonly shared platforms. So practically all German MPs will have to consider cohesion and unity within their parliamentary groups (also referred to as 'faction discipline' or 'faction solidarity') as an inevitable 'means towards an end' and as an important guideline of individual behaviour.[4] Therefore the profession of being an MP takes the form of a 'team sport' in Germany: MPs mostly co-operate within competing teams. Additionally, German MPs usually strive for a position in the executive branch of government, with the latter often being viewed not as an alternative to, but as the crowning event of, a parliamentary career.

*Professionalisation and Division of Labour Within a 'Work Parliament'*

In Germany, parliamentarism takes the form of 'work parliamentarism' rather than of 'debating parliamentarism'. Severe clashes between competing parliamentary groups on policy issues are staged mainly for attentive publics and constituencies outside parliament, whereas the internal workings of parliament are dominated by (competitive or co-operative) pragmatism in dealing with policy issues. Many MPs find this to be an important role conflict: they have to practice different types of parliamentary behaviour depending on whether it is directed at external or at internal addressees. In addition, the 'rules of the game' that yield successful results regarding the issue-oriented everyday work within parliament differ from those that lead to high levels of popularity and public recognition. So the decision to pursue either the one or the other set of rules more rigorously shapes the further development of one's individual role.

Furthermore, the character of German parliaments as work parliaments makes the key decision-making positions within parliament the most critical casting moulds of legislative roles. This is especially true for the following positions: committee chairman; chairperson of a working group within a parliamentary group;[5] spokesperson of a parliamentary group on a committee; spokesperson or policy expert on a specific policy area of a parliamentary group; rapporteur on an (important) piece of legislation. Parliamentary colleagues attach quite specific (though mostly informal) role expectations to these positions. An MP has to live up to those expectations and to undergo a challenging process of professionalisation if he intends to be promoted within the hierarchy of his parliamentary group.

Quite a few German MPs are assuming such political leadership responsibilities, even though 'only' on some lower or medium level of politics. Fifteen per cent of the German MPs are committee chairpersons; 33 per cent chair a working group formed by their parliamentary group; 53 per cent are spokespersons for a specific policy area; 28 per cent are members of a parliamentary group's executive committee; and six per cent are members of the presidium of a parliament. Hence, the position of backbencher MPs without *any* political influence is seldom found in German parliamentarism. Small parliamentary groups simply cannot afford to have backbenchers,[6] and those found in larger parliamentary groups will usually derive considerable political standing from a 'heavyweight' position in their electoral districts.

These findings notwithstanding, 31 per cent of the German MPs think that most of their fellow MPs do not have a lot of say in their parliamentary groups, whereas only 30 per cent clearly reject that statement. Low levels of MPs' perceived individual influence do not occur as a consequence of small authoritarian leadership groups dominating, within each parliamentary group, an oppressed and obedient mass of backbenchers. Rather, parliamentary groups (and the larger ones in particular) are highly differentiated entities with high levels of internal division of labour. Therefore an individual MP, acting by himself, cannot gain very much influence, whereas the leadership of the parliamentary group, given its capacity of reaching compromises and of forging majorities, has an advantage that an individual MP simply cannot compete with.

Formal votes within a parliamentary group are most frequently preceded by informal agreements. They relate to decisions both on policy issues and on who is to serve in a given position. Therefore, contested votes do not occur very often.[7] Likewise, the elections held within each parliamentary group (usually twice within a four-year legislative term) are not primarily important because of changes in leadership positions. Rather, the *anticipation* of these elections has a significant impact on role behaviour, since only those MPs can keep, or improve, their positions who act both in agreement with the broad medium ranks of their colleagues and keep in touch with the rank-and-file of the parliamentary group. This mechanism helps to select those individuals to important positions who display team-work and team leadership qualities.

## German MPs are Party Leaders

German MPs have strong ties to their parties, the main reason being the system of (personalised) proportional representation employed at German parliamentary elections. On the one hand, a candidate can expect to be elected to parliament if his party places him high up on its state party list. This usually requires his longstanding prior party activities in the course of which close ties between the representative and his party are established.[8] On the other hand, a seat in parliament is won by those candidates who prevail over their rival candidates in single-member electoral districts under the condition of relative majority vote.[9] Of course, only candidates presented by parties that are well established in the constituency have a chance of being elected this way. Therefore, such seats will almost exclusively be won by candidates well tried and experienced in strong party organisations where they have also proven to be capable of prevailing over rivals within their party. Either way, a German MP who is up to retaining his seat in parliament has to maintain a powerful standing within his party ranks.

As a result, not even ten per cent of all German MPs hold *no* party functions at all,[10] whereas 20 per cent hold positions on the local, 38 per cent on the district, and 20 per cent on the state (or national) party leadership bodies. On balance, a little less than two-thirds of all German MPs hold positions as chairpersons or as members of the executive committees on the different organisational levels of their party. Hence, it is no surprise that 77 per cent of the MPs subscribe to the notion that the party is a representative's 'political home' to whom he owes solidarity and loyalty (opposed: five per cent). Accordingly, 49 per cent agree with the statement that a representative should vote along with his party lines even if that might cost him some political support in his electoral district (opposed: 17 per cent). Such loyalty appears to come easy since only 15 per cent of the MPs think that their party restricts individual freedom of decision (opposed: 47 per cent).[11] Indeed, only 21 per cent of those surveyed report that there are frequent conflicts between their own policy positions and those of their parties, whereas a notable 46 per cent of them say such conflicts occurred (relatively) seldom. Thus, it is no real contradiction in terms for a representative simultaneously to exercise a free mandate[12] and – as a party leader on at least the regional level – to remain loyal to his party.

In fact, German political parties are mostly headed by *parliamentarians*, and usually the role of a German MP cannot be separated from that of an (at least informal) party leader.[13] Combining the role of an MP with that of a party leader makes sense not only from the viewpoint of the individual representative, but it is also functional for the governmental system as a whole. The reason is that in Germany parties constitute the central political actors and serve as the main addressees of the people's voting decision. Therefore, they have to closely link and co-ordinate their internal decision-making processes with those of the legislative (and governmental) institutions if there is to be a commonly pursued and well-tuned overall political course adhered to by the party as a whole, by its parliamentary groups and, if they hold a parliamentary majority, by 'their' governments. Obviously the best method of managing this co-ordinative task is to let the same politicians bear political responsibility in both their parties and in parliament (or even in the executive branch of government). That way they can be held accountable, by the punishment of losing the support of their party, for legislative decisions and executive branch policies. As a matter of course, this is a central control mechanism in democratic politics.

### Role-Shaping Effects of Interest Groups

In German politics, strong interest groups are important political actors and role partners of MPs. According to rules of procedures, interest groups must be consulted when new bills are drafted. Moreover, parliamentary specialists in given policy areas cannot afford to neglect the expert knowledge provided by interest groups, since doing so would leave MPs to rely solely on the information offered by government sources.[14] Given these reasons, German MPs are frequently and routinely exposed to contacts with relevant interest groups within the context of their legislative policy areas of specialisation. They claim, however, that the interest groups' influence on their own policy positions is moderate at most: 52 per cent of the MPs deny that interest groups have a strong impact on their own decisions, whereas only 11 per cent confirm any strong impact. Likewise, 55 per cent reject the statement that representatives can be talked into reversing their initial policy stances by lobbyists (with 14 per cent accepting that statement). In any event, conflicts between MPs and interest groups occur quite frequently: 49 per cent of the representatives report such conflicts, while only 24 per cent say they are seldom at odds with interest groups. Nevertheless, no more than 26 per cent of the MPs would favour efforts to restrain the political influence of interest groups and associations, but 39 per cent think that calling for such efforts would be wrong.

Besides, close personal ties of MPs with interest groups are a longstanding tradition within German parliamentarism. It is part of the rules of good conduct for a Social Democrat (and for many Christian Democrats) to be a union member. And, in the course of one's political career leading into parliament, dealing with interest groups and associations is clearly an essential part of the professional socialisation along the way. About ten per cent of the German representatives are recruited directly from different kinds of associations, anyway, and 54 per cent of the MPs credit themselves with previous experience of working for an association (hardly any such experience: 24 per cent).[15] So it does not come as a surprise that the MPs' areas of policy specialisation in parliament often follow their associational linkages.[16] In particular, the German parliaments' committees on agriculture are virtually 'owned' by associations of the agricultural sector.

### Role-Shaping Effects of Constituency Work

In west Germany, the way into parliament is normally paved with a necessity of engaging extensively in the activities of civil society and its 'pre-political space'. The ties established in this process usually remain stable even after winning the mandate.[17] Thirty nine per cent of German MPs actually belong to leadership bodies of associations, clubs or citizens' initiatives on the district level, 41 per cent have some functions as members of advisory councils or committees, 27 per cent are active in foundations and patrons' associations and so on. Twenty four per cent serve on expert commissions and on other panels and bodies of the pre-political space, 19 per cent are involved in the fields of education, culture, and the arts, and 15 per cent are engaged in charitable or philanthrophic organisations. Those functions create numerous occasions for an MP's presence in the pre-political space of his electoral district.[18] In addition, 29 per cent of the German MPs also hold a seat in a city or a community council, and 22 per cent serve on district councils.[19]

Given these close linkages with the civil society of the electoral district, it is obvious that for an MP the constituency work is a critical part of holding his office. Consequently, the representatives devote about one-third of their working hours to constituency work.[20] In fact, hardly any representative belonging to one of the big parties (that is, the CDU/CSU or the SPD) can afford to reject the numerous requests from his constituency to appear as a guest at meetings, special events, factory openings and so on at the local level. This is still somewhat less true in eastern Germany, but results from a recent study suggest that processes of adjustment to west German standards are clearly under way in eastern Germany.[21]

What forms an MP's constituency work will take depends largely on the specific shape of the electoral district he takes care of, and its civil society. In addition to the differences still existing between Germany's western and eastern parts (with the latter being characterised by a still underdeveloped civil society), the contrast between city and rural areas is significant. The presence of the MP at numerous social events and at lots of festivities and celebrations organised by local clubs and societies is sought predominantly in rural areas. Participating in these events is very time-consuming, yet they provide excellent opportunities for an MP to make highly visible public appearances in his electoral district. By contrast, the MPs from (big) cities are faced with clearly less 'direct representative duties'. But the downside to the trade-off is that these MPs have a much harder time than their colleagues from rural areas to get their names and their pictures into the newspapers on a regular basis. Whereas small parties or parliamentary groups simply do not have enough MPs to engage in broad-based constituency work, a considerable number of the MPs from the bigger parliamentary groups can afford to focus predominantly on constituency work.[22] At this point, an MP's personal preferences begin to shape central elements of his role as a representative.

*The Formation of East German Parliamentarism as an Example of the Role-Shaping Effects of the Political Systems' Structure and Functioning*

The different casting moulds of the roles of representatives discussed in this article so far are apparently all rooted in the overall structure of the German representative democracy. Obviously, the political system itself provides schemes of orientation and of behaviour that an individual MP can *choose* from, but that he cannot *alter* in any significant way. Thus, MPs' actual roles must be considered predefined by the institutional setting and the functional logic of the system. They cannot be attributed immediately to an MP's individual personality or character. Rather, 'roles of representatives' should be viewed as a given framework an MP enters into, acts within, and adapts to if he wants to succeed in politics. Doing so, the functional logic of the legislative system will shape and trim his role orientations and role behaviour.

Nowhere can this be observed more clearly than in the formation process of east German parliamentarism. After German reunification, the west German parliamentary system of government, as well as the party, interest group and media systems, were simply transferred to the former GDR. By adopting west German law and importing west German manpower and know-how, the new institutions were implemented first, and subsequently the new east German position holders were trained on the job. Therefore, basically the same role orientations known from west German parliamentarism could be discerned among east German MPs as early as in 1991/92, although eastern Germany's new political elite had completely different socialisational and cultural backgrounds. The process of assimilation had progressed even further by 1994.[23] Most of the significant differences between east and west German representatives that remain intact until today exist exactly in those areas where the functional logic of the newly erected system simply could not exert its intrinsic effects. That is true with respect to the insufficient linkages of east German parliaments and parliamentarians with the not yet fully reconstructed civil society in eastern Germany; with regard to the abnormally high legislative workload in east German state legislatures; and with respect to some individual values and attitudes deeply rooted in the east German political culture.

COUNTER-ROLES AND ROLE PARTNERS

The important counter-roles and role partners of German MPs can be grouped into nine categories. *First*, central counter-roles can be found in the executive branch of government and in its subordinated administrative agencies: the role partners of the majority parliamentary groups' chairpersons include the head of the government and the politically most important cabinet members; the chairpersons of the parliamentary committees have 'their' departmental ministers as their most important role partners; and the relevant division heads, deputy heads and subject specialists within the respective governmental departments constitute the role partners of the specialised parliamentary policy experts.

*Second*, and in part determined individually by their specific parliamentary functions, the MPs find their most important role partners within their own parliamentary group and among their colleagues from other parties' parliamentary groups. The chairpersons of the factions' working groups aggregate the expert reports submitted to them by MPs specialising in the given policy areas; and the role partners of those chairpersons include the members of their parliamentary group's executive committee and the chairpersons of the parliamentary committees relevant to the given policy area. Also, policy area specialists and officeholders of one parliamentary group enter into informal routines of co-operation with their counterparts from other parliamentary groups. This, of course, leads to particularly closely connected counter-roles between *coalition* parliamentary groups.

*Third*, the district chairpersons and the members of the party's district executive committee within an MP's electoral district are important role partners, and so are the chairpersons of the parties' specialised working groups, provided their fields of expertise match, or relate to, an MPs' own area of policy specialisation. Since German representatives tend to be regional party leaders, their important role partners also include the leaders of their parties' higher organisational levels. And because the latter usually hold specialised parliamentary or executive branch functions as well, and since these positions may also be held in some other state or its parliament, the resulting overall structure of counter roles turns out to be extraordinarily complex.[24]

*Fourth*, the officials from interest groups of all kinds rank among the important role partners of MPs. In any event, that is true for the interest groups engaging in an MP's primary policy area of specialisation. The higher the level of politics an MP operates in, the more comprehensive and stable the contacts with interest groups will become, until they finally comprise the leading persons of all important interest groups. Neo-corporatist negotiation processes between top-ranking parliamentarians, members of the government, and the leaders of the most powerful interest groups constitute the most spectacular manifestation of such role patterns.[25]

*Fifth*, their own staff members are some of the most important role partners of MPs. Many staff members are simultaneously schedule co-ordinators, gate-keepers, policy consultants, like-minded political comrades, and personal friends.

*Sixth*, the mayors and council commissioners on the community or district levels, and the heads of administrative agencies in the electoral district are important role partners for MPs' constituency work. This is especially true for representatives of state legislatures, because in Germany the principal responsibility for local politics rests with the federal states.

*Seventh*, the chairpersons of local associations, clubs and societies, the sponsors of cultural events in the constituency, the local leaders of social and charitable institutions, and quite often the spokespersons of regional citizens' initiatives are important role partners of the MPs. All of them may become instrumental in helping the MP to establish or to consolidate further his contacts and his links with the civil society of his constituency. They will invite him to attend some of their meetings, social events and festivities, thereby creating opportunities for the MP to make public appearances and enabling him to demonstrate that he continues to be firmly rooted in his constituency and that he still is responsive to the peoples' concerns.

*Eighth*, the role of a journalist constitutes an important counter-role to that of a parliamentarian. An MP simply has to keep in contact with the chief editors and with the most influencial staff writers of the newspapers based in his constituency if he seeks sufficient news coverage. In addition, the MP's office at the seat of the parliament has to co-operate with the reporters and officials representing the big national news media, providing them with press releases and targeted information on current policy issues the MP engages in. In addition, top-ranking MPs tend to enter into nearly 'symbiotic relations' with top-level journalists.

The *ninth* category of counter-roles relates to MPs' contacts with individual citizens. The average citizen does not actually care about his representative very much, and usually he does not notice the MP's efforts to establish grassroots contacts. That neglect does not come as a surprise, since only a small share of ordinary citizens bother to participate in those social and cultural events that provide MPs with access to 'ordinary people'. An even smaller number of citizens actually *does* establish contacts with an MP, but mostly they will confront him with individual problems and expect help in those matters. So the role of a citizen – as a counter-role to that of a representative – is significant rather as a normative concept than in practice. In actual political life, therefore, intermediary organisations are the central linking elements between MPs and civil society, and they, not individual contacts, constitute the *de facto* grassroots basis of the legislative system.[26]

## ROLE ORIENTATIONS AND ROLE BEHAVIOUR

The basic pattern of German MPs' role orientations was studied in 1989 and in 1991/92, when open-ended interviews with a total of 265 MPs from the federal state of Bavaria (54), from eastern Germany (183), and from West Berlin (28) were conducted.[27] They included the question already posed by Wahlke *et al.*:[28] 'How would you describe the job of a legislator, what are the most important things he should do?' The activities named by the MPs as forming the most important aspects of their roles could be grouped into seven categories (see Figure 1): (a) participating in the legislative process; (b) making a contribution to scrutiny of government; (c) collecting and processing information provided by numerous sources and contacts; (d) representing citizens' concerns in parliament ('responsiveness'); (e) exercising political leadership *vis-à-vis* the citizens; (f) providing services to citizens and to their constituency; and (g) fulfilling a 'linkage function', that is, serving as intermediaries between parliament and society.

FIGURE 1

GERMAN PARLIAMENTARIANS' BASIC PATTERN OF ROLE ORIENTATIONS

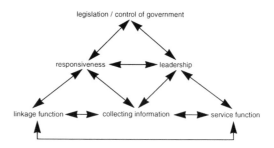

Based on these results, the *intensity* of role orientations was studied in the 1994 survey of all German MPs. Always employing five-point rating scales, the corresponding role behaviour was also assessed.[29] Table 1 lists the means calculated from those scales with respect to both role orientations and role behaviour.[30] The figures presented in the table confirm the findings from the qualitative interview studies, since all role orientations discerned earlier obviously prove to be important. Legislative work in parliament and the scrutiny of government, combined with a readiness to fulfil a 'linkage function', to absorb information extensively and to utilise the knowledge stemming from it in order to turn citizens' concerns into policies dominates

TABLE 1

ROLE ORIENTATIONS AND ROLE BEHAVIOUR OF GERMAN PARLIAMENTARIANS

| | Role orientation West | | Role orientation East | | Role behaviour West | | Role behaviour East | | Role orientation combined | | Role behaviour combined | |
|---|---|---|---|---|---|---|---|---|---|---|---|---|
| | mean | n | mean | n | mean | n | mean | n | mean | n | mean | n |
| *Activities devoted to the control of government* | 1.2 | 311 | 1.3 | 108 | 1.7 | 455 | 1.7 | 160 | 1.2 | 419 | 1.7 | 615 |
| *Participation in the process of legislative work* | 1.4 | 313 | 1.5 | 108 | 2.3 | 454 | 1.7 | 106 | 1.4 | 421 | 2.1 | 614 |
| *Earning political trust: for oneself, party, parliament, political system* | 1.3 | 156 | 1.6 | 56 | – | | – | | 1.4 | 121 | – | |
| *Collecting information from various sources and contacts* | 1.5 | 442 | 1.6 | 155 | 1.9 | 598 | 1.8 | 205 | 1.5 | 597 | 1.9 | 803 |
| *Representation of citizens' concerns in parliament* | 1.6 | 600 | 1.5 | 208 | see below | | see below | | 1.5 | 808 | see below | |
| *'Linkage function' between citizens and parliament* | 1.8 | 443 | 2.1 | 155 | see below | | see below | | 1.9 | 598 | see below | |
|   *Maintaining contacts with the people 'at home' by doing constituency work* | – | | – | | 1.8 | 600 | 1.8 | 203 | – | | 1.8 | 803 |
| *Strengthening the political role of one's party* | 2.0 | 157 | 2.3 | 56 | – | | – | | 2.1 | 213 | – | |
| *Exercising political leadership towards the citizens* | 2.0 | 598 | 2.7 | 207 | see below | | see below | | 2.2 | 804 | see below | |
|   *Negotiations aiming at co-ordination and compromise* | – | | – | | 1.9 | 598 | 2.0 | 202 | – | | 2.0 | 800 |
|   *Exerting influence on the public on local and regional levels* | – | | – | | 2.5 | 599 | 2.8 | 205 | – | | 2.6 | 804 |
|   *Preparing policy concepts and devising strategies; getting them accepted in one's party* | – | | – | | 2.6 | 458 | 2.6 | 159 | – | | 2.6 | 617 |
| *Implementing the policy goals of one's party* | 2.2 | 157 | 2.4 | 56 | – | | – | | 2.3 | 213 | – | |
| *Providing services to citizens, interest groups and local governments* | 2.3 | 444 | 2.5 | 155 | see below | | see below | | 2.3 | 599 | see below | |
|   *Case work for individual citizens* | – | | – | | 2.4 | 595 | 2.6 | 205 | – | | 2.5 | 800 |
|   *Case work for communities and districts* | – | | – | | 2.6 | 590 | 2.6 | 202 | – | | 2.6 | 792 |
|   *Case work for economic interests in the electoral district* | – | | – | | 2.7 | 589 | 2.5 | 205 | – | | 2.6 | 794 |
|   *Case work for interest groups* | – | | – | | 3.0 | 598 | 2.8 | 203 | – | | 2.9 | 801 |
| *Pursuing personal policy preferences* | 2.8 | 157 | 3.0 | 56 | – | | – | | 2.9 | 213 | – | |
| *Focus between parliamentary work 1 vs. constituency work 5* | 2.7 | 433 | 2.7 | 149 | 2.6 | 567 | 2.4 | 201 | 2.7 | 583 | 2.6 | 769 |
| *Importance attributed to case work for individual citizens* | 2.8 | 290 | 2.9 | 109 | 2.8 | 292 | 2.9 | 102 | 2.8 | 392 | 2.8 | 394 |
| *Importance attributed to case work for the electoral district as a whole* | 2.7 | 289 | 2.6 | 101 | 2.8 | 286 | 2.9 | 101 | 2.8 | 390 | 2.8 | 387 |
| *The MP – a 'professional'?* | 1.4 | 156 | 1.7 | 56 | 2.5 | 302 | 3.0 | 110 | 1.5 | 212 | 2.6 | 412 |

*Notes:* Means are based on five-point rating scales used to evaluate statements or descriptions presented to the respondents. Codes: '1' = strong, '5' = weak (unless noted otherwise). The number of cases depends on how many of the four versions of the questionnaire an indicator was included in. Due to rounding errors at weighing, the number of cases among east and west German MPs do not always add up to exactly the total number of cases.

German MPs' role orientations. Neither leadership functions nor case work are normatively neglected. Within that context, legislators regard the securing of political trust and of system legitimacy as priority goals. The MPs also seek to balance generally the attention given to their parliamentary and to their constituency work.

As far as role orientations are concerned, significant differences between west and east German parliamentarians are exceptions. Where the functional logic of the new system could unfold freely, it entailed assimilating effects. It must be admitted that, in normative terms, east German MPs place a significantly smaller emphasis on efforts of political leadership and on increasing their party's political influence; but this still seems to be a reaction to party rule as it was experienced in the GDR. Another difference is east German MPs' normative neglect of their 'linkage function'. It should go back to the unusually weak 'pull effects' emanating from eastern Germany's still underdeveloped civil society.[31] A third striking difference between east and west German parliamentarians concerns the role of a 'professional politician'. Both east and west German MPs, but especially the latter, view holding the office of a representative as a 'real profession'. But all of them, and the east German MPs in particular, are quite reluctant to refer to *themselves* as professional politicians. The fact that most west German MPs do not admit to being professionals seems to be a sign of lacking self-confidence and lacking professional pride, since they undoubtedly *are* professionals, having undergone complex selection processes within their parties and having adjusted and lived up to professional work standards expected from them as parliamentarians. The east German MPs' reservations are, however, understandable, since after German reunification many of them became parliamentarians more or less by accident, and since some of them even voiced their readiness to give up their parliamentary careers after their first term in office.

Generally, the representatives' role behaviour is lagging behind their normative role orientations. Such tensions between normative orientations and reality are quite common both in everyday life and in politics. The most significant differences can be found with regard to work in parliament, where the very high normative emphasis on duties in the legislative arena is not fully matched by role behaviour. The reason might be that role *orientations* are very much an echo of traditional views, whereas the reported role *behaviour* is shaped by one's actual position within an altered parliamentary environment with its modernised communication and interaction structures. Other than that, a detailed look at the variables capturing role behaviour reveals that role orientations match role behaviour quite well. This finding is confirmed by the figures presented in Table 2, where bivariate correlations between attitudinal and behavioural variables are shown.

There are particularly strong correlations where role orientations and role behaviour were measured based on the same statements. This is the case with scrutiny of government, legislative work and collecting information. There are also strong correlations relating to the priorities placed on parliamentary versus constituency work, and with regard to casework and services offered to the constituency.[32] There are weaker correlations between each of the role orientations of 'providing services to citizens and to local communities', 'representing citizens' concerns in parliament ('responsiveness')', 'political leadership', and 'linkage function', on the one hand, and the respective indicators of behaviour on the other hand. But (with a single exception relating to east German MPs) *all correlations are positive*, and they are mostly not too weak.[33]

So it is safe to conclude that role orientations and role behaviour of German representatives match each other quite well. It is true that there are some deviances between their normative role orientations and their actual role behaviour, as is shown by the differences of the means in Table 1 and by the correlation coefficients in Table 2 that are far from 1.0. But we have to acknowledge that there is a multitude of intervening and potentially distorting variables, and therefore any perfect match would come as a surprise. So would any lack of congruence. The reason is that the functional logic of the overall system has far-reaching impacts not only on the role behaviour of any MP who is up to political success, but also on the MPs' role orientations, since such legislators quickly develop a common sense understanding of the system's central functional and structural requirements important to them.[34]

## 'REPRESENTATIONAL ROLES' AND ROLE CONFLICTS

There has been a long debate on 'representational roles' for many years. Its focus was *whose representatives* the MPs perceived themselves to be *primarily*, and whether or not such alleged role orientation had any impact on actual role behaviour. The findings on this subject have been neither unanimous nor convincing.[35] Therefore the figures on 'representational roles' in Table 3 require complex interpretation.

According to the means shown in Table 3, the primary concern of German MPs is to be advocates of the public interest and to side with positions supportive of the common good.[36] A close second to that priority, they view themselves as representing the interests of the people, followed by that of their voters and that of their parties. Supporting the positions of interest groups is the least favoured response. On balance, German MPs view themselves as 'trustees' holding a free mandate, and they would not like to be constrained in their discretion, that is, to act as 'delegates' with a

TABLE 2

CORRELATIONS BETWEEN ROLE ORIENTATIONS AND ROLE BEHAVIOUR

| Role element | West gamma | n | East gamma | n | combined gamma | n |
|---|---|---|---|---|---|---|
| A.  Correlations between identically formulated indicators of role orientation / behaviour | | | | | | |
| Control of government by means of various activities | .64 | 305 | .41 | 154 | .57 | 411 |
| Participation in the process of legislative work | .50 | 305 | .46 | 106 | .45 | 411 |
| Collecting information from various sources/ contacts | .41 | 435 | .41 | 154 | .41 | 589 |
| Focus between parliamentary work vs. constituency work | .62 | 413 | .69 | 146 | .62 | 559 |
| Importance attributed to case work for citizens | .67 | 290 | .67 | 102 | .67 | 391 |
| Importance attributed to case work for the electoral district | .72 | 286 | .59 | 101 | .69 | 387 |
| B.  Correlations between differently formulated or indirect indicators | | | | | | |
| 1. Providing services to citizens, interest groups and local governments with | | | | | | |
| a)  case work for | | | | | | |
| – individual citizens | .49 | 433 | .62 | 152 | .53 | 588 |
| – communities or districts | .42 | 430 | .33 | 152 | .39 | 581 |
| – economic interests in the electoral district | .27 | 429 | .21 | 154 | .24 | 583 |
| – interest groups | .32 | 437 | .25 | 153 | .29 | 589 |
| b)  practical importance of case work for citizens | .38 | 292 | .37 | 102 | .38 | 393 |
| c)  practical importance of case work for electoral district | .36 | 285 | .21 | 101 | .33 | 386 |
| 2. Representation of citizens' concerns in parliament with | | | | | | |
| a)  case work for | | | | | | |
| – individual citizens | .41 | 589 | .18 | 205 | .35 | 793 |
| – communities or districts | .26 | 584 | .44 | 202 | .30 | 786 |
| – economic interests in the electoral district | .30 | 583 | .07 | 205 | .25 | 788 |
| – interest groups | .19 | 592 | .49 | 203 | .26 | 795 |
| b)  practical importance of case work for citizens | .20 | 291 | -.12 | 102 | .13 | 393 |
| c)  practical importance of case work for electoral district | .15 | 284 | .06 | 101 | .12 | 385 |
| 3. Exercising political leadership towards the citizens with | | | | | | |
| a)  negotiations aiming at coordination and compromise | .16 | 589 | .19 | 201 | .17 | 790 |
| b)  exerting influence on the public on local and regional  level | .14 | 590 | .03 | 204 | .14 | 794 |
| c)  preparing policy concepts and devising strategies; getting them accepted in one's party | .19 | 450 | .23 | 159 | .18 | 608 |
| 4. 'Linkage function' between citizens and parliament with ... maintaining contacts with the people 'at home' by doing constituency work | .32 | 437 | .35 | 153 | .33 | 590 |
| 5. The MP – a 'professional'? | .56 | 155 | .51 | 56 | .56 | 211 |

Notes:  The gamma-coefficients are based on the variables listed in Table 1. The number of cases depends on how many of the four versions of the questionnaire an indicator was included in. Due to rounding errors at weighing, the number of cases among east and west German MPs do not always add up to exactly the total number of cases.

TABLE 3

THE 'REPRESENTATIONAL ROLES' OF GERMAN PARLIAMENTARIANS

| Role orientation | West | | East | | Combined | |
|---|---|---|---|---|---|---|
| | mean | n | mean | n | mean | n |
| Representative of the public interest/the common good | 1.6 | 597 | 1.8 | 206 | 1.7 | 803 |
| 'Trustee' | 1.8 | 152 | 1.8 | 55 | 1.8 | 207 |
| Free (1) vs. binding ('imperative') mandate (5) | 1.8 | 449 | 2.1 | 149 | 1.9 | 597 |
| Representative of the citizens in the electoral district | 2.2 | 595 | 2.0 | 207 | 2.1 | 802 |
| Representative of one's party's voters | 2.5 | 595 | 2.1 | 206 | 2.4 | 800 |
| Representative of one's party | 2.8 | 595 | 2.9 | 206 | 2.8 | 797 |
| Representative of close interest groups | 3.5 | 592 | 3.3 | 206 | 3.5 | 798 |
| 'Delegate' | 3.6 | 149 | 3.3 | 51 | 3.5 | 199 |
| When in conflict, decision in favour of: (1) the public interest, (5) constituency interests | 2.3 | 293 | 2.5 | 102 | 2.4 | 395 |

*Notes:* Means are based on five-point rating scales used to evaluate statements or descriptions presented to the respondents. Codes: '1' = strong, '5' = weak (unless noted otherwise). The number of cases depends on how many of the four versions of the questionnaire an indicator was included in. Due to rounding errors at weighing, the number of cases among east and west German MPs do not always add up to exactly the total number of cases.

'binding' or 'imperative' mandate. Indeed, the free mandate-type of a representative's role orientation is the only conceivable arrangement that allows for *both* an orientation towards pursuing the public interest *and* for acting in accordance with a clear sense of obligation towards the people in the electoral district. Within the normative framework of a 'free mandate' there is also no room for a real contradiction between both attitudes. This is shown in Table 4, which displays the bivariate correlations between the indicators of the different 'representational roles'.

Three important findings flow from these data. *First*, 'trustee' and 'delegate' are no mutually exclusive role orientations for German MPs. In a sense, all of them are 'politicos'. There is, however, a basic 'normative feeling', since the correlations of the 'representational roles' of 'trustee' or 'delegate' with the self-placement on the free/binding-mandate scale are absolutely clear. This basic 'normative feeling' seems to go back to those famous traditional (and popular) discussions of this topic which nobody can avoid when thinking about the role of an MP.

*Second*, as part of this basic 'normative feeling', the role orientation of being rather a 'trustee' with a free mandate is clearly accompanied by a tendency towards giving priority to the public interest and the common

TABLE 4

CORRELATIONS AMONG THE 'REPRESENTATIONAL ROLES'
OF GERMAN PARLIAMENTARIANS

| | | Repre-sentative of the voters | Repre-sentative of the citizens | Repre-sentative of one's party | Repre-sentative of interest groups | Repre-sentative of public interest | 'Trustee' | 'Delegate' | Free (1) vs. binding / imperative mandate (5) |
|---|---|---|---|---|---|---|---|---|---|
| Representative of the citizens | West: | .24 | | | | | | | |
| | East: | .00 | | | | | | | |
| | comb.: | .19 | | | | | | | |
| Representative of one's party | West: | .45 | .03 | | | | | | |
| | East: | .45 | .12 | | | | | | |
| | comb.: | .43 | .05 | | | | | | |
| Representative of interest groups | West: | .26 | .12 | .43 | | | | | |
| | East: | .24 | .16. | .47 | | | | | |
| | comb.: | .26 | .14 | .44 | | | | | |
| Representative of the public interest | West: | -.17 | .07 | -.08 | -.09 | | | | |
| | East: | -.13 | -.11 | -.02 | -.16 | | | | |
| | comb.: | -.19 | .01 | -.06 | -.12 | | | | |
| 'Trustee' | West: | -.04 | .18 | -.01 | -.07 | .45 | | | |
| | East: | -.06 | .19 | -.29 | -.30 | .26 | | | |
| | comb.: | .01 | .18 | -.08 | -.05 | .39 | | | |
| 'Delegate' | West: | .38 | .36 | .28 | .41 | -.23 | .01 | | |
| | East: | .04 | .29 | .31 | .45 | -.08 | .09 | | |
| | comb.: | .33 | .35 | .29 | .44 | -.20 | .01 | | |
| Free (1) vs. binding /imperative mandate (5) | West: | -.14 | .16 | -.23 | -.25 | .40 | .23 | -.35 | |
| | East: | .02 | -.21 | -.19 | -.24 | .06 | .53 | -.52 | |
| | comb.: | -.13 | .05 | -.20 | -.26 | .33 | .31 | -.41 | |
| In conflict, decision in favour of: (1) the public interest, (5) constituency interests | West: | -.13 | -.25 | -.02 | -.01 | .29 | -.00 | -.15 | .15 |
| | East: | .08 | -.33 | .22 | -.02 | .31 | .05 | -.39 | .26 |
| | comb.: | -.10 | -.27 | .05 | -.09 | .30 | .01 | -.20 | .19 |

*Notes:* The gamma-coefficients are based on the variables listed in Table 3. The number of cases depends on how many of the four versions of the questionnaire an indicator was included in. Due to rounding errors at weighing, the number of cases among east and west German MPs do not always add up to exactly the total number of cases.

good. By contrast, 'delegates' will prefer siding with interest groups, citizens, voters or parties. On balance, a role orientation towards serving the public interest will generally be perceived as standing in contrast with a role orientation towards serving the positions of special interest groups, groups of voters and so on. Here Rousseau's theorems on the irreconciliability of fostering particular interests *and* of striving for the *volonté générale* find their echo in common sense theories.

*Thirdly*, there are no contradictions between siding with citizens, voters, parties and interest groups. A German MP wants to represent the interests of *all* these target groups combined, when trying to do his job in a professional way. And usually he *can* act in this way, since conflicts with these role partners are not too frequent, as is shown in Table 5.

TABLE 5

GERMAN PARLIAMENTARIANS' FIELDS OF CONFLICT

| Frequency of ... | West | | East | | combined | |
|---|---|---|---|---|---|---|
| | *mean* | *n* | *mean* | *n* | *mean* | *n* |
| a.  Conflicts of a parliamentarian with ... | | | | | | |
| – interest groups | 2.8 | 296 | 2.6 | 102 | 2.7 | 397 |
| – his party | 3.3 | 297 | 3.2 | 102 | 3.3 | 399 |
| – his constituency in general | 3.3 | 295 | 2.9 | 102 | 3.3 | 396 |
| b.  Conflicts between constituency interests and the public interest/common good | 3.3 | 295 | 2.9 | 102 | 3.2 | 397 |

*Notes:* Means are based on five-point rating scales. Codes: '1' = very often, '5' = almost never. Due to rounding errors at weighing, the number of cases among east and west German MPs do not always add up to exactly the total number of cases.

Conflicts between an MP and his party or his constituency in general are infrequent; they occur from time to time, but rarely. Conflicts between broader general interests and interests of the constituency are of slightly higher importance, but do not weigh heavily either. Only conflicts between representatives and interest groups break out rather more frequently.[37] This latter finding is plausible since (unlike the 'constituency in general') interest groups are well organised to articulate their claims efficiently, and since (unlike with regard to parties) MPs usually have little say in the internal decision-making processes of interest groups. On the whole, German representatives are indeed exposed to *potential* conflicts that, in Hanna Pitkin's theory of representation,[38] form the necessary prerequisite for representation. And they apparently succeed in accommodating these conflicts, thereby making representation emerge.

Other forms of role conflict occur where mutual role expectations do not match. Parliamentary newcomers, for example, tend to perceive the division of labour practised within their parliamentary groups as too restrictive to their individual scope of action, whereas senior members of parliament value exactly that 'restricting' division of labour as a precondition for effective work in a parliamentary group. Another role conflict occurs when a party – like Bündnis 90/Die Grünen – establishes an incompatibility between a seat in parliament and party leadership positions. That division entails an MP being kept from the possibility of routinely tuning decision-making processes in the one political arena to those in the other. Further role conflict is caused by the media system: MPs have to choose between holding office as a solid, but hardly publicly noticed, policy expert, or to produce newsworthy events at nearly any cost, even if this prevents any serious work. An MP's frequent constituency appearances, for example, will give him news coverage in the local papers, but will lead to a waste of working time which could better be used for other purposes.[39] Representatives are expected to act as ombudsmen with far more rigour than they feel should be required of them.[40] Finally, it is extremely difficult to combine the role of an MP with a partnership role in private life.[41] So it is not surprising that personal crises and addictive habits, well-known indicators of role stress, are not uncommon among German representatives.[42]

## PARLIAMENTARY SOCIALISATION

Practically all German MPs report that professional socialisation is happening by practising the profession, that is, by 'training on the job', and by observing and copying the way experienced parliamentary colleagues exercise their roles as representatives. Though basic political skills are already acquired in the course of the initial steps on the political career ladder before election as an MP, a parliamentary newcomer will find himself faced with a set of demands and challenges quite unfamiliar to him at first.[43] The following skills especially seem to require practical personal experience: individual time management and sound allocation of work on parliamentary, constituency and party duties; acting both as a specialised policy expert in parliament and as a generalist in the constituency; handling public relations and media affairs; adapting to the informal modes and rules of parliamentary work. An MP simply must accept the fact that he will make some beginner's mistakes and suffer some avoidable political defeats upon first entering his role as a representative, since practical experience can be gained only in a 'trial and error' fashion.[44] Successfully adapting to the functional logic of the legislative system on the part of individual MPs will collectively lead to the reproduction of long-established matters of course and to an amazing continuity of parliamentary practices and customs passed on from one generation of MPs to the next. Such socialisation effects can be interpreted negatively as a 'regrettable imitation and continuation of overcome structures' by parliamentary newcomers.[45] But it seems more adequate to understand them as efficient ways to engender team spirit and to transfer tried skills, or as reliable means of securing the experiences made in the past by institutionally preserving them.

Based on detailed analyses of the 1994 data, the significant socialisation effects of German MPs can be summarised as follows.[46] The longer an MP serves in office, the less likely he is to continue to work in his original job, and the more likely he is to consider himself as a professional politician. Of course, MPs advance to more important roles in parliament and in their parties over time. This career progress is accompanied by easier access to the national and the electronic news media. Likewise, access to and the processing of information that is necessary for the work becomes much more efficient over time. The proportion of time spent on committee work will increase over the years, while the relative time spent on constituency work and on local party work will decrease.[47]

Nevertheless, the chances of re-election increase over time.[48] So Fenno's findings about the interplay of parliamentary and constituency careers are confirmed.[49] In addition, long-term MPs are less likely to view themselves in a 'delegate' way, that is, as direct representatives of the citizens' concerns. They will rather hold their office in a 'trustee' way, keeping the elements of responsiveness and of leadership well balanced. And while continuing to be quite well attuned to the citizens' concerns in practice, senior MPs are also confident in making their own individual judgements. To arrive at this type of role orientation and role behaviour is certainly no bad lesson learnt from experience, since nothing could better match the functional logic of representative democracy.

NOTES

1. In this article, roles are considered (a) as patterns of behaviour the holder of a certain social position exposes; (b) as patterns of attitudes shaped by a position holder's everyday activities and their circumstantial conditions; (c) as systems of concerted expectations linking role actors to their counterparts; and (d) as shared schemes of interpretation. Roles tie social actors into common contexts, which is why there is a counter-role to almost every conceivable role. Combined, roles and counter-roles form social structures that may then be further formalised into organisations or institutions. One can enter into such roles, and often one can also exit them without risking their dismemberment.

2. There has been a lot of research on German MPs and their roles; see the recent *monographs* by D. Herzog, H. Rebenstorf, C. Werner and B. Weßels, *Abgeordnete und Bürger. Ergebnisse einer Befragung der Mitglieder des 11. Deutschen Bundestages und der Bevölkerung* (Opladen: Westdeutscher Verlag, 1990); S. Holl, *Landtagsabgeordnete in Baden-Württemberg. Sozialprofil, Rekrutierung, Selbstbild* (Kehl: Engel, 1989); H. Maier, H. Rausch, E. Hübner and H. Oberreuter, *Parlament und Parlamentsreform. Zum Selbstverständnis des fünften Deutschen Bundestages* (Munich: Vogel, 1979, second rev. edn.); W.J. Patzelt, *Abgeordnete und Repräsentation. Amtsverständnis und Wahlkreisarbeit*

(Passau: Rothe, 1993); id., *Abgeordnete und ihr Beruf. Interviews, Umfragen, Analysen* (Berlin: Akademie, 1995); H. Puhe and H.G. Würzberg, *Lust und Frust. Das Informationsverhalten des deutschen Abgeordneten* (Köln: Informedia, 1989); R. Paprotny, *Der Alltag der niedersächsischen Landtagsabgeordneten. Ergebnisse einer qualitativen und quantitativen Befragung der Mitglieder der 12. Wahlperiode* (Hannover: Niedersächsische Landeszentrale für politische Bildung, 1995). See also H.-U. Derlien and S. Lock, 'Eine neue politische Elite? Rekrutierung und Karrieren der Abgeordneten in den fünf neuen Landtagen', *Zeitschrift für Parlamentsfragen*, 1 (1994), pp.61–94; R. Hrbek and C.-C. Schweitzer, 'Die Deutschen Europa-Parlamentarier. Ergebnisse einer Befragung der deutschen Mitglieder des Europäischen Parlaments', *Aus Politik und Zeitgeschichte*, 3 (1989), pp.3–18; E.-P. Müller, 'Der Bundestag ist gebildeter geworden. Zur Entwicklung des Bildungsstandes der Bundestagsabgeordneten seit 1949', *Zeitschrift für Parlamentsfragen*, 19 (1988), pp.200–219; H. Oberreuter, 'Landtage im Spannungsfeld zwischen Bürgerinitiative und Parteiloyalität', in H.A. Kremer (ed.), *Das Selbstverständnis des Landesparlamentarismus* (Munich: Bayerischer Landtag, 1987); id., 'Role of Parliamentarians and their Relationship with their Electors', *Human Rights Law Journal*, 9 (1988), pp.413–26; E. Rose and J. Hofmann-Göttig, 'Selbstverständnis und politische Wertungen der Bundestagsabgeordneten. Ergebnisse repräsentativer Umfragen', *Zeitschrift für Parlamentsfragen*, 1 (1982), pp.62–84; B. Scholz, 'Bundestag und Volkskammer. Meinungsprofile von Abgeordneten im Vergleich', in D. Herzog, H. Rebenstorf and B. Weßels (eds.), *Parlament und Gesellschaft. Eine Funktionsanalyse der repräsentativen Demokratie* (Opladen: Westdeutscher Verlag, 1993); W.J. Patzelt, 'Legislators of New Parliaments: The Case of East Germany', in L.D. Longley (ed.), *Working Papers on Comparative Legislative Studies* (Appleton: Research Committee of Legislative Specialists, Lawrence University, 1994); slightly modified in A. Agh (ed.), *The Emergence of East Central European Parliaments: The First Steps* (Budapest: Hungarian Centre of Democratic Studies); id., 'Deutschlands Abgeordnete: Profil eines Berufsstandes, der weit besser ist als sein Ruf', *Zeitschrift für Parlamentsfragen*, 27 (1996), pp.462–502.

3. The German national and state governments are all elected by the respective parliaments. In case only the head of the government (who will subsequently appoint his cabinet) is elected by parliament, that election is preceded by a *de facto* binding agreement on the composition of the cabinet as part of a 'coalition agreement'. Minority governments without a permanent parliamentary majority have thus far always been viewed as exceptions that should be avoided. In the past, they only existed for very short periods of time in the wake of governmental crises, until the federal state of Saxony-Anhalt entered into such an experiment in 1994.

4. Only 26 per cent of the German MPs, most of them members of permanent opposition parties, would consider the 'loosening up of party or faction discipline' to be an adequate way of improving the work and the effectiveness of their parliament. By contrast, 46 per cent do not think that would be a good approach. These and all other data presented in this article are taken from a study of German representatives conducted by the author in early 1994. All of the more than 2,800 German MPs on the state and national levels, and of the European Parliament, were surveyed on how they perceive their parliamentary roles, how they actually exert their mandates, and how they are linked to their constituencies and to society. The return rate ranged at about only one-third (n=856), mainly because a lot of elections were held on the European, national and state levels in 1994. Since four different, thematically specialised versions of the questionnaire were used (with each of them sent to a random sample of a quarter of those surveyed), the number of cases for individual variables ranges at about one-fourth of the total number of cases. All results will exclude the responses of 30 members of the European Parliament; the remaining responses of 177 MPs of the German national parliament (Bundestag) and of 638 MPs of the state legislatures will be analysed together. There are some significant differences with regard to role orientations and role behaviour, but those are, by and large, confined to the facts that state MPs are more strongly linked to local governments; that they perceive themselves to be more direct representatives of their voters; and that they place a higher practical value on supporting the positions of interest groups. Other than that, they often view becoming an MP on the national level as a

'continuation' of their parliamentary careers started in the state legislatures, holding that such a change would imply only a change of location, but none regarding their overall job. In the light of all these considerations, it is possible to arrive at meaningful findings with regard to 'the' German MP (that is, not just limited to the members of the Bundestag). The figures reported in this article are mostly based on five-point rating scales, where each of the two 'outer' categories were collapsed. The values completing 100 per cent fall into the middle category: 'partly agree, partly disagree' or 'somewhat'.

5. The variety of parliamentary committees is reflected within those working groups of each parliamentary group.

6. While almost no MP of the smaller parliamentary groups can escape the obligation of assuming some of the somewhat 'more important' roles (for example, becoming the spokesperson for a specific policy area), the larger parliamentary groups practise an extensive degree of division of labour and, consequently, of hierarchical differentiation. In the latter case, fast careers are a rare exception, since climbing the career ladder usually requires some proof of efficiency over a longer period of time.

7. If they do occur, however, some form of prior mismanagement must have happened, for example, violations of the (informal) incumbency or the seniority principles. Another example would be someone who seeks re-election even though he has lost the support of the majority of his colleagues.

8. Seventy seven per cent of the German MPs report long-term party activities and the assumption of different party functions before a seat in parliament was sought; 15 per cent responded 'was not the case'.

9. Most of these candidates are placed on the party list as well, so as to guarantee a seat even when defeated in the electoral district.

10. Being re-elected to parliament without formal party leadership functions is highly exceptional.

11. This result is quite understandable, since 77 per cent of German MPs report to be intensively engaged in forming party politics and platforms. Only five per cent say that this is 'less so' or 'not the case'.

12. Cf. Tables 3 and 4.

13. There are only rare exceptions to that rule. For example, Bündnis 90/Die Grünen have formally decided that a parliamentary mandate is incompatible with holding party functions. But they have in the meantime become painfully aware that not allowing such double functions exposes their MPs to very tiring role conflicts, and that it leads to severe frictions and to decreasing political effectiveness. Thus, though attempting to play the role of representatives against the functional logic of the legislative system appears to be possible over a medium time-span, it proves to be counterproductive already in the short run.

14. Not surprisingly, German MPs view interest groups in a favourable light: 77 per cent of the representatives regard interest groups as an important source of information for their political work; 58 per cent state that interest groups have a significant impact on their work, and 41 per cent of those surveyed say they consider interest groups to be valuable indicators of public opinion. More generally, 54 per cent of the MPs think that, as constitutive elements of an open society's pluralist principles, it is not only legitimate but indeed desirable that interest groups seek to influence political parties, with 53 per cent approving of attempts to influence representatives and parliaments, and 47 per cent in favour of lobbying efforts directed at the government.

15. Forty six per cent of the MPs think such work experience with associations is important and useful, only 14 per cent consider it not very important.

16. Forty six per cent of the German MPs belong to associations of the social sector (for example, welfare organisations or women's associations), 39 per cent are members of associations in the fields of culture and the arts, education and science. Some further percentage figures on the MPs' associational memberships can be broken down by sector as follows: environmental groups (20 per cent), leisure activities associations (34 per cent), church associations (19 per cent), labour unions (44 per cent), medium and small business associations (14 per cent), employers' associations (six per cent), associations of freelancing professions (ten per cent), other professional associations (14 per cent).

17. This holds true unless severe time constraints on the part of the MP arise, for example, caused by his election to a leadership position within his parliamentary group, or by his appointment to a position in the executive branch of parliament.

18. The practical experience gained from serving in such functions is considered to be important by 59 per cent of the representatives ('not so important': six per cent), and 66 per cent of the MPs fully credit themselves for having made that kind of experience ('rather not': 14 per cent).

19. Seventy per cent of the German MPs acquired some experience with local politics prior to the time they were elected to office ('less so': 22 per cent), with 70 per cent regarding the work experience stemming from those functions as useful and important ('less so': five per cent). Prior to his election to parliament, the average German MP has served on community or city councils for a little over six years, and on district councils for a little over three years.

20. Half of the time is spent on parliamentary work, and the remainder is spent on other obligations that go along with holding office as a representative.

21. See W.J. Patzelt (in co-operation with R. Schirmer), *Repräsentanten und Repräsentation in den neuen Bundesländern* (Dresden: Technische Universität, 1996); and Patzelt and Schirmer, 'Parlamentarismusgründung in den neuen Bundesländern'.

22. Not all of the political heavyweights in the constituency are necessarily backbenchers in parliament. Furthermore, it should be noted that most of the differences between MPs elected via the direct mandate and those elected via a party list can be found in the ways they carry out their constituency work: the representatives elected via direct mandate are more closely linked with local politics and with the civil society in their constituency. This difference is, however, not intrinsically defined by the type of mandate, but is mainly due to the fact that the smaller parties have no, or only very few, MPs elected by direct mandate. With practically all of them elected via party lists, those smaller parties' MPs find themselves in a local political environment dominated by rival political parties, in which there are fewer (and qualitatively different) opportunities for constituency work.

23. Cf. Patzelt, 'Legislators of New Parliaments'; id., 'Repräsentanten und Repräsentation in den neuen Bundesländern'; Patzelt and Schirmer, 'Parlamentarismusgründung in den neuen Bundesländern'.

24. An MP can also draw on additional support from his party in several different forms. Among these the support relating to technical organisational matters is especially important, and 75 per cent of the MPs state that such help is provided frequently. Sixty three per cent of the MPs also cite the moral support offered by their parties as occurring frequently. Fifty eight per cent say they often receive detailed information from their parties, and 51 per cent state that, in response to prior requests for information on specific policy matters, their parties frequently come in handy with well-prepared briefing papers to enable the MP to launch a clearly focused policy initiative.

25. MPs also enjoy different forms of support from interest groups. The most important is that interest groups provide them with detailed expert information; 74 per cent of the MPs cite this as occurring frequently. Getting edited briefing papers from interest groups that position and prepare the MP to launch a clearly focused policy initiative also constitutes an important form of support (45 per cent of the MPs report this to happen frequently), and so does 'moral support' offered for MPs' political work (44 per cent). By contrast, help with technical or organisational matters has no significance with regard to interest groups: only six per cent of the MPs state that interest groups frequently help them organise political events ('rarely': 78 per cent), and only a small portion of the MPs report receiving cash donations ('happens frequently': three per cent; 'rarely': ten per cent) or gifts in kind ('frequently': two per cent; 'rarely': 93 per cent).

26. The concrete networks of counter-roles in the area of an MP's *legislative* work take a different shape than those of his *constituency* work. For a detailed analysis of those differences see Patzelt, 'Deutschlands Abgeordnete', pp. 60–68.

27. But cf. Herzog *et al.*, *Abgeordnete und Bürger*.

28. See J.C. Wahlke, H. Eulau and L.C. Ferguson, *The Legislative System. Explorations in Legislative Behavior* (New York: Wiley, 1962).

29. Early findings from a participant observation study currently conducted by the author on the

role behaviour of MPs during constituency work suggest that assessments of both role orientations and role behaviour offered by MPs can *widely* be considered as valid.

30. In addition to the role orientations detected in 1989 and 1991/92, some further descriptions of role orientations were included in the 1994 survey. Behavioural variables are often based on indirect indicators.

31. It should be noted that east German MPs ascribe a markedly higher significance to their parliamentary and legislative work than do the MPs from western Germany. This is due to the fact that the new east German state legislatures have been predominantly occupied by legislative work, since there was a strong need for new laws in eastern Germany during the initial years after German reunification. In addition, the east German MPs had not yet clearly realised that engaging in extraparliamentary activities is an essential part of a representative's job.

32. Since the latter role elements were captured by directly consecutive items in the questionnaire, the possibility of biased responses (with inflating effects on the correlations) cannot be ruled out here.

33. The weakest correlations occur where the behavioural indicators are too specific to allow for capturing the effects of role orientations on role behaviour adequately. This is especially the case with regard to political leadership. And since 'representing citizen concerns' implies much more than just *case work* and service or allocation responsiveness, even these small coefficients need not stir doubts concerning the general validity of the findings.

34. In this context, it is an important finding that the correlations remain very similar even when contrasting east German with west German MPs. Significant differences are found only in those areas where the reconstruction process of east German parliamentarism allows for a clear causal explanation. In the initial years after reunification, citizens' concerns were predominantly articulated by the local communities and by interest groups, since these intermediary institutions were among the first resuming their functions. At the same time, MPs from eastern Germany did not yet consider case work and services offered to the constituency as intrinsic functions of representatives, and they have continued to underestimate their duties in the field of public relations to the present day. Therefore it can be claimed that these differences between east and west Germany are also remarkable examples of both the role-shaping power of the overall system and of its limits, since in both parts of the country the same legislative system has been implemented.

35. For a thorough discussion of this topic and for further bibliographical notes see W.J. Patzelt, 'Rollen und Rollenorientierungen deutscher Parlamentarier. Probleme und Ergebnisse der Forschung', in *Jahrbuch des österreichischen Parlaments* (Vienna: Manz, 1997).

36. When faced with conflicts between constituency interests and more general national or state-level interests, 60 per cent of the MPs say they would give preference to the latter over the former, whereas only 20 per cent responded inversely.

37. Correlation analyses display strong relationships between the different sources of conflict.

38. See H.F. Pitkin, *The Concept of Representation* (Berkeley: University of California Press, 1967), esp. pp.209ff.

39. Fifty two per cent of the German MPs hold that there are too many such 'representational duties' for German representatives ('not the case': 24 per cent), and 37 per cent even call these duties 'burdensome'.

40. Indeed 61 per cent of the German MPs state they have too little time to reflect upon political problems thoroughly (not the case: 11 per cent), and 53 per cent feel they have too little time to collect and absorb the information they need to do their job (not the case: 12 per cent).

41. Ninety seven per cent of the German MPs think that for a representative there is too little time for private or family life, and 82 per cent of the MPs report that they feel the poor compatability of political role with private or family life to be burdensome.

42. Fifty three per cent of the German MPs think the way representatives are nowadays expected to exercise their mandates poses health threats to them (not the case: 21 per cent); 74, 59, and 55 per cent respectively say that the stress stemming from the demands on their time and on their physical and psychological strength is burdensome.

43. That is why a lot of representatives think that long-term prior work experience as a staff member to an MP is an excellent way of preparing oneself to assume a parliamentary

mandate.

44. The basic maxim to guide those learning processes can be stated as 'I am right or wrong on the grounds of who agrees with me'. Following that guiding principle, the MPs act both as 'hidden apprentices' and as 'practical methodologists' who – regardless of academic theories – seek to acquire the practical know-how of parliamentary work. In doing so, they are under considerable stress of performance, and therefore the common sense theories arrived at should offer quite an accurate picture of the practical working of parliament and of the personally relevant parts of its functional logic. Hence, analyses of parliamentary socialisation and of MPs' everyday activities, conducted from an ethnomethodological research perspective, seem to be very useful. For details on the ethnomethodological approach see W.J. Patzelt, *Grundlagen der Ethnomethodologie. Theorie, Empirie und politikwissenschaftlicher Nutzen einer Soziologie des Alltags* (Munich: Fink, 1987); for legislative research (implicitly) carried out in this perspective see R.F. Fenno, 'U.S. House Members in their Constituencies: An Exploration', *American Political Science Review*, 71 (1977), pp.883–917; id., *Home Style: House Members in their Districts* (Boston: Little, Brown, 1978); H. Gottweis, *Die Welt der Gesetzgebung. Rechtsalltag in Österreich* (Vienna: Böhlau, 1989); R. Mayntz and F. Neidhardt, 'Parlamentskultur: Handlungsorientierungen von Bundestagsabgeordneten – eine empirisch explorative Studie', *Zeitschrift für Parlamentsfragen*, 20 (1989), pp.370–87.

45. For an example see B. Badura and Jürgen Reese, *Jungparlamentarier in Bonn. Ihre Sozialisation im Deutschen Bundestag* (Stuttgart: Frommann-Holzboog, 1976).

46. The following findings are based on complex analyses of covariance. Only data of west German MPs were included. In 1994 they had spent a little more than nine years in parliament on average. East German MPs, however, had spent only a little more than three years in parliament in 1994, which is not long enough for an analysis of long-term socialisation effects.

47. The smaller amount of time spent in the constituency is partly due to less time spent on attending events and on contacts with individual citizens. In addition, long-term MPs are less likely to hold additional political functions on the local level.

48. This statement is based on self-assessments of the representatives who ran for re-election in 1994.

49. See Fenno, *Home Style*, pp.171–224.

# The Political Roles of Danish MPs

## ERIK DAMGAARD

This article reviews the fairly limited research on the roles of Danish MPs. Analytically, one may distinguish between roles relating to representation and to decision making. Party is the primary focus of representation, although electoral districts and interest groups are also important to several MPs. In terms of representational style, MPs differ according to party affiliation: party delegate views dominate in leftist parties, whereas trustee convictions dominate in the parties of the centre and right. Decision-making roles generally include subject-matter specialisation. The more specific role behaviour of MPs depends very much upon whether their party is in government or opposition.

## INTRODUCTION

The Danish system of government is parliamentary democracy. The cabinet (government) is responsible to parliament, which can vote a government out of office. On the other hand, the government may dissolve parliament at almost any time. Political parties are very important with respect to the formation and termination of governments, the legislative process, and elections to parliament. In legal constitutional terms Danish MPs are sovereign individuals, but in practice they are certainly also party agents.

### Government Formation

The formal rules on government formation are almost nonexistent; the constitution only states that a government must leave office if a motion of no-confidence is adopted, unless the government calls elections. Informal norms on government formation have developed since the early twentieth century (cabinet responsibility was introduced in 1901). Parties and party leaders are crucial actors in the formation process, which can be quite complicated because the party system, especially since the early 1970s, has been rather fragmented, as explained below. In recent years, the parties have usually not been able to agree on the formation of majority coalitions. Thus, since 1971 only one short-lived (January 1993 to September 1994) majority coalition has been formed.

Erik Damgaard is Professor of Government in the Department of Political Science, University of Aarhus, Denmark.

This means that for decades Danish governments have been over-whelmingly of the minority type, either single-party or minority coalition governments. Generally, these governments have not been very strong or stable. They terminated because they were defeated in important matters, could not enact their policies, or had their support from opposition parties withdrawn.[1]

The other side of the coin is that opposition parties have been able to exert considerable influence in policy making. They were able to defeat government proposals on numerous occasions and, if they could agree among themselves, they could even enact their own policies against the will of governing parties.[2] In this sense, opposition parties and MPs had real and visible policy influence. To some extent this is still true, although the current pattern of opposition party power is one of influence through compromises with the minority coalition formed in September 1994 by Social Democrats, Radical Liberals and Centre Democrats.

*The Party System*

The traditional Danish party system consisted of a nucleus of four 'old' parties and a small and a changing number of other parties.[3] The four old parties – Social Democrats, Radical Liberals, (Agrarian) Liberals and Conservatives – more or less dominated political life until the late 1960s, especially in parliament and government. At the 1966 election the Socialist People's Party entered parliament as a fifth significant party capable of influencing government formation and policy making in many cases. The 1973 election produced no less than five parties in addition to the five just mentioned.

Two of them – the Justice Party and the Communists – had in fact been represented in previous periods that in both cases ended in 1960. The two parties again lost their representation in 1979 and 1981, respectively. However, three newly formed parties entered parliament for the first time in 1973: the Christian People's Party which survived in parliament until 1994 after having participated in different government coalitions in 1982–88 and 1993–94; the Centre Democrats which participated in government coalitions in 1982–88 and 1993–; and the Progress Party which, according to the dominant parties, was a party of protest that should not be allowed to participate in any government, but by its sheer presence it was nevertheless sometimes able to influence government formation and policy making. From the mid-1970s to the mid-1980s a small Left Socialist party was also represented in parliament. In 1994 a new small left-wing party, the Unity List, obtained parliamentary representation.

Put another way, the Danish parliament has been composed of eight to 11 parties since 1973. Among these parties were, during the whole period, the four old parties, the Socialist People's Party, the Centre Democrats and the Progress Party. The current minority coalition is made up of Social Democrats, Radical Liberals and Centre Democrats. It has two opposition parties to the left (Unity List, Socialist People's Party) and three to the right (Conservatives, Liberals, Progress Party).

The electoral system is an important condition for the representation of that many parties. Although technically perhaps a bit complicated to explain, the PR system applied in Denmark basically assures that parties obtaining at least two per cent of the national vote get seats in parliament.[4] As there are 179 members to be elected (out of which four from Greenland and the Faroe Islands), the smallest parties may have only four to five seats. But even tiny parties, especially if located in the political centre, can be crucial for majority formation and thus sometimes quite influential.

MPS' ROLES

A role is the pattern of behaviour and cluster of attitudes expected of persons occupying some position in a social structure, and political roles are thus the behaviour and attitudes associated with political positions.[5] The authors of *The Legislative System* defined a role as 'a coherent set of "norms" of behaviour which are thought by those involved in the interactions being viewed, to apply to all persons who occupy the position of legislator'.[6] It was assumed that legislators adapt their behaviour to the relevant norms.

Danish research on the roles of MPs in this sense is still fairly limited, and some of the studies are rather old, but probably not obsolete. Nevertheless, one may distinguish between roles relating to representation and decision making, respectively, although in practice they are interconnected. The former role types concern the focus and style of political representation, including constituency relationships, while the latter deal with various aspects of parliamentary work in general.

REPRESENTATION

*Focus of Representation*

Studies based on informal interviews with a limited number of MPs and on questionnaires to all members of parliament have investigated the relative importance of party versus electoral district as foci of representation.[7] In a questionnaire study, the members were asked whether they primarily considered themselves as representatives of their constituency, their party, or both to roughly the same degree. The response rate was two-thirds of the MPs who were not ministers of government. The main finding is clearly that members of parliament primarily consider themselves to be representatives of their parties. However, a substantial proportion of the members think that they represent the district as well as the party, and a small number of MPs even gives priority to the district (see Table 1).

TABLE 1

FOCUS OF REPRESENTATION BY PARTY (%)

| Party/Parties | Constituency | Constituency and party | Party | (N) |
|---|---|---|---|---|
| Left Wing* | 0 | 0 | 100 | (12) |
| Social Democrats | 13 | 50 | 37 | (38) |
| Centre Parties** | 6 | 55 | 39 | (18) |
| Liberals | 14 | 50 | 36 | (14) |
| Conservatives | 0 | 83 | 17 | (12) |
| Progress Party | 9 | 36 | 55 | (11) |
| Total | 9 | 44 | 47 | (105) |

*Notes:*   *   Left Socialists, Socialist People's Party.
       **   Radical Liberals, Justice Party, Centre Democrats, Christian People's Party.

Thus, there are differences in the extent to which the district is the representational focus of MPs. Interestingly, these differences turned out to be correlated with reported behavioural variations in a number of respects. For example, MPs who at least to some extent emphasise the importance of the district are more likely than those only mentioning party to have fixed hours for surgeries, to promote matters of local interest, and to give interviews to local media (see Table 2).

TABLE 2

FOCUS OF REPRESENTATION AND REPORTED CONSTITUENCY
RELATIONSHIPS (%)

| Focus | Fixed time for surgeries | Promote local matters | Local contacts to min.* | Interviews in local newspapers** | (N) |
|---|---|---|---|---|---|
| Constituency | 56 | 100 | 56 | 78 | (8-9) |
| Constituency and party | 26 | 63 | 26 | 59 | (37-50) |
| Party | 20 | 35 | 19 | 44 | (42-50) |
| Total | 26 | 53 | 26 | 54 | (92-105) |

*Notes:*   *   Percentage indicates communications from constituency as most important reason for MPs contacts to ministries.
       **   MPs interviewed at least monthly in local newspaper.

MPs may also consider interest groups as important foci of representation, and in the questionnaire study about half of the members answered that they attempted to represent at least one interest organisation.

The study further showed that there was a fair correspondence between the organisations mentioned and those with which MPs reported to be in regular contact. However, MPs are generally much more willing to report contacts to interest organisations in a number of areas than to claim that they represent special interest groups. In a similar way, a vast majority of MPs thinks that the most important task of political parties is to promote common societal interests, while only a minority thinks that the main purpose of parties should be to represent the interests of distinct social groups (see Table 3).

TABLE 3

MPS' ATTITUDES ON MOST IMPORTANT TASK OF PARTIES IN TERMS OF REPRESENTATION (%)

| Party/Parties | Represent distinct social groups | Broker among various interests | Promote common societal interests | (N) |
|---|---|---|---|---|
| Left Wing* | 75 | 8 | 17 | (12) |
| Social Democrats | 35 | 6 | 59 | (34) |
| Centre Parties** | 0 | 6 | 94 | (18) |
| Liberals | 0 | 0 | 100 | (13) |
| Conservatives | 0 | 0 | 100 | (12) |
| Progress Party | 0 | 0 | 100 | (11) |
| Total | 21 | 4 | 75 | (100) |

*Notes:*   \*   Left Socialists, Socialist People's Party.
        \*\*   Radical Liberals, Justice Party, Centre Democrats, Christians People's Party.

## *Style of Representation*

Although party affiliation generally permeates representational attitudes and activities, see below, it is relevant to ask questions about how an MP should vote in cases of conflicts (a) between his/her own conviction and the party posititon, and (b) between own conviction and the position of the majority of his or her voters.

Questions on the latter type of conflict refer to the classic trustee/delegate issue in political representation. According to the Danish constitution, MPs are solely bound by their own consciences and not by any directions given by their electors. The questionnaire data show that the members overwhelmingly agree that their own opinion should prevail in voting in cases of conflict with voter opinions. In this sense Danish MPs are trustees.

But what ought to happen if the conviction of a member conflicts with the party line? According to a voter survey conducted simultaneously with the MP questionnaire, Members of Parliament should vote their conviction at the expense of party policy. But this is not really what the MPs generally think. Although a small majority of MPs agreed with the proposal, the opinions were basically divided along, and to some extent within, party lines (see Table 4)

TABLE 4

HOW SHOULD MPS VOTE IN CASES OF CONFLICT BETWEEN OWN CONVICTION AND PARTY POSITION OR POSITION OF MAJORITY OF HIS/HER VOTERS? BALANCE OF OPINIONS

| Party/Parties | Own conviction (+)/ party position (-) | Own conviction (+)/ voter position (-) | (N) |
|---|---|---|---|
| Left Wing* | -80 | 56 | (9-10) |
| Social Democrats | -16 | 62 | (26-32) |
| Centre Parties** | 86 | 100 | (15-18) |
| Liberals | 60 | 84 | (10-13) |
| Conservatives | 64 | 100 | (11-12) |
| Progress Party | 16 | 64 | (11) |
| All MPs | 16 | 76 | (83-95) |
| All Voters | 64 | 17 | (1857) |

Notes:  *   Left Socialists, Socialist People's Party.
       **  Radical Liberals, Justice Party, Centre Democrats, Christians People's Party.

## Party Variation

The variations in representational style orientations just mentioned divide the several centre, liberal and conservative parties from the parties to their left and right (Socialist People's Party, Social Democrats, Progress Party). The centre, liberal and conservative groups of MPs display strong individualistic attitudes while the Socialists strongly advocate the primacy of party. The Social Democrats and Progress Party MPs are internally split on the issue.

A number of inter-party differences is also found in terms of representational focus. Thus the Socialist People's Party Members of Parliament uniformly claim that they are mainly party representatives while several members of all other groups claim that the district is also important. Furthermore, most members of the Socialist group, and a fair share of the Social Democrats, think that the most important task of parties is to represent distinct social groups, whereas all other MPs emphasise representation of common societal interests. A similar divide exists in answers to the question on whether MPs attempt to represent particular interest groups: the Socialists and the Social Democrats tend to mention a number of groups as foci of representation, whereas other MPs were quite reluctant to do so.

However, this difference does not exclude the fact that members of all parties have regular contacts to various interest groups and organisations.

Thus the Social Democrats and the Socialists have close contacts with labour and white collar organisations, whereas the liberal and conservative parties maintain close contacts with employers', agricultural and industrial organisations. The former parliamentary groups also have well-developed connections with the organisations of, for example, environment protection, consumers, welfare and health.[8]

### Representational Profiles of Parties

The main patterns of the aspects of political representation briefly described above may be summarised in the following way: there is a socialist profile best represented as a pure type by the Socialist People's Party, a liberal-conservative profile best represented by the Conservative People's Party, and a social democratic profile combining features from both these rather pure profiles.

The Socialist MP basically considers himself to be a representative of a party working to promote the interests of distinct social groups to which he and his fellows have close contacts. The party programme, and not a concern with the interests of the electoral district, is important for parliamentary decision making. The party position, and not individual convictions, shall determine voting decisions in Parliament.

Conservative MPs are not only party representatives but also representatives of their electoral constituencies. Parties should not cater for special groups but promote common societal interests. A Conservative claims not to represent special groups but can nevertheless maintain contacts to several of them, including those of employers and business. The party line is of course important in decision making, but in cases of conflict the conviction of individual MPs should be decisive.

The Social Democratic group (the largest in parliament since 1924) combines elements of the two types. Like the Conservatives, Social Democrats emphasise constituency as well as party, but their contacts to interest groups and claimed attempts to represent special groups are closer to the Socialist model. Some of the Social Democrats think, as the Socialists, that the primary purpose of parties is to represent distinct social groups, but most of them claim, like the Conservatives, that parties should promote the common interests of society.

### DECISION MAKING

To understand the patterns of legislative behaviour it is important to be aware of the parliamentary structure in which they occur. The parliamentary organisation to some extent moulds the roles of MPs seeking re-election and advancement within the hierarchy of party positions.

*The Setting*

As already emphasised, party affiliation is crucial to individual MPs in parliamentary work. Several studies based on legislative voting data have shown that the party groups generally are highly disciplined.[9] The very uniform legislative voting behaviour of party group members gives some reason to question the empirical validity of the individualistic style orientation described above on the basis of questionnaire data. There seems to be a discrepancy between what some MPs ideally think should be decisive and what actually happens. However, it is also true that deviations from the party line do occur in some matters, not least in those involving moral judgements and local interests. The latter kind of deviations may obviously reflect a district role orientation, but unfortunately there are no Danish studies empirically linking role orientations to observable behaviour.

The parliamentary party groups are important instruments for division of tasks among its members, including committee memberships and spokesman roles, and for co-ordination of their activities. The leadership of the party groups has crucial functions in these respects, but leadership roles in Denmark have so far not been empirically studied by any rigorous or systematic method.

The system of some 20 permanent specialised committees, established in the early 1970s to scrutinise bills and control government activities, obviously also structures the behaviour of MPs. Henrik Jensen thus shows that the division of tasks within the party groups reflects the committee structure.[10]

Finally, Danish MPs have in recent years acquired access to reasonable, although not extravagant, personnel resources and technical facilities in the performance of their job.[11] This is one of the causes of a general development in recent decades which has led to the creation of professional MPs in Denmark. Other changes contributing to the development include a gradual expansion of the time needed to perform the job, increases of MP salaries to finance that time, and an ever-increasing need for specialised information and knowledge to cope with the problems of contemporary society.

Since the 1950s, roughly speaking, such gradual changes have transformed the Danish Parliament (and many other parliaments in democracies of the modern world) from being one composed of part-time, amateur members managing with modest *per diems* and personal resources, towards one composed of full-time employed and paid members with a need for specialisation and various supporting services.

*Specialisation*

A conspicuous finding in a number of studies is that parliamentary behaviour is specialised in terms of policy area. All MPs to some extent perform specialised roles in the committees and on the floor of Parliament.

A comprehensive investigation of the composition of Danish committees, based on official records and biographical information, found that MPs tend to get committee assignments corresponding to the policy area with which they are familiar from previous education or experience. The study even concluded that 'legislative policy in the various areas to a high extent is controlled by groups of legislators characterized by special relationships with the segments of society most directly affected'.[12] This is still true, as demonstrated in the major new study by Henrik Jensen mentioned above, but of course this is not to say that committee members of different parties always agree among themselves.

When MPs were asked about the reasons for membership of a particular committee, the typical answer given was a 'general interest' in the policy area in question. Several MPs also pointed to special expertise and relevant occupational background.[13] Henrik Jensen obtained similar results in his questionnaire. However, both questionnaire studies just mentioned also showed that membership of committees is sometimes explained by the needs of the party groups to have members on all committees (and not only on those which are attractive to most MPs).

A second finding of the 1977 study concerns the stability of committee memberships over time. It turned out that four-fifths of those who could reasonably be expected to stay on in a committee actually did so. Furthermore, those who continued in the committee were more likely to have a sectoral affiliation than those who left.

The 1977 study also revealed a clear difference with respect to the roles of male and female MPs in the sense that women were 'overrepresented' on some committees (for example, church, culture, education, welfare, legal affairs) and 'underrepresented' on others (for example, agriculture, taxation, economy, market relations). A more recent study shows that such differences between 'reproductive' and 'productive' committee areas still exists.[14] Interestingly, however, this role difference has diminished considerably since the mid-1970s, which also is a period in which the percentage of female MPs has increased from 16 to about 33.

Subject-matter specialisation in the floor activities of MPs was also documented by the 1977 study. It found that a clear majority of participations in plenary debates were performed by party spokesmen in the various areas, and that the spokesmen were normally members of the committees having jurisdiction over the relevant policy areas. In addition, it showed that 'private' participations in debates (that is, participation not associated with the role of party spokesman) dealt with topics within the jurisdiction of committees to which the members belonged.

But the 1977 analysis of floor participation could also conclude that a fair number of interventions in debates and of questions asked were obviously motivated by a concern with district interests in matters not necessarily involving the committees of which the speakers were members. Thus there are clear signs of the district as focus for representational activities on the floor of Parliament.

## Government and Opposition

In analyses of MP roles, a distinction between parties in government and opposition is mandatory. In many ways, but certainly not all, the roles of individual MPs change dramatically with shifts of governments. The Danish political culture is basically one of bargaining and compromise among several parties. Yet, the adversarial government/opposition style is also very much alive. It is almost as if consensus is sought in a great many areas in order to allow for a fierce fight among the major parties about government positions.

It is true that district interests, for example, do not change because a new government is formed. But the behaviour of MPs in most other areas is certainly affected by governmental changes. Opposition leaders and backbenchers use the parliamentary instruments available to further their goals, of course. But members of government parties also must co-operate, and sometimes comply, with the ministers of their parties in parliamentary work.

The role behaviour of government and opposition party members is therefore quite different. Opposition party MPs have to propose private member's bills and resolutions, whereas MPs of government parties may talk to their colleagues in government about desired initiatives, and so on.

Such differences in role behaviour have been demonstrated in various studies. Some of the most recent analyses deal with the questioning activity of MPs. Plenary questions, for example, are almost only asked by opposition members. When the government changes party composition, the party affiliation of questioners in parliament also changes, even overnight. Questions asked in committees follow the same patterns.[15] The two investigations referred to further gave support for a 'distance-from-power' hypothesis in the sense that not only opposition party members but especially members of left- and right-wing opposition parties were most active in questioning activity. Members of governing parties, and of parties co-operating more or less with the government, do not feel a need for using formal questioning procedures to such an extent, as they can use other channels of influence.

## Role Typologies

From several empirical studies typologies of MPs' roles have been, or could be, developed concerning some aspects of representational and decision-making roles.[16] The only attempt to define MPs' roles in the most general sense, however, was made recently by Torben Jensen, who argued that an MP will develop a deliberate 'political style' to cope with the innumerable forces pulling at him with a view to acquire relevant information and to secure power and influence. On the basis of in-depth personal interviews he claims that Danish MPs basically employ three pure strategies (networks, media, matter-of-factness) that can be combined into eight empirical types.[17]

Typologies of MP roles are interesting because they may enhance the understanding of legislative behaviour through simplification of complicated matters. The creation of typologies should therefore be encouraged, but the endeavour is presumably bound to be constrained by contextual factors. Universal typologies will almost inevitably be very abstract and thus limited in terms of empirical content.

## CONCLUDING REMARKS

In conclusion it is suggested that the political roles of MPs be investigated by all methods available. There is no best or optimal method for all purposes. Hence, data from public documents and records, questionnaires, elite and in-depth interviews, standardised interviews, participant observation, and so on should be used. The most important thing is to remember that the appropriateness of methods is contingent upon the research purpose and the questions asked.

Concerning explanations of the role differences, the Danish experiences suggest that at least the following variables should be taken into account: government versus opposition, election system, party ideology, size and organisation of parliamentary party, and gender.

Again, however, it must be stressed that any advance in the comparative analysis of MPs' roles requires a deliberate specification of the dimensions or aspects of role attitudes and behaviour that ought to be studied as the general concept of the MPs' role is far too vague to give any direction to empirical research.

## NOTES

1. See E. Damgaard, 'Termination of Danish Government Coalitions: Theoretical and Empirical Aspects', *Scandinavian Political Studies*, 17 (1994), pp.193–211.
2. These aspects are dealt with in E. Damgaard, 'Denmark: Experiments in Parliamentary Government', in E. Damgaard (ed.), *Parliamentary Change in the Nordic Countries* (Oslo: Scandinavian University Press, 1992); and E. Damgaard and P. Svensson, 'Who Governs? Parties and Policies in Denmark', *European Journal of Political Research*, 17 (1989), pp.731–45.
3. Overviews may be found in M.N. Pedersen, 'The Danish "Working Multiparty System": Breakdown or Adaptation?', in H. Daalder (ed.), *Party Systems in Denmark, Austria,*

*Switzerland, The Netherlands and Belgium* (London: Frances Pinter, 1987); and E. Damgaard, 'Stability and Change in the Danish Party System over Half a Century', *Scandinavian Political Studies*, 9 (1974), pp.104–25.

4. An authoritative account of the Danish election system is J. Elklit, 'Simpler than Its Reputation: The Electoral System in Denmark since 1920', *Electoral Studies*, 12 (1993), pp.41–57.

5. Cf. Geoffrey Roberts and Alistair Edwards, *A New Dictionary of Political Analysis* (London: Edward Arnold, 1951).

6. J.C. Walke, H. Eulau, W. Buchanan and L.C. Ferguson, *The Legislative System* (New York: John Wiley, 1962), p.8.

7. E. Damgaard, *Folketingsmedlemmer på arbejde* (Aarhus: Forlaget Politica, 1979); and E. Damgaard, *Partigrupper, repræsentation og styring* (Copenhagen: Schultz, 1982). Tables 1–4 above are based on the latter study.

8. E. Damgaard, 'The Public Sector in a Democratic Order. Problems and Non-Solutions in the Danish Case', *Scandinavian Political Studies*, 5 (New Series, 1982), pp.337–58.

9. The studies include M.N. Pedersen, 'Consensus and Conflict in the Danish Folketing', *Scandinavian Political Studies*, 2 (1967), pp.143–66; E. Damgaard, 'Party Coalitions in Danish Law-Making', *European Journal of Political Research*, 1 (1973), pp.33–66; P. Svensson, 'Party Cohesion in the Danish Parliament during the 1970's, *Scandinavian Political Studies*, 5 (New Series, 1982), pp.17–42; E. Damgaard and P. Svensson, 'Who Governs? Parties and Policies in Denmark', *European Journal of Political Research*, 17 (1989), pp.731–45; H.C. Mikkelsen, 'Udviklingen i partisammenholdet', *Politica*, 26 (1994), pp.25–31.

10. H. Jensen, *Arenaer eller aktører? En analyse af Folketingets stående udvalg* (Frederiksberg: Samfundslitteratur, 1994).

11. Cf. E. Damgaard (ed.), *Parliamentary Changes in the Nordic Countries* (Oslo: Scandinavian University Press, 1992). In 1995 these resources were further expanded.

12. E. Damgaard, *Folketinget under forandring* (Copenhagen: Samfundsvidenskabeligt Forlag, 1977), p.301.

13. E. Damgaard, *Partigrupper, repræsentation og styring* (Copenhagen: Schultz, 1982).

14. E. Refsgaard, 'Tæt ved toppen. Kvinders placering i Folketingets arbejds- og magtdeling 1965–1990', in D. Dahlerup and K. Hvidt (eds.), *Kvinder på Tinge* (Copenhagen: Rosinante, 1990).

15. E. Damgaard, 'Parliamentary Questions and Control in Denmark', in M. Wiberg (ed.), *Parliamentary Control in the Nordic Countries* (Helsinki: Finnish Political Science Association, 1994); and H. Jensen, 'Committees as Actors or Arenas? Putting Questions to the Danish Standing Committees', in M. Wiberg (ed.), *Parliamentary Control in the Nordic Countries*, pp.77–102.

16. For example, E. Damgaard, *Folketinget under forandring* (1977); *Folketingsmedlemmer på arbejde* (Aarhus: Forlaget Politica, 1979); 'The Function of Parliament in the Danish Political System', *Legislative Studies Quarterly*, 5 (1980), pp.101–21; *Partigrupper, repræsentation og styring* (1982); H.J. Nielsen, 'Politikersamtalerne', in J.G. Andersen et al., *Vi og vore politikere* (Copenhagen: Rockwool, 1992).

17. T.K. Jensen, *Politik i praxis. Aspekter af danske folketingsmedlemmers politiske kultur og livsverden* (Frederiksberg: Samfundslitteratur, 1993); T.K. Jensen, 'Knowledge, Strategy or Prudence. Political Style and Political Rationality among Danish Members of Parliament' (Paper, IPSA Congress, Berlin, 1994).

# Roles, Structures and Behaviour: Norwegian Parliamentarians in the Nineties

## KNUT HEIDAR

The empirical analysis presented in this article gives little reason for disregarding traditional images of the representatives of the Norwegian Storting as egalitarian minded, party based and district orientated. We found few trustees, but many delegates. There were also more MPs of the partisan and constituency varieties than policy advocates and parliamentary men. The most frequent role in the Norwegian Storting, however, was the 'no role' type. Judged on the basis of the history of the Storting as well as the literature describing it, that is more likely to be the truth than an incomprehensible paradox, as the egalitarian nature of the asssembly and the low level of parliamentary institutionalisation is not the best of circumstances for generating firm role models.

In the following I shall present some structures, behavioural characteristics and prospective roles within the Norwegian Storting. Can certain 'roles' be identified as being more central to Norwegian MPs than others? In seeking the role profile of the Storting, I shall focus on some general role types – in particular the classics of Wahlke *et al.* and those suggested in the recent work by Donald D. Searing. Before turning to the empirical discussion, however, some comments on role analysis are warranted. In the next section I will present the main institutional features of the Storting – with its potential for 'formalised roles' – and the major behavioural traits identified in the academic literature. The fourth section will describe the recruitment process and the background of Norwegian MPs from the perspective of socialisation potential. Using a recent (1996) survey of Storting representatives the fifth section will turn to some actual role mapping.

ROLES

The classic literature on parliaments and parliamentarians is full of discussions on tasks, functions and roles.[1] These are conceptualised in very different

Knut Heidar is a Professor in the Department of Political Science at the University of Oslo, Norway. He would like to thank the participants at the Vienna Conference organised by Wolfgang C. Müller in April 1995 for their comments and suggestions. He would also like to acknowledge colleagues at the Storting Survey, Henry Valen and Hanne Marthe Narud, and Frode Berglund who prepared the data for analysis and Johnny Arnesen who did the computer work.

ways and at different levels of analysis, and the 'functions' of parliaments within political systems are not necessarily identical to the 'roles' of individual parliamentarians.[2] Clearly there are links between the levels, and without deviating much from a standard list of functions some prospective parliamentary roles can be extracted.

## 1. Representative Tasks

Identifying conflicts/defining debates, interest articulation, safety-valve for dissatisfaction/complaints and mobilising, informing and educating the electorate. In the Wahlke et al. tradition one can distinguish between the style and focus of representative roles.[3] In particular the 'delegate' role will serve the representative needs of the institution. According to Donald Searing's list of main parliamentary backbench roles, we can also distinguish the 'constituency member' as the main character type aspiring to represent.[4]

## 2. Parliamentary Tasks

Electing a government, controlling the government, developing government alternatives and recruiting, socialising and training government ministers. In Searing's world at Westminster, we find the 'parliamentary man' and to some extent also the 'ministerial aspirants' – later to be recast as 'partisan' – in this category.

## 3. Decision-Making Tasks

Deciding on legislation, deciding on state budgets, reducing conflict and making compromises. Decision making is the main domain of Searing's 'policy advocates'. But those who would like to represent also seek to be present in the decision-making arena.

In order to trace the theoretically interesting behavioural guidelines labelled 'roles', we have to start at the analytical level: What can 'role analysis' do for us? The standard answer is that it should help us to understand why people act as they do, and thus help to predict behaviour. Role analysis is based on the assumption that the internalised norms which constitute a particular role restrict the actor's 'behavioural space'. If the role norms specify a certain action, the likelihood of that action being carried out increases.

Two alternative models explaining behaviour (both currently more in fashion than role theory) would – in their purest forms – argue that the behavioural guidelines can be found either in the actor's structural context/institutional setting or in his/her rational calculation of interests. In principle, there are no absolute barriers between role theory, institutional analysis and rational choice theory. Each of these points to alternative motivational forces – norms, rules and interests – which may be combined analytically in numerous ways. The borders between the models depend on the degree to which one purifies one motive at the expense of the others, or – perhaps more conveniently – defines one type of motivation as 'really' belonging to the other. Institutional structure may, for example, merely provide the actor with the goal or incentive which is to be maximised through action. The pragmatic adaptation of role theory – to be utilised here – would be to argue that 'roles' present us with a convenient *summary* of the actors' goals and attitudes in a way which shapes behaviour. Roles in this sense will supply a useful analytical tool for explaining parliamentary behaviour, but will not erect a clear boundary against the institutional or the rational choice approach.

We should, however, be on guard against using role types as a substitute description. If role shifting becomes excessive, that is, when an actor always changes his or her role when moving from one context to another, the analytical value of these role types decreases. To explain that an MP is acting differently as a committee member, on the House floor or in the party group by enlisting different roles for the different settings, is of little analytical value. We could explain the differences just as easily by drawing attention to the changing context. Role analysis would in this case only be an alternative or substitute description. Drawing a line between role shift and role change is not easy, but role change would have to delve more deeply into the normative structure of the actor. In other words, roles must represent certain robust characteristics if they are to add something worthwhile to the analytical approach.

Both Wahlke *et al.*'s classic role types (delegate, trustee and national/district orientation) and Searing's backbench roles clearly qualify in terms of robustness. It should be noted, however, that they are at different levels of abstraction (robustness) with the delegate role enlisting fewer connotations than the policy advocate. This makes the first more analytically daring than the latter, but also more prone to empirical refutation. Whatever their empirical merits, however, both add an analytical cutting edge to a study. Their usefulness must nevertheless be judged on the basis of the empirical insights they generate in understanding/explaining the problem analysed.

## THE STORTING: THE STRUCTURES AND THE PERSONNEL

Having just argued that the usefulness of different role conceptions depends on the problem addressed, however, I will have to admit that no particular behavioural pattern will be discussed in the following. I shall instead present the main structures and behavioural characteristic of the Storting as they are reported in the academic literature.

Roles are shaped by the intertwined effects of structure and culture. Structure is the easiest element to discuss. In general terms, the assertion that organisation, that is, structure, is important in shaping the representatives in the Norwegian Storting is an argument put forth in particular by Hernes and Olsen.[5] Armed with the theoretical tools of Coleman's theory of collective decisions, Gudmund Hernes asks how the functioning of the Storting affects its decision-making process and he claims to explain one-third of the variation in socio-metric choices of the representatives ('who are your closest collaborators') on the basis of structural factors embedded in the committee system of the Storting.[6] Johan P. Olsen does not quantify the institutional impact, but surveys structural variables such as resources and work organisation to evaluate changes in the overall power of the Storting.[7] The structural/institutional approach is also generally pursued by the academic lawyers who are the traditional craftsmen within this domain. Their aim, however, is to excavate the operative, legally binding guidelines for the Storting – whether in the statute book or uncodified. In these terms Per Stavang describes the rules for when a government must go and when it can stay on.[8]

*Parliamentary Politics*

Parliamentary research in Norway is limited, predominantly empirical and based on relatively few data sources. It is also strongly influenced by what King calls the 'Montesquieu formula', that is, a preoccupation with parliament–executive relations.[9] The decline-of-parliament thesis has been the major research hypothesis as well as the recurring conclusion of most studies since the 1960s, although the diagnoses provided more nuance during the 1980s.

The parliamentary breakthrough in Norwegian politics came in 1884. According to the Constitution, the basic formal powers of the Storting include law making, deciding allocations on the state budget and controlling the government. The parliamentarians are elected every fourth year (fixed terms) in multiple-member constituencies according to proportional representation (modified Laguë). Since 1884 the proper balance of power between the Storting and the government has been a recurring topic in political debate. During the inter-war period the political problem was often argued to be that of excessive Storting government ('*Stortingsregjereri*'). The majority governments of the post-war period reversed this balance, but during the 1970s the tide again turned.

Later studies have focused on the divergent forces at work. David Arter has argued, with reference to all the Nordic parliaments, that their policy impact has been reduced. But he too – during the 1970s and 1980s – saw a 'modest revival' in their power position due to the decline of social democratic parties, the occurrence of minority governments and the rise of new-issue political action groups.[10] Johan P. Olsen reported an increase in the importance of the Storting in Norwegian politics during this period,[11] a view supported in later studies.[12] This development was considered to be the result not only of the rise of minority governments, but also of the increase in administrative resources. Hernes and Nergaard focused not so much upon the balance of power between parliament and executive as on the degree to which this is a more or less integrated system.[13] In this approach the 'ebb and flow' of the Storting as an arena of conflict or compromise was just as important for the democratic operation of the system as the relative power of the two institutions.

The two-block character of Storting politics was generally the norm between 1963 and 1990. The Labour Party has been the main pillar of the 'socialist block' since 1945, while the centre-right parties by and large have made up the 'bourgeois', or 'non-socialist', alternative. But even if the left–right dimension is crucial in explaining non-socialist coalition formation and termination in Norway, the explanatory potential increases substantially when more than one dimension – like centre versus periphery – is considered.[14]

*The Speaker's Conference*

Formally the Storting is under the supervision of the Speaker's Conference. This has six members, the presidents and vice-presidents of the three sections into which the Storting is divided: the whole house and its two chambers (Odelsting and Lagting). The Speaker's Conference works on generalist premises and guards the institution of the Storting as a whole – with restrictions flowing from its party proportional composition and inclination towards unanimous decisions. In comparative terms the power of the Speaker is weak, which is often taken as an illustration of the minor part played by hierarchy in the Norwegian parliament.[15] In so far as seniority and hierarchy are operative, they work inside the party groups rather than as elements of the Storting's organisational structure.

*The Committees*

The 14 permanent committees provide the main arena for developing specialist skills within the Storting. Each representative is a member of one – and only one – committee.[16] The committees are divided by functions mirroring by and large the governmental ministries. According to Hernes they constitute the main political arenas within the Storting.[17] The committees are for compromise, while the open debates in the house are for confrontation.[18] Most representatives claim only to have the capacity to follow issues handled within their own committee closely. For other business, they have to trust party colleagues (if any) in the other committees.[19] The lobbying activities in the Storting naturally focus on the committees and on the representatives as committee members.[20]

Hernes also reports that, over time, the representatives both gain control over what interests them *and* subsequently become interested in the things over which they gain control. When the MPs acquire more varied committee experience, the erstwhile 'localist' representatives can turn into 'cosmopolitans'. The party groups are in control of the committee memberships (within the overall package won by party), and the leadership makes use of that power to distribute reward and punishment.[21]

Committee work not only enhances specialisation and provides a setting for compromise on concrete issues, it also serves to integrate the opposition into the power structures of the state. Rokkan's thesis (1966) that opposition survived because it had access to power not in parliament, but through the corporate channel, must – at least under a system of minority parliamentarism – be revised to include the Storting arena.[22] Studying informal contacts, Hernes and Nergaard found a tight-knit cross-party network.[23] The interaction was, as expected, highest between the ruling party(ies) and the government, but the opposition also had its channels to the government. This constituted an 'informally integrated power system' where, Rokkan revised: 'opposition is also position'.[24]

*The Party Groups*

The main and most effective counterforce against specialisation and sectoral interests within the Storting are the party groups.[25] These groups are by some taken to be *the* centre of power within the Norwegian parliamentary system.[26] Within these groups there are hierarchical structures. For example, formally it is the group meeting that decides on committee placements – although in reality this is decided by the group leadership.[27] Party positions on important and controversial issues are prepared by the group board – although formally decided after debates at group meetings.

Individual representatives are expected to abide by the party group decision when an issue comes up for a vote in the house. Roll-call analysis primarily shows the high degree of party discipline found in the Norwegian Parliament. Studies both in the early 1970s[28] and in the mid-1980s[29] give high figures. Bjurulf and Glans reported that as much as 90–96 per cent of the votes (1969–74) were without any party splits, while Shaffer gave an 84 per cent figure for the 1985–86 session. In terms of dimensionality (as measured through these vote analyses) the left–right dimension presents the best description of the political conflicts between the Storting parties in both periods, although in the latter an urban–rural dimension could also be recognised.

A representative *may* dissent, but the norm is that this must be cleared with the leadership in advance. The party leadership may also show different degrees of 'understanding' towards dissenting members, depending on the nature of the issue. Dissent on local issues are the easiest for the leadership to tolerate. The same applies to strongly held ethical views – particularly if they are not explicitly answered in the party programme. But if an issue is addressed in the party programme, a representative can only dissent if he or she has submitted a reservation on this issue *before* the nomination. In short, the committees produce similarities, the party groups reinforce differences.

*Plenary Sessions*

Few believe that it would be possible to influence a decision or to alter the voting with a speech from the Storting rostrum.[30] These speeches usually have a different purpose and are addressed to a wider audience. There have been attempts to discuss the general debates in the Storting in terms of its closeness to the 'Habermasian' norms of 'democratic dialogue' – openness, rationality and responsibility.[31] The conclusion is – no surprise – that the general debates have a long way to go before they fulfil these requirements. They are seen as rather closed (presenting points of views decided elsewhere), conflictual (arguments presented in black and white) and guided by party loyalties.[32]

The 'Question Hour' is primarily the arena of the opposition.[33] The backbenchers are also more active in presenting questions than the party leadership. Furthermore, representatives of the small parties question the ministers more often than the representatives of the large parties, and those with an electorally less secure mandate more often than those with secure mandates. The propensity to ask particular parliamentary questions is clearly related to committee membership as well as to constituency background. This committee link increases in importance with committee tenure, but is inversely related to general seniority in the Storting.[34]

The availability of administrative assistance for the MPs has increased substantially since the 1960s.[35] Although Norwegian MPs remain far less well served than, for example, the MPs in the Swedish Riksdag or the US Congress, there has been an increase in secretarial assistance (both in terms of political and administrative help), office facilities and money. Note, however, that these resources are for the most part controlled by the party groups, not by the individual representatives.

ROOTS: WHO AND HOW

The modest, straightforward appearance/role of the father of the nation figure, Einar Gerhardsen (Prime Minister 1945–51/1955–65), would not have been credible without his own modest background. Generally post-war parliamentarians in Norway belonged to the social elite.[36] Later recruitment studies have also emphasised the importance of political experience and the trend toward a higher degree of political professionalisation.[37] In particular, the extent to which local councils are the training ground for future parliamentarians is unique to Norway. These studies also make the point that, in comparative terms, the Storting is one of the most egalitarian parliaments around.[38] An important characteristic of Norwegian MPs today is also the high degree to which they are recruited from the public rather than the private sector.[39]

Nominations to party lists presented at the Storting election are highly decentralised.[40] The constituency parties (in the 19 counties making up the electoral districts) are in charge, and the selection criteria are very much defined to serve local needs. This means that ticket balancing is a question of representing the various districts within the county, reflecting the organisational strength of the local party units as well as that of significant local organisations (trade unions, and so on). They also seek a fair gender balance, particularly after several parties (since the mid-1970s) started to practice quotas on election lists. Lastly there is no doubt also a need to balance the different political fractions or tendencies within the constituency party.[41]

The importance of local ties is abundantly reflected in studies of parliamentary behaviour and opinion. The political practice of building local or regional alliances to promote local/regional interests, regardless of ideological inclination or party label, is time honoured and not particularly Norwegian. But research stresses the strength of this practice within the Norwegian Storting. Governments seldom fall on such issues, however; they adjust. It is part of the tradition that the governments accept their fate in these matters. The party whip is rarely used when strong local/district interests are at stake, and, if attempted, the chances are that it will not work – like in the Storting vote on the location of a new airport in 1988.[42] Roll-call analysis easily picks up the breakdown in party unity on matters of strong local interest.[43] Parliamentarians also list constituency initiatives as the reason for many of the contacts they have with bureaucracy and ministers.[44] The issues raised by representatives at 'Question Hour' very much reflect local interests. In more general terms, Hernes describes the process as one in which representatives from 'deprived districts' are inclined to exchange influence on national issues for influence over issues of local importance.[45] The 'centre–periphery axis' in politics is, not accidentally, among the export articles of Norwegian political science.[46]

AUDITION

The behavioural and attitudinal characteristics of the Norwegian MPs emerging from the Storting research can be summarised as egalitarian, district oriented and party based. *Egalitarian* because of the weakness of hierarchy and seniority rights as well as the slim powers of the Speaker's Conference and the comparatively modest social elitism of the representatives recruited. *District oriented* because of the decentralised nomination process, the importance of the centre–periphery conflict and the political legitimacy of pursuing local interests even against the party whip. *Party-based* because of the high party clustering seen in roll-call analyses as well as the pivotal position of the party groups within the Storting.

Issuing role predictions on the basis of this would seem doubtful if we did not have some general role models from which to depart. In the following we shall first seek to differentiate between the style and focus of Norwegian MPs. In the tradition following Wahlke *et al.* (1957) we would expect that the *delegates* far outnumbered the *trustees* in the Storting. We would also expect that the *district oriented* dominated over the *nation oriented.* Our second task will be to see if some of Searing's role types are present in the Storting. Given the nature of his types, however, which are closer to the descriptive 'task-motivation' approach, I will exchange his 'ministerial aspirant' with the 'partisan' type.[47] This swap in role types is due both to the egalitarian culture of the Storting (which probably will make it difficult to find the ministerial aspirant by employing the empirical material available, even when he or she actually exists) and to the importance attributed to the party in the Storting literature.[48] Here our expectations will be that the 'partisan' and the 'constituency member' will be the main role types of Norwegian parliamentarians, while the 'policy advocate' and the 'parliament man' (whichever sex) will be more rare.

The data presented below have been collected during the spring of 1996 under a joint project with Norwegian as well as Nordic collaborators.[49] The survey, mostly with fixed response sets, had a response rate of 88 per cent, that is, 145 out of 165 MPs returned the questionnaire.

*Style and Focus*

In terms of *representative style* three questions can be used to seek out the 'trustee', the 'delegate' and the mixed type (called 'politico' by Wahlke *et al.*). The first question reported stems from a battery where the representative was asked to mark six different '*Storting tasks*' on a five-point scale from 'very important' to 'not at all important'. One such task was 'to mirror the opinions of the electorate in important questions'. In Table 1A we see that 19 per cent thought this to be very important, while nine per cent considered it either 'not really' or 'not at all' important. Next we asked about several tasks relating to them personally as MPs. One of these '*personal tasks*' was to 'argue the opinions they personally considered important'. The response set here was 'very', 'fairly', 'not particularly' or 'not at all' important. Twenty five per cent of Norwegian MPs felt it was very important to present opinions they themselves felt were important to the public. Our third indicator of representative style is also a personal task evaluation. Sixty nine per cent considered it very important to 'argue the policies of their party' and no one thought that was not really/not at all important.

TABLE 1

STYLE – DELEGATE OR TRUSTEE

*Table 1A*: Responses indicating representative style. Percentages and weights ( ).

|  | Very important | Fairly important | Neither / Nor | Not particularly important | Not at all important | Total | N |
|---|---|---|---|---|---|---|---|
| Mirror electorates' opinions | 19 (3) | 50 (2) | 22 (1) | 8 (0) | 1 (0) | 100 | 143 |
| Argue personal opinions | 25 (0) | 60 (1) | – | 13 (2) | 2 (3) | 100 | 143 |
| Argue party's policies | 68 (3) | 31 (2) | – | 1 (1) | 0 (0) | 100 | 143 |

Response rate (N=165): 87%

*Table 1B*: Delegate, Politico or Trustee Style according to Party. Percentages.

|  | Mixed Parties* | Left Socialist | Labour | Centre | Christian | Conservative | Progress | Total |
|---|---|---|---|---|---|---|---|---|
| Trustee (2-3) | 17 | 27 | 2 | 7 | 0 | 13 | 33 | 8 |
| Politico (4-5) | 66 | 46 | 41 | 41 | 30 | 66 | 50 | 46 |
| Delegate (6-8) | 17 | 27 | 57 | 52 | 70 | 21 | 17 | 46 |
| Total % | 100 | 100 | 100 | 100 | 100 | 100 | 100 | 100 |
| N | 6 | 11 | 59 | 27 | 10 | 24 | 6 | 143 |

Response rate (N=165): 87%

*Note*: * Free Democrats, Liberal Party and Red Election Alliance.

To find the 'trustees' and the 'delegates' we subsequently graded each question from 0 to 3 – with 3 consistently being the most delegate-like answer.[50] An MP who considered it to be 'very important' to mirror the electorate's opinions viewed personal opinions as 'not at all important' and felt that arguing the policies of their party was 'very important' would have got nine points – which no respondent actually got. In Table 1B the distribution of the 'trustees' (2–3 points), the 'politicos' (4–5) points and the 'delegates' (6–8 points) is presented – overall and according to party.[51] As expected, we find that the delegate role dominates among the Storting representatives. Forty six per cent emerged with the delegate profile in contrast to the eight per cent 'trustees'. The mixed group of politicos was, however, the largest group in the Storting.

Turning to party differences the trustees make a U-shape along the left–right scale. (We disregard those to be found in the mixed parties bag of Free Democrats, Liberals and Red Election Alliance.[52]) Traditional text-book knowledge would lead us to expect that the old caucus parties of the right would bring forward more of the Burkean trustee type than the left-wing parties. Comparing the two traditional main parties of left and right in Norwegian politics, Labour and the Conservative, the text-book is right – even if there are more delegates than trustees among conservative MPs. The 'new left' Socialist Left Party, however, does not fit this image with an equal balance of trustees and delegates in the party group.

As for *representative focus*, the main question is whether we will find the expected degree of strong local ties among Norwegian parliamentarians. Again three questions – presented in Table 2A – give us a basis for excavating the 'district-oriented' versus the 'nation-oriented' representatives. The first question is from the battery on Storting tasks and queries about the importance of the Storting 'making major decisions for the general development in society'. An unsurprising 86 per cent considered that to be 'very important'. The next two questions deal with individual level tasks. Twenty nine per cent indicated that it was 'very important' to 'work with the problems of individual voters who turned to them'. Lastly, 14 per cent actually thought it was 'not particularly important' to 'articulate the interests/opinions of their own region/county'.

Weighting each answer from 0 to 3 gives again a theoretical scale from 0 to 9. In practice it varies from 3 to 8. To model the 'national-oriented' MP we allow a loss of one point on each question, covering all respondents getting at least six points. MPs would qualify if they think that decisions of major importance were very important to the Storting and indicate *either* that requests from individual voters *or* that arguing district interests was 'not particularly important'. Table 2B shows that 17 per cent had a national focus in this sense. As for district orientation we allow for one additional

TABLE 2

FOCUS – NATION OR DISTRICT

*Table 2A*: Responses indicating representative style. Percentages and weights ( ).

| | Very important | Fairly important | Neither / Nor | Not particularly important | Not at all important | Total | N |
|---|---|---|---|---|---|---|---|
| Mirror major societal decisions | 86 (3) | 14 (2) | 0 (1) | 0 (0) | 0 (0) | 100 | 141 |
| Handle requests from individual voters | 29 (0) | 58 (1) | – | 12 (2) | 1 (3) | 100 | 141 |
| Argue interests of own district | 23 (0) | 62 (1) | – | 14 (2) | 1 (3) | 100 | 141 |

Response rate (N=165): 85%

*Table 2B*: District, Mixed and National Focus according to Party. Percentages.

| | Mixed Parties* | Left Socialist | Labour | Centre | Christian | Conser- vative | Progress | Total |
|---|---|---|---|---|---|---|---|---|
| District (3-4) | 33 | 27 | 52 | 52 | 20 | 58 | 40 | 48 |
| Mixed (5) | 17 | 27 | 36 | 30 | 70 | 29 | 60 | 36 |
| National (6-8) | 50 | 46 | 12 | 19 | 10 | 13 | 0 | 17 |
| Total % | 100 | 100 | 100 | 100 | 100 | 100 | 100 | 100 |
| N | 6 | 11 | 58 | 27 | 10 | 24 | 5 | 141 |

Response rate (N=165): 85%

*Note*: * Free Democrats, Liberal Party and Red Election Alliance.

point lost, that is, counting those with a total score of 3 or 4. The reason for this is that only two response options are actually used in the responses to the first question (making major societal decisions). This is either 'very' (86 per cent) or 'fairly' (14 per cent) important to all MPs.[53] This calculus gives a percentage of district-oriented representatives of 47 and a mixed category of 36.[54] The result clearly does not violate established conceptions regarding where the representative focus of Norwegian parliamentarians lies. But even with this operationalisation the district representatives are not a majority in the Storting.

## The World of the Storting

'Political roles ... are particular patterns of interrelated *goals, attitudes*, and *behaviors* that are characteristic of people in particular positions.'[55] According to Donald Searing these three terms are used by politicians and political scientists alike to make sense of 'Westminster's world'. We do not have his rich, in-depth personal interviews which would be necessary to cover all aspects of the political roles in the Storting. Instead, we shall have to resort to the rather crude method of classification based on a combination of survey questions.[56]

Career goals and incentives are at the motivational core of Searing's roles. What can we learn about such goals from the survey questions available to us? The role types developed below are operationally mainly based on attitudes. Starting with our newly brewed 'partisans' type, the party is their arena more than parliament. In public they advocate party policies and in the Storting they act on behalf of their party. The partisans should think it 'very important' for themselves as MPs to argue their party's policies. Not wanting the mouthpieces to qualify (paying easy money to the party norms), we also set the additional requirement for partisans to want the norms for parliamentary work to be 'much' or 'somewhat' stricter when it comes to leaks from internal party discussions. In Table 3A we see that 26 per cent qualified for the partisan role given this operationalisation.

TABLE 3A

ROLE VARIATION IN THE STORTING

| | Types in full* | | Types without mixed cases | |
|---|---|---|---|---|
| | % | N | % | N |
| Partisan | 26 | 36 | 15 | 21 |
| Policy Advocates | 9 | 13 | 8 | 11 |
| Constituency Member | 23 | 32 | 11 | 15 |
| Parliament Man | 6 | 8 | 3 | 4 |
| Mixed | – | – | 14 | 19 |
| No Role | 49 | 71 | 49 | 71 |
| Total | 114 | – | 100 | 141 |

Response rate (N = 165): 85%
*Notes:* * Here all representatives satisfying 'the role requirements' are included under each role type. Since 14 per cent qualify for two roles or more, the total 'percentages' will exceed 100.

**Partisan**: Considers it 'very important' to 'argue ones party's policies' (cf. Table 1A) *and* states that the party norms should be 'much' or 'somewhat' 'stricter than today' in 'not leaking internal party discussions'.

**Policy Advocates**: Do *not* consider 'argue own, party's policies' 'very important' (cf. Table 1A), but ticks *at least one* 'very important' in arguing ten special group interests. ('To argue the interest of': The young,the pensioners, the wage earners, industry, the women, the farmers, teetotalists, the 'new Norwegian' language, the refugees, and the Christians.)

**Constituency Member**: Considers it 'very important' to argue the interest of own region/electoral district (cf. Table 2A).

**Parliament Man**: Considers it 'very important' for the Storting both to 'control the work of the government and the ministers' *and* to 'be the central arena for political debate' *and* to 'take initiative when an issue does not receive attention from the government.

To find the 'policy advocate' – who views his parliamentarian task primarily as pursuing selected causes in order to influence decisions – we first excluded the MP who stated that to argue the party's policies was 'very important', that is, one component in the partisan type. Then we looked at the ten subsequent questions (within the same battery) dealing with special group interests (see Table 3A). The MPs who had only stated that party policies were not 'very' important, but subsequently ticked off *at least one* of the special group interests as 'very important' qualified as a policy advocate. This was nine per cent of the Storting representatives.

The operationalisation of 'constituency member' is very simple and comprises those who consider it 'very important' to 'argue the interests and opinions of their own region/electoral district'. Thirty two MPs or 23 per cent gave this answer. 'Parliament Man' (actually more women than men) was a rather exclusive group within the Norwegian Storting, with a six per cent following. Operationally these were the MPs who ticked off 'very important' on three general Storting tasks: to supervise the work of the government and the ministers, to be the central arena for political debate, and for the Storting to take an initiative when some issues did not receive attention from the government.

Taken together, the role mix of the Storting is fairly close to what we would expect. But then our expectations also guided our operationalisations and hence contributed in creating the role frequencies. Table 3A also shows that 49 per cent of the representatives did not fall neatly into one of the four role types. There can be a substantive as well as a methodological reason for this. Firstly it may actually be the case that half the MPs do not take on a particular role. Role analysis presupposes that the actor internalises a particular cluster of norms *and* that these 'role constructs' capture fairly neat groupings of actors/MPs. One worrying possibility is, however, that norm clusters do not make up neat categories of actors. It may be the case that norm distribution is far messier in real life than in role theories. An alternative interpretation is that our four role types just do not capture the right clusters. Methodologically the reason may be that we do not have the right kind of data or questions to catch these roles among the Storting representatives. But why does every MP 'need' to adopt a role? Two arguments against this may be, first, that the degree to which role adoption takes place at all may be a derivative of the political system as such. And, second, that narrowly defined roles (with a sharp analytical cutting edge in terms of predicting behaviour) are less likely to generate a high number of actors who are actually living out that role.

Operationalisation of role types are based on what seems reasonable from the data and questions available, and are in this sense arbitrary. There are, however, limits to the arbitrariness in terms of the questions and responses employed. There are also limits in the sense that it all becomes meaningless if the criteria are set so narrowly that no MPs are found to fill a role, or – alternatively – so broadly that most representatives qualify or qualify for more than one role. Table 3A shows that 14 per cent of the Storting MPs actually have two different roles, and in the combination matrix (Table 3B) we see that this in particular is the result of the duplication of partisans and constituency members. In the context of Norwegian parliamentary politics this should come as no surprise. We would expect a number of MPs to be devoted representatives both of their party and of their district. There are in other words no particular problems hidden in this special role combination. It rather adds to the validity of the types and their operationalisation.[57]

TABLE 3B

COMBINATION MATRIX (%) N=141

|  | Partisan | Policy Advocates | Constituency Members | Parliamentary Man | Total |
|---|---|---|---|---|---|
| Partisan | 15 |  | 10 | 1 | 26 |
| Policy Advocates |  | 8 | 1 |  | 9 |
| Constituency Members | 10 | 1 | 11 | 1 | 23 |
| Parliamentary Man | 1 |  | 1 | 3 | 6* |

* Six per cent in total due to rounding errors.

TABLE 3C

ROLE VARIATION ACCORDING TO PARTY (%)

|  | Mixed Parties* | Left Socialist | Labour | Centre | Christian | Conservative | Progress | Total |
|---|---|---|---|---|---|---|---|---|
| Partisan | 17 | 27 | 34 | 15 | 0 | 36 | 0 | 26 |
| Policy Advocate | 0 | 18 | 7 | 4 | 20 | 15 | 17 | 9 |
| Constituency Member | 0 | 18 | 24 | 30 | 10 | 32 | 0 | 23 |
| Parliament Man | 0 | 0 | 3 | 15 | 0 | 5 | 17 | 6 |
| No Role | 83 | 46 | 48 | 48 | 80 | 36 | 67 | 50 |
| Total % | 100 | 109 | 116 | 112 | 110 | 124 | 101 | 114 |
| N | 6 | 11 | 59 | 27 | 10 | 22 | 6 | 141 |

Response rate (N=165): 85%

Note: * Free Democrates, Liberal Party and Red Election Alliance.

Table 3C shows role according to party. The figures are small, however, and it only makes sense to comment on the largest parties. We would expect Labour to be the party of the partisans, the Conservatives the party of parliament man, while the Centre Party would be the home of the constituency members. This is wrong according to Table 3C. The partisans dominate both of the two (traditionally) main parties,[58] Labour and the Conservatives. The constituency member makes up about one-third of the party group in both the Centre Party and the Conservative Party. Lastly, there are very few parliament men among the Conservatives; in fact both the Centre and the Progress parties have a larger relative share. Perhaps the party factor is no longer as instrumental in shaping roles as assumed in the old Duvergerian tradition? There may by other factors shaping roles today than ideology (hard to get at now) and the mass party tradition. Although not a theme here, it turns out that education differentiates much better between the role types than party. The higher the representative's education the more likely we are to find a policy advocate and the less likely to find a partisan.

## SUMMARY

Provided that one accepts the adjustments as well as the measurements of Searing's role types as suggested above, the most frequent role to be found in the Norwegian Storting is the 'no-role' type. Judged on the basis of the history of the Storting as well as the literature describing it, that is more likely to be the truth than a paradox. The egalitarian nature of the assembly and the low level of parliamentary institutionalisation is not the best of circumstances for generating firm role models.

The empirical analysis presented in this article gives little reason for disregarding traditional images of the Storting representatives as egalitarian minded, party based and district oriented. We found few trustees, but many delegates. There were also more MPs from the partisan and constituency varieties than policy advocates and parliament men. In terms of the three parliamentary tasks discussed in the introduction to this article, the representative tasks are clearly best served by the Storting personnel, next comes the parliamentary functions and in the third place the decision-making role of the Storting. We are also left, however, with an impression of complexity: half the assembly did not fall into neat role categories and the role combinations – in particular the partisan and the constituency types – made up an additional 14 per cent. The analytical value of a role analysis which describes or prescribes a limited set of roles in parliaments must therefore be balanced against the dangers of oversimplification. But that, one may argue, is the balancing act facing political science in general.

## NOTES

1. P. Norton (ed.), *Legislatures* (Oxford: Oxford University Press, 1990).
2. K. von Beyme, 'The Role of Deputies in West Germany', in E.N. Suleiman (ed.), *Parliaments and Parliamentarians in Democratic Politics* (New York: Holmes and Meier, 1986), pp.154–75.
3. J.C. Wahlke, H. Eulau, W. Buchanan and L.C. Fergusen, *The Legislative System: Explorations in Legislative Behavior* (New York: Wiley, 1962). See Saalfeld and Müller's introduction in this volume.
4. D.D. Searing, *Westminster's World. Understanding Political Roles* (Cambridge, MA: Harvard University Press, 1994).
5. G. Hernes, *Interest, Influence, and Cooperation. A Study of the Norwegian Parliament* (Ph.D. dissertation, The Johns Hopkins University, 1971); J.P. Olsen, *Organized Democracy* (Oslo: Universitetsforlaget, 1983).
6. G. Hernes, 'Stortingets komitésystem og maktfordelingen i partigruppene', *Tidsskrift for samfunnsforskning*, 14 (1973).
7. Olsen, *Organized Democracy*.
8. P. Stavang, 'Parlamentarismen i Noreg', *Tidsskrift for Rettsvitenskap*, 89 (1976).
9. A. King, 'Modes of Executive–Legislative Relations: Great-Britain, France and West-Germany', *Legislative Studies Quarterly*, 1 (1976), pp.11–36.
10. D. Arter, *The Nordic Parliaments. A Comparative Analysis* (London: C. Hurst and Co., 1984), pp.415–16.
11. Olsen, *Organized Democracy*.
12. H. Rommetvedt, 'Norway: From Consensual Majority Parliamentarism to Dissensual Minority Parliamentarism'; and E. Damgaard, 'Parliamentary Change in the Nordic Countries', in E. Damgaard (ed.), *Parliamentary Change in the Nordic Countries* (Oslo: Scandinavian University Press, 1992).
13. G. Hernes and K. Nergaard, *Oss i mellom* (Oslo: FAFO, 1989).
14. H.M. Narud, 'Issue Saliency, Policy Distances and Coalition Bargaining', *West European Politics*, 18 (1995).
15. Olsen, *Organized Democracies*, p.62; K. Strøm, 'Forskjellsbehandling og pragmatisme i norsk parlamentarisme: Stortinget i et komparativt perspektiv', *Norsk Statsvitenskapelig Tidsskrift*, 1 (1985), p.12.
16. We have to make an exception for the enlarged foreign affairs committee.
17. G. Hernes, *Makt og styring* (Oslo: Gyldendal, 1983), p.138.
18. Hernes and Nergaard, *Oss i mellom*, p.192.
19. Hernes, *Makt og styring*, p.142–5.
20. K. Nergaard, *Parti, komite og kontakt. En analyse av stortingsrepresentantenes kontakt med interesseorganisasjonene* (MA thesis, Department of Political Science, University of Oslo, 1987); and T. Nordby, *Korporatisme på norsk 1920–1990* (Oslo: Universitetsforlaget, 1994).
21. G. Hernes, 'Interests and the Structure of Influence: Some Aspects of the Norwegian Storting of the 1960s', in W.O. Aydelotte (ed.), *The History of Parliamentary Behavior* (Princeton, NJ: Princeton University Press, 1977), p.296.
22. S. Rokkan, 'Norway: Numerical Democracy and Corporate Pluralism', in R.A. Dahl (ed.), *Political Oppositions in Western Democracies* (New Haven, CT: Yale University Press, 1966).
23. Hernes and Nergaard, *Oss I mellom*.
24. Hernes and Nergaard, *Oss I mellom*, pp.166 and 219; also H. Rommetvedt, *Partiavstand og partikoalisjoner* (Stavanger: Rogalandforskning, 1991), p.312.
25. P. Stavang, *Parlamentarisme og maktbalanse* (Oslo: Universitetsforlaget, 1964), chapter 7.
26. E. Moe, 'Stortinget', in T. Nordby (ed.), *Stortinget og regjering 1945–1985. Institutsjoner og rekruttering* (Oslo: Kunnskapsforlaget, 1985), p.26.
27. K. Heidar, 'Partigruppene på Stortinget', *Norsk Statsvitenskapelig Tidsskrift*, 11 (1995).
28. B. Bjurulf and I. Glans, 'Från tvåblockssystem till fraktionalisering. Partigruppers och ledamöters röstning i norska stortinget 1969–1974', *Statsvetenskaplig Tidsskrift*, 3 (1976).
29. W.R. Shaffer, 'Interparty Spatial Relationships in Norwegian Storting Roll Call Votes',

*Scandinavian Political Studies*, 14 (1991).
30. Stavang, *Parlamentarisme og maktbalanse*, p.100.
31. Ø. Christensen, *Det norske storting som diskusjonsforum* (Oslo: MA thesis, Department of Political Science, University of Oslo, 1987).
32. Christensen, *Det norske storting som diskusjonsforum*, p.99.
33. S. Kuhnle and L. Svåsand, 'Spørreordningene og politiske profiler i Stortinget 1977–1981', in O. Berg and A. Underdal (eds.), *Fra valg til vedtak* (Oslo: Aschehaug, 1984); L.C. Blichner and J.P. Olsen, *Spørsmål i Stortinget. Sikkerhetsventil i petroliumspolitikken* (Oslo: Universitetsforlaget, 1986); B.E. Rasch, 'Question Time in the Norwegian Storting – Theoretical and Empirical Considerations', in M. Wiberg (ed.), *Parliamentary Control in the Nordic Countries. Forms of Questioning and Behavioural Trends* (Helsinki: The Finnish Political Science Association, 1994).
34. H.C. Høyer, *Organisasjonstilknytning og aktivitet: en analyse av sammenhengen mellom stortingsrepresentantenes fagkommiteplassering og deres debattdeltakelse i Stortinget* (Oslo: MA thesis, Department of Political Science, University of Oslo, 1984).
35. J.W. Grythe, *Utviklingen av sekretariatsfunksjoner i Stortinget: En beskrivelse og drøfting av mulige forklaringer og konsekvenser* (Oslo: MA thesis, Department of Political Science, University of Oslo, 1984); H. Rommetvedt, 'Personellressurser, aktivitetsnivå og innflytelsesmuligheter i et Storting i vekst' (Bergen: LOS-Senteret, 1995).
36. O. Hellevik, *Stortinget – en sosial elite?* (Oslo: Pax, 1969).
37. K. Eliassen, 'Rekrutteringen til Stortinget og regjeringen 1945–1985', in T. Nordby (ed.), *Stortinget og regjering 1945–1985, Institutsjoner og rekruttering* (Oslo: Kunnskapsforlaget, 1985), p.112.
38. Olsen, *Organized Democracy*, p.52; Eliassen, 'Rekrutteringen til Stortinget', p.116.
39. Hernes, *Makt og sstyring*, p.158.
40. H. Valen, 'The Recruitment of Parliamentary Nominees in Norway', *Scandinavian Political Studies*, 1 (1966); H. Valen, 'Norway: Decentralization and Group Representation', in M. Gallagher and M. Marsh (eds.), *Candidate Selection in Comparative Perspective. The Secret Garden of Politics* (London: Sage, 1988).
41. A. Skare, *Nominasjoner. Kandidatutvelgelsens politiske innhold. Politisk utvelging og politiske endringer* (Oslo: MA thesis, Department of Political Science, University of Oslo, 1994).
42. S.S. Nilson, 'Flyplass-saken, et styringsproblem', in K. Midgaard (ed.), *Oppstyr og styring rundt flyplass. Hurum, Fornebu, Gardermoen* (Oslo: Lifo, 1990).
43. Burulf and Glans, 'Från tråblocksystem till fractionalisering', pp.241–50.
44. Hernes and Nergaard, *Oss i mellom*, pp.201–9.
45. Hernes, 'Interests and the Structure of Influence', p.288.
46. S. Rokkan, *Citizens, Elections, Parties* (Oslo: Universitetsforlaget, 1970).
47. In the old days this role type would (without much error) have been labelled 'party man'.
48. See also Rudy B. Andeweg's trichotomy in 'Role Specialization or Role Shifting' in this issue: parliamentarian, partisan and advocate – where the partisan type is based on interaction between MPs and ministers as party representatives. The partisan type is what I call 'Party Man' and this may indeed be a strategy for ministerial appointments in the parties with a governmental potential.
49. The Norwegian group in charge of the Storting survey consists of Hanne Marthe Narud and Henry Valen of the Institute for Social Research, Oslo and the author. This is financed by the Norwegian Research Council. Political candidate Frode Berglund has assisted in coding and the making of the data file, and cand.mag. Jonny Arnesen has done the SPSS analysis necessary to produce the tables found in this article. See also Knut Heidar, Hanne Marthe Narud, Henry Valen and Frode Berglund, 'Rapport om data og datainnsamling for spørreskjemaundersøkelse med stortingsrepresentantene 1996' (Oslo: Department of Political Science, University of Oslo and Institute for Social Research, 1996). The project is also part of a Nordic research collaboration in 'Nordleg', financed by the Nordic research council collaboration in NOS-S, with researchers from the universities of Gothenborg, Aarhus, Tampere and Reykjavik.
50. Mirror electorate's opinions: VI=3, FI=2, NNI=1, rest=0.

Personal opinions: VI=0, FI=1, NRI=2, NAAI=3.
Party's policy: VI=3, FI=2, NRI=1, NAAI=0.
On the two latter questions the category 'neither important nor unimportant' did not exist.

51. The cut-off points were set *a priori* on the basis that it would be 'fair' for a delegate to lose one point on each question, and for a trustee to add one point on each. Clearly this 'fairness' is debatable, but it is a debate which cannot be avoided by methodological niceties. In theory the scale could vary from 0 to 9 summary points, in practice it varied from 2 to 8.

52. This category has no meaning on the left–right scale, but the parties had to be grouped together to protect the anonymity of the respondents.

53. A representative would accordingly qualify to the status of 'district oriented' if stating that societal decisions were very important and at the same time opting for the 'fairly important' response *either* on individual requests *or* on district interests.

54. If administrating the stricter requirement of not more than three points, the share of district representatives drops to nine per cent. This should also be compared to the 23 per cent stating that arguing the interests of district is very important.

55. Searing, *Westminster's World*, p.18.

56. Crude – but definitely more cost effective. The point is, of course – as the good elementary book on methodology will tell us – to avoid reading more into the results than warranted by the methods generating them.

57. Nor does anyone qualify for more than two roles.

58. The Centre Party has one representative more than the Conservative in the 1993–97 Storting. In the 1980s the Conservative Party was about three times as large as the Centre Party in the Storting.

# Role Specialisation or Role Switching? Dutch MPs between Electorate and Executive

## RUDY B. ANDEWEG

In studies of the Dutch Parliament, the only political roles that have been studied explicitly are the representative roles defined by Wahlke and Eulau in the context of the US presidential system. The main drawbacks of this role typology for the study of MPs in parliamentary systems is that it ignores political parties, and that the roles deal only with the interactions between MP and electorate, not with the interactions between MP and government. This article seeks to remedy this situation by defining three roles ('parliamentarian', 'partisan' and 'advocate'). Although the emphasis has shifted over the years from one role orientation to the other, all three roles seem to co-exist. Such a co-existence of roles can be accounted for by different MPs specialising in different roles, or by all MPs switching from one role to another in different contexts. On the basis of interview data the article reaches the conclusion that role switching may be more important, although there is also some evidence of role specialisation.

It is the defining characteristic of a parliamentary, as opposed to a presidential, system of government, that the survival of the government is dependent upon the support of the majority in parliament.[1] Being elected by the governed, MPs are expected to control the government. As a consequence of this linchpin position, MPs maintain relations with citizens as well as with ministers. Any analysis of the roles of MPs in parliamentary systems must take into account these two faces of parliamentary life, and must combine 'representation' and 'executive–legislative relations'.

However, the study of parliamentary roles has been heavily influenced by the American literature, written in the context not of the more common parliamentary system, but in that of the rather exceptional presidential system of government. The separation of powers does not assign to parliament the same linchpin position between electorate and executive as is found in parliamentary systems. As a consequence, American political scientists have concentrated primarily on the repertoire of representative

Rudy B. Andeweg is Professor of Political Science and Dean of the Faculty of Social and Behavioural Sciences at Leyden University, The Netherlands.

roles. Using data from parliamentary studies in the Netherlands,[2] I shall discuss the reception of the American role models, attempt to develop an alternative role model, and discuss the extent to which MPs specialise in a single role, or take on different roles in different contexts.

## FOCUS AND STYLE: THE LIMITS OF AN AMERICAN IMPORT

Of all American scholars working in this field, Wahlke and Eulau, through their model of representative roles, have had the greatest impact on their European colleagues.[3] They distinguish between the focus and the style of representation. The focus of representation refers to the question who is represented: a local constituency, the nation, and so on. The style of representation refers to what Pitkin has coined 'the mandate-independence controversy';[4] to the question whether the MP should act as a delegate, putting the instructions from his constituents above his own judgement, or as a 'Burkean' trustee, who is expected to follow his own judgement.

For a longitudinal impression of the foci of representation of Dutch MPs, we can use the answers MPs gave to the open-ended question 'What do you regard as the most important tasks you have to perform as an MP?'. Table 1 gives the distribution of the representative tasks that were mentioned, broken down according to the focus of representation.[5]

TABLE 1

MOST IMPORTANT TASK OF AN MP, 1972–90 (%)

|  | 1972 | 1979 | 1990 |
|---|---|---|---|
| Representing 'the' voters | 10 | 12 | 7 |
| Representing 'own' voters or party | 4 | 13 | 10 |
| Representing a specific group, organisation, or category | 3 | 2 | 4 |
| Representing a region | 3 | 0 | 0 |
| Representing specific views | 3 | 3 | 6 |
| All representative tasks as percentage of all tasks mentioned | 23 | 30 | 27 |

Table 1 has three striking features. The first is the relatively low percentage of representative tasks among the tasks that were spontaneously mentioned as most important. MPs could mention more than one task, and many MPs mentioned tasks other than representation ('policy making', 'legislation', 'supervising government', and so on), some of them not referring to any form of representation at all. The same pattern emerges in the answers by MPs to the open-ended question what the voters see as the most important task that they, the MPs, ought to perform: a mere eight per cent of the tasks mentioned can be classified as 'representation', compared to 24 per cent for 'supervising the government' (1990 Parliamentary Study). In other words, both according to their own views and according to their perception of their voters' expectations, representation ranks among the most important tasks of an MP, but without in any way overshadowing other tasks such as activities involving executive–legislative relations.

The second striking feature of Table 1 is the apparent absence of geographical representation. The constituency is the most important focus of representation in most American studies, but also in studies of representative roles in many other countries. The explanation is a simple one: since 1917, the Dutch electoral system is a variety of proportional representation in which the whole country is treated as a single electoral district, and voters are presented with national party lists.[6] However, until recently all major parties had decentralised the nomination procedure, sometimes with the explicit purpose of giving an MP the responsibility for communication with a particular part of the country.[7] There is some evidence that this may have resulted in the recognition by MPs of region as a secondary focus of representation. In response to the question 'Do you perhaps also see yourself as a representative of a particular region in addition to being a representative of a political party?' (1990 survey), 54 per cent gave an affirmative answer. However, the facts remain that they did not mention regional representation spontaneously, but had to be prompted, and that for very few of them does it have behavioural consequences: only 18 per cent claim to discuss regional interests with MPs from other parties, coming from the same region, at least several times per month.

The third deviation from the American pattern is again less idiosyncratic to the Dutch case. Table 1 shows that representing one's party or 'own' voters is the most important rival of the whole nation as the focus of representation. This is true for most if not all political systems outside the US, and the failure to incorporate party into models of representation is the most serious weakness of the American import.[8] Parties are weaker and more heterogeneous in the US Congress, whether for historical reasons or because the government's survival is not dependent on the continued support of a parliamentary majority. Dutch political parties are well developed, and in general the position on the party list contributes more to a candidate's election than his or her popularity or rapport with a particular segment of the electorate. Voters may feel represented by a party, rather than by an individual MP. Seen from the perspective of the voters, it can be argued, therefore, that political parties have replaced individual MPs as the principal representative actors. From the perspective of an MP, however, it makes more sense to see the party as one of several potential foci of representation. Although the only 'politically correct' answer to the question of the focus of representation is '"the" voters' (Art. 50 of the

Constitution: 'The States General represent the whole Dutch people'), according to Table 1, there does seem to be a shift away from representing 'the' voters to representing 'my' voters or my party. In the 1990 survey a closed question was specifically designed to ascertain the MP's focus of representation: 'Do you consider yourself primarily a representative of the members of your party, of the voters of your party, or of all voters?' (see Table 2).

TABLE 2

FOCUS OF REPRESENTATION, 1990 (%)

| | |
|---|---|
| Representing the members of my party | 5 |
| Representing the voters of my party | 63 |
| Representing all voters | 32 |
| **N** | **136** |

The second dimension of the Wahlke and Eulau role model refers to the nature of the relationship between the representative and the focus of representation. In the Dutch Parliamentary Studies, MPs were asked 'Suppose that an MP feels that his party's voters think differently about a particular issue than he does, what do you think he should do? Should he cast his vote in Parliament according to the views of his party's voters, or according to his own views?' MPs who advocate adherence to the party voters' views can be regarded as delegates, those who argue that the MP should stick to his own judgement are trustees, and those for whom it depends on the issue form the category of 'politicos' (see Table 3).

TABLE 3

STYLE OF REPRESENTATION WITH PARTY VOTERS AS FOCUS, 1972–90

| | 1972 | 1979 | 1990 |
|---|---|---|---|
| Delegates | 7 | 7 | 9 |
| Politicos | 22 | 29 | 34 |
| Trustees | 71 | 64 | 57 |

It seems that, at least since 1972, the Burkean model is gradually losing ground, not to the instructed delegate, but to the politico for whom 'it depends' whether he follows his party's voters or not. The same development can be seen in the relations between an MP and his parliamentary party. The question whether an MP should stick to his own judgement or not was repeated, but now in the context of a conflict not with the party voters, but with the parliamentary party (see Table 4). Over the last two decades, fewer MPs think that they should put their own judgement above that of the parliamentary party, but here we see an increase not only in the percentage of politicos, but also in that of delegates.

TABLE 4

STYLE OF REPRESENTATION WITH PARLIAMENTARY PARTY
AS FOCUS, 1972–90

|  | 1972 | 1979 | 1990 |
|---|---|---|---|
| Delegates | 7 | 14 | 20 |
| Politicos | 53 | 65 | 69 |
| Trustees | 40 | 22 | 11 |

There are at least two complementary explanations for the ascendancy of the party as focus of representation. First, after 1965, the salaries of MPs were increased so that the need of having a job in addition to a seat in parliament disappeared: membership of parliament has become a full-time profession. This, however, also made MPs financially more dependent on those in charge of their renomination: the party. This financial dependence may have translated in greater political dependence. Second, in that same period, electoral dealignment caused more heated competition between the parties, which in turn led to more party discipline, both in parliament and in the (coalition) cabinet.[9]

The strengthening grip of the party at the expense of the individual and independent MP, as illustrated with the aid of the Wahlke/Eulau model, is an important development that needs to be taken into account in any analysis of the roles of MPs. The fact that we have to treat the parliamentary party as the focus of representation to do so, however, illustrates a weakness of the American import. Is not the parliamentary party the representative of the electoral party, rather than a focus of representation in its own right? We need a role model that gives party its proper place. The increase in the number of 'politicos' among the MPs adds to the unease about the model, because this representative role seems little more than an attractive label for what is otherwise known as the missing value 'don't know'.

## FROM EXECUTIVE–LEGISLATIVE RELATIONS TO PARLIAMENTARY ROLES

From this application of the Wahlke/Eulau model to the Dutch case, it is clear that in a parliamentary system, the analysis of parliamentary roles needs to take into account the impact of political parties and of executive–legislative relations on the lives of MPs. A useful starting point for the search for such roles is Anthony King's typology of 'modes of executive–legislative relations', as it was developed in order to incorporate the impact of parties into the study of executive–legislative relations.[10] King distinguishes five modes: a non-party mode for the interactions between government and parliament as such; an intra-party mode for the relations between governments and governing party backbenchers; an inter-party mode for the relations between government and different parties; an opposition mode for the relations between government and opposition; and a cross-party mode for the relations between government and a parliamentary committee. King's typology has been used to analyse executive–legislative relations in Austria, Germany, and the Netherlands,[11] but not without modifications. In order to eliminate some of the remaining ambiguities in King's definitions of his modes, we have argued elsewhere that it is possible to simplify the typology to three basic modes of executive–legislative relations:[12]

(1)  a non-party mode in which members of 'the' government interact with members of 'the' parliament. This is the classic two-body image of executive–legislative relations, in which parliament is an *institution*, checking or balancing the institution of government.

(2)  an inter-party mode in which ministers and MPs from one party interact with ministers and MPs (or, if it is an opposition party: only MPs) from another party. Within this mode, two sub-modes can be distinguished:

(2a) (only in the case of a multi-party or factionalised one-party government) an intra-coalition mode in which ministers and MPs from one governing party or faction interact with ministers and MPs from another governing party or faction.

(2b) an opposition mode in which ministers and MPs belonging to the governing majority interact with opposition MPs.

The image evoked by the inter-party mode is not one of two bodies engaged in institutional checks and balances, but of the parliamentary/governmental complex as an *arena* in which the ideological struggle between political parties is fought out.

(3)  a cross-party mode in which ministers and MPs combine to interact on the basis of cross-party interests. Here a third image comes to mind, different from both the institution and the arena image: that of the parliamentary/governmental complex as a *marketplace* where social interests are traded in fierce competition.

Just as Wahlke and Eulau's representative roles stood for different patterns of relations with voters, these three patterns of relations between MPs and ministers result in different parliamentary roles of MPs. Although these roles are derived from modes of executive–legislative relations, they are representative roles at the same time, as the focus of representation is a different one for each of the three roles: in the non-party mode, the MP sees his role as a 'parliamentarian', feels loyalty to the institution of parliament, representing 'the' people with the crown; in the inter-party mode, the MP sees himself as a 'partisan', loyal to his political party and its programme, representing his party's voters in a democratic competition with MPs and ministers from other parties; and in the cross-party mode, an MP defines his role as an 'advocate', representing a particular regional or sectoral (but non-partisan) interest, forming alliances with MPs and ministers, regardless of party, who are defending similar or compatible interests, and competing with the representatives of other interests or with the generalists who try to coordinate policies or enforce budgetary discipline.

The most puzzling difference between the two typologies is the absence of the 'partisan' in Searing's analysis. Even the most superficial knowledge of the British House of Commons would lead to the conclusion that its political parties are, if anything, more dominant than their counterparts in the Dutch Parliament. The solution to this puzzle can be found in one of

Although we shall proceed to discuss evidence for the existence of the three roles in the Dutch Parliament, it must be admitted that these roles are developed deductively. In his recent work on roles in the British House of Commons, Searing argues that it is preferable to let the roles emerge from MPs talking about their experiences.[13] It is useful to compare the outcomes of these two approaches. Searing distinguishes 'policy advocates', 'ministerial aspirants', 'constituency members', and 'parliament men' as backbench roles. The similarity between his 'policy advocate' (especially the 'specialist' subtype) and our 'advocate', and between his 'parliament man' (especially the sub-type of the 'Good House of Commons Man') and our 'parliamentarian' is striking and goes beyond the identical labelling. The absence of the 'constituency member' in our typology of roles is easily accounted for by the absence of geographical representation in the Dutch electoral system. For systems where geographical representation is important, this role can be incorporated into the typology as part of the cross-party mode. The absence of 'ministerial aspirants' in our typology is also explained by a Dutch idiosyncracy: recruitment of non-parliamentarians or even non-politicians as ministers has been quite common in the Netherlands,[14] and the constitution prohibits the combination of a ministerial portfolio and a seat in parliament. Moreover, 'ministerial aspirant' is not a parliamentary role as such, but rather a form of anticipatory socialisation into the role of minister, the counter-role to our 'parliamentarian'.

The most puzzling difference between the two typologies is the absence of the 'partisan' in Searing's analysis. Even the most superficial knowledge of the British House of Commons would lead to the conclusion that its political parties are, if anything, more dominant than their counterparts in the Dutch Parliament. The solution to this puzzle can be found in one of

Searing's final footnotes: 'What does not appear at all in our typology, but appears often in typologies published by both MPs and political commentators, is the "role" of the Party Politician or Party Loyalist. This is obviously one of the most important dispositions on the backbenches. But it is a *disposition*, not a role, a disposition like "delegate" or "trustee", a disposition that functions like a decision rule and can be applied by MPs *in any role*.'[15] Here I disagree with Searing, and not only because the distinction between role and disposition is confusing, especially with respect to Wahlke and Eulau's delegates and trustees. It seems unlikely that 'party' is a decision rule for one of Searing's 'constituency members' conducting a surgery. The correlation between the increase of 'policy advocates' in the House of Commons and the decrease of party cohesion in the division lobbies also gives rise to the hypothesis that party is not a general decision rule for 'policy advocates'. If we were to add the 'partisan' to Searing's list of backbench roles, the two typologies become very similar.

## CHANGES OVER TIME

The typology of role orientations can be used to analyse developments in parliamentary culture. Although we do not have survey evidence for the whole history of the Dutch Parliament, each of the three role orientations ('parliamentarian' (non-party mode), 'partisan' (inter-party mode), and 'advocate' (cross-party mode)) is likely to have dominated for a particular period.[16] The label 'non-party mode' implies that before the arrival of disciplined mass parties, the role of 'parliamentarian' probably dominated. This period started with the introduction of ministerial responsibility in 1848 and ended with the widening of the suffrage and concomitant forma-tion of political parties between 1870 and 1920. In those years only 32 per cent of all cabinet ministers were recruited from among the MPs compared to (excluding the period of German occupation) 41 per cent since (53 per cent since 1967).[17] Resignations of ministers or cabinets because of conflicts with parliament were not unusual: between 1848 and 1918 35 individual ministers and 12 cabinets were forced to step down. Since then only ten individual ministers and seven cabinets met with that fate.

Between 1920 and 1965, parties were in existence, but the 'partisan' role orientation was not as dominant as one would expect. Most cabinets were based on oversized coalitions, so that party discipline was not vital to the survival of the government. In order to provide some stability to the then deeply divided, 'pillarised', country, the political elites tacitly adhered to the rule 'let the government govern'.[18] Instead of the development of an inter-party mode, a cross-party mode became visible. Such a mode, and its concomitant role orientation of 'advocate', may have existed before 1917 when the electoral system required a candidate to be elected by absolute majority in a constituency. This may have caused MPs to act as advocates of their district (like Searing's 'constituency members'). Even if the role of 'advocate' existed before 1917, its content changed with the electoral reform of that year. Under the new electoral system, parties present lists of candidates. Some parties, and especially Christian-Democratic parties, underscored their appeal to a socio-economic cross-section of the electorate by putting candidates on their list who represented various interest groups. The growth of neo-corporatist policy-making networks after the Second World War also contributed to this role conception. In addition, the committee system of the Dutch Parliament gradually changed during the first half of the twentieth century from non-specialised standing committees to specialised select committees. All these factors together have facilitated the emergence of the role of 'advocate' in the sense of a representative of a particular social interest.

From 1965 onwards, the role of 'partisan' came to dominate life in the Dutch Second Chamber. Depillarisation of the electorate increased the number of floating voters, and election campaigns became fierce battles for the undecided voters, rather than a ritual mobilisation of the party faithful. For their electoral promises to be turned into governmental policies, it became necessary for the parties to discipline their MPs and ministers more than in the past. As we saw, more ministers were recruited from parliament, and fewer were sent down by parliament. The coalition agreement became a detailed policy document, binding both ministers and MPs of the parties in the governing coalition. From 1972, a governing party's ministers and parliamentary leadership meet each week on the eve of the weekly Cabinet meeting, to prepare that Cabinet's agenda. Party discipline has increased significantly, although it is difficult to gauge actual party cohesion in parliamentary votes accurately as roll calls are rare and dissenters therefore are not registered. The extent of party discipline is such that it even extends to putting a written question to a minister, which, constitutionally, is the right of *individual* MPs. In the 1990 Parliamentary Study 44 per cent of the MPs reported asking prior permission for a written question from the parliamentary party chairperson, 15 per cent from the parliamentary party's executive, and 43 per cent from a parliamentary party committee (with some MPs apparently asking permission from several authorities within the parliamentary party). In Tables 1 and 2 we already saw that the party has become the dominant focus of representation.

ROLE SPECIALISATION OR ROLE SWITCHING?

Despite this development from 'parliamentarian' to 'advocate' to 'partisan' in the role orientations of Dutch MPs, there is considerable evidence that the 'partisan' has not replaced the 'parliamentarian' or the 'advocate' completely, but that all three to some extent seem to coexist.

Role orientations have an empirical as well as a normative side, and especially the role of 'parliamentarian' is still seen by MPs as the most appropriate one. When asked 'who does judge government policy', 40 per cent of the MPs referred to the (opposition) parties and 50 per cent to 'parliament as a whole', but when asked 'who should judge government policy', the (opposition) parties were mentioned by only one per cent, and 95 per cent opted for parliament as a whole. Recently, a committee of all parliamentary party leaders testified to the normative preference for the 'parliamentarian' by complaining that too often MPs use self-restraint in co-legislation and supervision of the government (classical elements of a 'parliamentarian' role) because of complicity in the government's policies, whether from feeling bound by the coalition agreement (part of the 'partisan role' for an MP in the governing coalition), or from having been involved in sectoral policy making (typical of the 'advocate' role).[19]

Apparently, these parliamentary leaders believe that all three role orientations coexist empirically. Some Dutch commentators have predicted the return of the 'parliamentarian', as the waning of ideological differences renders the 'partisan' struggle sterile, and as the fiscal crisis of the state makes the role of 'advocate' of social interests less rewarding.[20] Indeed, there has been a marked revival of parliamentary inquiries and investigating committees in the 1990s to support this prediction. In addition, it is worth remembering that Tables 1 and 2 showed the party and the party's voters to be the dominant, but not the only foci of representation. In Table 2, one-third of all MPs still claimed to represent 'the' voters: the focus of representation of the 'parliamentarian', and in Table 1 four per cent spontaneously mentioned representing a specific group or interest as an MP's most important task, which indicates an 'advocate' role orientation. This four per cent probably underestimates the number of 'advocates', as this is the least politically correct of the three role orientations, just as the number of 'parliamentarians' is probably overestimated.

There are two rival explanations for the continued occurrence of 'parliamentarian' and 'advocate' role orientations in addition to that of the 'partisan' in contemporary Dutch parliaments: either different MPs choose different role orientations, or each individual MP has all three roles in his or her repertoire, and continually switches from one role to another.

*Role Specialisation?*

The case in favour of role specialisation has been argued most recently by Donald Searing in his aforementioned work on the UK Parliament.[21] Searing distinguishes between 'position roles' and 'preference roles'. Position roles are practically forced upon the incumbents of positions that are very demanding, for example, leadership positions; incumbents of less demanding positions, for example, backbench positions, have more freedom to choose their own role orientation. These roles are 'preference roles', and Searing's motivational approach to role theory argues that MPs are driven by different motivations, and that these different motivations in turn lead to different role preferences.

There are signs that such role specialisation does occur in the Dutch Second Chamber. In the first place, it is interesting to note that the focus of representation varies considerably by party. In the 1990 Parliamentary Study MPs from the left most often mention their party's voters as focus of representation (100 per cent of Green Left MPs, 83 per cent of progressive Liberal (D66) MPs, 75 per cent of Labour (PvdA) MPs, but 54 per cent of Christian-Democrat (CDA) MPs, and only 32 per cent of conservative Liberal (VVD) MPs). Second, some answers to the question about an MP's most important task also support the specialisation hypothesis. The following examples from the 1990 Parliamentary Study indicate specialisation in the role of 'parliamentarian':

> 'Representation, of all voters. When I write a letter, I do so as a Member of the Second Chamber and not as a member of a particular political party.'

> 'Being a true representative, an independent representative of the people.'

The following MPs appear to describe themselves as 'partisans':

> 'To propagate what the people who voted for your party think; to realise as much as possible of the election manifesto.'

> 'You are there as a member of your party, also to realise specific political goals.'

Finally, these are examples of, more veiled, answers of 'advocates':

> 'In the first place to carry out the tasks that ensue from my specialisation, but on the basis of what those people whom I represent think. It is not only what the people within the party think, but also what people, in particular in my district, think about my specialisation. That may well lead to conflicts with the parliamentary party.'

> 'To voice the demands and desires of certain groups within the population whom you represent within your policy area.'

However, the same question also prompted answers that indicate that MPs may hold more than one role orientation, such as 'parliamentarian' and 'partisan':

> 'To control the government, to check – free from party interests – whether the country is governed well. Second, and of equal importance, to exercise influence in order to realise as many of my party's aims as possible.'

or 'parliamentarian', 'partisan', and 'advocate':

> 'To keep in touch with the voters, and with the party you represent, and with the relevant policy sector.'

It is therefore worth taking a closer look at the second hypothesis, that MPs constantly switch from one role to another.

*Role Switching?*

It is curious that Searing does not seriously consider this hypothesis. It has, after all, deep roots in the study of representative roles. Back in 1962, Eulau argued: 'Of course even logically contradictory role orientations may be held without the experience of conflict. The legislator may take roles seriatim, one role in one connection but not in another, without any feeling that a problem of consistency is involved.'[22] And after a study of congruence of constituency and legislator opinion on civil rights, social welfare and foreign policy, Miller and Stokes concluded in 1963:

> The findings of this analysis heavily underscore the fact that no single tradition of representation fully accords with the realities of American legislative politics. The American system *is* a mixture, to which Burkean, instructed-delegate, and responsible party models all can be said to have contributed elements. Moreover, variations in the representative relation are most likely to occur as we move from one policy domain to another. No single generalised configuration of attitudes and perceptions links Representative with constituency but several distinct patterns, and which of them is invoked depends very much on the issue involved.[23]

Even where Searing discusses the problem of role conflicts (for example, of ministers who are caught between the conflicting expectations of their ministerial colleagues and civil servants, of their party's backbenchers, and of their constituents), he maintains that politicians resolve such role conflicts by choosing a generalised response on the basis of their own preferences.[24]

However, Searing does not deny that MPs possess a whole repertoire of roles. After assigning scores for each of his role orientations to all his respondents, he argues the case for 'role specialisation' by referring to the fact 'that only 6.5 per cent of all backbenchers had ties among their composite scores. In other words, nearly all of them had only one top score'.[25] However, he admits that 'the remaining three scores were rarely negligible', '(t)he composite scores for the role of the Policy Advocate, for example, show that most backbenchers do dabble in this role', and '(m)uch the same pattern applies to the role of the Constituency Member: nearly everyone does some, but only a minority makes it a principal occupation'.[26] If nearly all MPs appear to play at least two other roles in addition to their specialisation, and if all of them also have a 'partisan disposition', it would seem to be an oversimplification to classify MPs on the basis of a single role orientation, just as odd as classifying great actors as either 'Hamlets', 'Uncle Vanyas' or 'Algy Moncrieffs'.

Other observers of the British Parliament do describe, however implicitly, occasions where individual MPs change roles, such as in Adonis' account of 'partisans' changing gear to become 'parliamentarians' in the context of departmental select committees:

> For the DSCs have engineered a partial but distinct institutional separation between the Commons' machinery for executive scrutiny on the one hand, and its forums for legislative and party political business on the other. The arenas for the latter are the chamber and standing committees ..., both alike battlegrounds in which the last and next general elections are perpetually fought. Departmental select committees are not worlds apart. The governing party has a majority on each committee, and MPs do not mysteriously shed their party colours on entering the committee corridor. But the select committees' modes of operation are fundamentally different from those pertaining in the other forums of the House. ... The behavioural distinctiveness of select committees is therefore essentially a matter of *situation*. For an MP is in a fundamentally different situation in a select committee to what he occupies in his other roles.[27]

In the Dutch Parliament the hypothesis that MPs change roles when the nature of the issue changes, finds support in the 1990 Parliamentary Study. In Table 4 we saw that for most MPs 'it depends' whether an MP should follow his parliamentary party or vote according to his own judgement when there is a conflict between these two. In an open-ended question they were asked on what it would depend which view should prevail. Here are some typical answers:

> 'Follow the parliamentary party, unless in case of ethical issues; indicate in advance that one is going to follow one's own opinion.'

'Follow the parliamentary party if it is important for the recognizability of the party; follow one's own opinion in all other matters, including those of conscience.'

'Follow the parliamentary party if the matter has been written into the coalition agreement and the MP has not objected to that section.'

'In principle: follow the parliamentary party; follow one's own opinion if one has made reservations about the election manifesto on that point in advance.'

'Follow one's own course if conscience plays a part; follow the parliamentary party if one has a different opinion, but it has been arranged in the coalition agreement or in the election manifesto, and no reservations have been made or it is not a matter of principle.'

The answers reveal a widespread consensus: the party prevails whenever the election manifesto or (in case of a governing party) the coalition agreement is involved. In those cases MPs are expected to be 'partisans'. If these two documents are silent on the issue under consideration, other roles may come into play.

We have explored the hypothesis of role switching by asking MPs to identify the best description of executive–legislative relations in different contexts from among the three modes that are related to our three role orientations.

TABLE 5

MPS' PERCEPTIONS OF EXECUTIVE–LEGISLATIVE RELATIONS, 1990

| | Best description of executive–legislative relations | | |
| --- | --- | --- | --- |
| | in general | in budget proceedings | during inquiries |
| Non-party mode ('parliamentarian' role) | 27 | 21 | **73** |
| Inter-party mode ('partisan' role) | **58** | 49 | 25 |
| Cross-party mode ('advocate' role) | 15 | **30** | 2 |

That most MPs play the role of 'partisan' most of the time is confirmed once more by the 58 per cent mentioning the inter-party mode as the generally dominant one in Table 5. Whenever a parliamentary inquiry is set up, or when parliament is debating some government fiasco, 73 per cent identify the non-party mode (with its role of 'parliamentarian') as the dominant pattern of interaction. The cross-party mode, with its role orientation of 'advocate', is mentioned most often in the context of budgetary proceedings, but, somewhat counter-intuitively, nearly half of the MPs feel that even then the 'partisans' set the tone.

However, as we have already mentioned, the role of advocate scores lowest in constitutional desirability, and this may have coloured our respondent's answers. Secondly, the question wording may have been too broad, including as it did both the committee stage and the plenary sessions. In the plenary debates MPs are most likely to be 'partisans', while there is more room for the 'advocate' role in committee meetings. In both the 1979 and the 1990 Parliamentary Surveys, about 80 per cent of the MPs fully agreed that 'as a rule, the parliamentary party allows one considerable freedom of manoeuvre in Parliamentary Committees', while less than five per cent disagreed. This allows MPs to operate as 'advocates' in committees. The influence of this role orientation often extends into the plenary session, but is then disguised as the 'partisan' role. In the 1972 and 1979 Parliamentary Surveys there was widespread agreement with the statement that 'as a rule, one votes according to the advice of the specialist': 80 per cent in the 1972 study and 91 per cent in the 1979 study fully agreed. This statement was not used in the 1990 study, but the answers to a question about the centre of gravity in the parliamentary party's decision-making process, asked in both the 1979 and 1990 studies, indicate that the influence of the specialists (that is, of our 'advocates') in the parliamentary party is increasing rather than decreasing. The importance of committees (of specialists) within the larger parliamentary parties appears to be increasing especially. The conservative Liberal party (VVD) is the only major party where the plenary meeting of the parliamentary party is still that party's centre of gravity (63 per cent) although its specialists are also influential (31 per cent). Apparently, the parliamentary party usually takes its cues from its specialist(s), and thus 'advocate' and 'partisan' roles become indistinguishable for the outside observer.

TABLE 6
DECISION-MAKING CENTRE WITHIN PARLIAMENTARY PARTY, 1979, 1990

|  | 1979 | 1990 |
| --- | --- | --- |
| Parliamentary party meeting | 50 | 26 |
| Parliamentary party leadership | 3 | 9 |
| Parliamentary party committees | 38 | 53 |
| Parliamentary party specialists | 8 | 13 |

So far, we have assumed that MPs automatically switch roles when dealing with different issues, or when entering different arenas: the role of 'partisan' is related to politically controversial issues on which the party has taken a position in its manifesto or in the coalition agreement. MPs play this role primarily in plenary sessions of the Second Chamber; the role of 'advocate' is related to issues that are more of a routine or technocratic nature, and this role can be observed primarily in the proceedings of the specialised select committees; the role of 'parliamentarian' is played primarily when dealing with governmental scandals and policy fiascoes, such as in parliamentary inquiry committees. Automatic, if more gradual, role shifts are also likely as parliament moves through the political business cycle: as elections draw nearer, MPs will more frequently put on their party hats.

However, role shifts may also be less automatic. Different MPs may define the issue context differently, with role conflicts as a consequence. As the nature of an MP's potential alliance varies with role (the party in his 'partisan' role, other parties' specialists in the same policy area in his 'advocate' role, all other MPs in his role of 'parliamentarian'), and as his prestige or reputation for power may also vary with role (the Speaker leading the 'parliamentarians', committee chairmen the 'advocates', parliamentary party leaders the 'partisans'), players may attempt to manipulate the choice of roles. In the case of a government scandal or fiasco, a minister may come under attack from MPs as 'parliamentarians'. To avoid a vote of no-confidence the minister will attempt to shift MPs to their 'partisan' roles, because this will enable the minister to appeal to the partisan loyalties of the governing majority. In such situations, MPs feel torn between the demands of these two roles. The Proceedings of the Dutch Parliament contain several examples of MPs publicly hesitating over which role to choose. In 1977, the Minister of Justice was accused of being responsible, through personal negligence, for the escape of a war criminal. The spokesman for one of the other parties in the governing coalition, in his role of 'parliamentarian' severely criticised the minister, but suddenly switched to his role as 'partisan' at the end of his speech:

> We have judged this minister as minister of Justice. He is more. He is the Deputy Prime Minister, he is a member of this coalition cabinet. As such he is a partner in compromises that we have made. That is what we have to consider. That is what is on the scales. If we weigh that, we can come to no other conclusion [than to refrain from censuring this minister]. (Proceedings of the Second Chamber, 1977, p.3418, my translation)

## CONCLUSION

In studies of the Dutch Parliament, the only political roles of MPs that have been studied explicitly are Wahlke and Eulau's representative roles. The main drawbacks of the Wahlke/Eulau role typology for the study of MPs in parliamentary systems is that the factor 'party' has no place in it, and that the roles deal only with the interactions between an MP and the electorate, not with the interactions between an MP and the government. On the basis of King's modes of executive–legislative relations, we developed three roles ('parliamentarian', 'partisan' and 'advocate') that stand for both different executive–legislative relations and different foci of representation. Each of these three roles probably dominated life in the Dutch Second Chamber during a particular period, but today the 'older' role orientations of 'parliamentarian' and 'advocate' can still be observed in addition to the now dominant 'partisan' role. The main research question now seems to be whether the coexistence of different roles is to be accounted for by different MPs specialising in different roles, or by all MPs switching from one role to another in different contexts. Searing's study of British MPs emphasises role specialisation. Our data for the Dutch Parliament suggest that role switching may be more important, although there is also some evidence of role specialisation.

It may be that both hypotheses are true, each in different institutional contexts. Role specialisation, for example, may occur more easily in large political institutions: the 659-member House of Commons, with its parliamentary parties of several hundred members, lends itself more easily to role specialisation than the 150-member Second Chamber, with its biggest parliamentary party currently containing 37 members.

To be able to choose between role specialisation and role shifting, or to be able to conclude in what context which explanation applies, we need better data than are currently available. In the Dutch Parliamentary Survey only one question explicitly inquired into the possibility of role switching. All the other evidence that we used from that study for this paper is the by-product of unrelated questions. For a much-needed comparative study of the political roles of MPs in parliamentary systems, we need to ask more and better questions in the Netherlands, as well as in other European countries.

NOTES

1. But see D.V. Verney, *The Analysis of Political Systems* (London: Routledge and Kegan Paul, 1979 [1959]), who lists no less than 11 characteristics.
2. These are studies of the background and attitudes of Dutch MPs, collected in surveys in 1968, 1972, 1979 and 1990, carried out as a joint effort of political scientists from various Dutch universities with financial support from the Dutch Science Foundation NWO. For more information on the latest study, see J.J.A. Thomassen *et al.*, *Dutch Members of Parliament 1990; Codebook* (Leiden: Leyden University, 1992).
3. First formulated in H. Eulau and J. Wahlke, 'The Role of the Representative: Some Empirical Observations on the Theory of Edmund Burke', *American Political Science Review*, 53 (1959), pp.742–56; and further developed in, among other publications, J.C. Wahlke,

H. Eulau, W. Buchanan and L.C. Ferguson, *The Legislative System: Explorations in Legislative Behavior* (New York: Wiley, 1962).

4.  H.F. Pitkin, *The Concept of Representation* (Berkeley: University of California Press, 1967).
5.  The Dutch Parliamentary Studies have interviewed members from both Houses of the Dutch Parliament. However, the analysis in this paper is confined to members of the more important Second Chamber.
6.  For technical reasons, the exact composition of the list may vary regionally, but this plays no role in campaigning or voting behaviour. Proposals to strengthen geographical representation through a reform of the electoral system are currently debated.
7.  R.A. Koole and M.H. Leijenaar, 'The Netherlands: The Predominance of Regionalism', in M. Gallagher and M. Marsh (eds.), *Candidate Selection in Comparative Perspective; The Secret Garden of Politics* (London: Sage, 1988); R. Hillebrand, *De Antichambre van het Parlement; kandidaatstelling in Nederlandse politieke partijen* (Leiden: DSWO Press, 1992) (with a summary in English).
8.  J. Thomassen, 'Empirical Research into Political Representation: Failing Democracy or Failing Models?', in M.K. Jennings and T.E. Mann (eds.), *Elections at Home and Abroad; Essays in Honor of Warren E. Miller* (Ann Arbor: University of Michigan Press, 1994).
9.  In the Dutch case, this development is part of the wider phenomenon of the 'de-pillarisation' of society. See for example R.B. Andeweg and G.A. Irwin, *Dutch Government and Politics* (London: Macmillan, 1993), chapters 2, 5 and 6.
10. A. King, 'Modes of Executive–Legislative Relations: Great Britain, France, and West-Germany', *Legislative Studies Quarterly*, 1 (1976), pp.11–36.
11. W.C. Müller, 'Executive–Legislative Relations in Austria: 1945–1992', *Legislative Studies Quarterly*, 18 (1993), pp.467–94; T. Saalfeld, 'The West German Bundestag after 40 Years: The Role of Parliament in a "Party Democracy"', in P. Norton (ed.), *Parliaments in Western Europe* (London: Cass, 1990); R.B. Andeweg, 'Executive–Legislative Relations in the Netherlands: Consecutive and Coexisting Patterns', *Legislative Studies Quarterly*, 17 (1992), pp.161–82.
12. R.B. Andeweg and L. Nijzink, 'Beyond the Two-Body Image: Relations between Ministers and MPs', in H. Döring (ed.), *Parliaments and Majority Rule in Western Europe* (New York: St Martin's Press, 1995), esp. pp.153–6.
13. D.D. Searing, *Westminster's World. Understanding Political Roles* (Cambridge, MA: Harvard University Press, 1994), pp.13, 26–8.
14. W.P. Secker, *Ministers in Beeld; de sociale en functionele herkomst van de Nederlandse ministers (1848–1990)* (Leiden: DSWO Press, 1991), pp.193–220 (the book contains a summary in English).
15. Searing, *Westminster's World*, p.486, note 16.
16. See Andeweg, 'Executive–Legislative Relations in the Netherlands', for a more extensive dicussion of these historical developments.
17. Secker, *Ministers in Beeld*, p.198.
18. A. Lijphart, *The Politics of Accommodation* (Berkeley: University of California Press, 2nd edn., 1975).
19. The Deetman Committee, *Rapport Bijzondere Commissie Vraagpunten*, Proceedings of the Second Chamber, 1990–1991, 21.427, n.2.
20. J.Th.J. van den Berg, D.J. Elzinga and J. Vis, *Parlement en Politiek* (The Hague: SDU, 1992), pp.200 *et seq.*
21. Searing, *Westminster's World*.
22. H. Eulau, 'The Network of Legislative Role Orientations', in Wahlke *et al.*, *The Legislative System*, p.384.
23. W.E. Miller and D.E. Stokes, 'Constituency Influence in Congress', *American Political Science Review*, 57 (1963), p.56.
24. Searing, *Westminster's World*, p.401.
25. Searing, *Westminster's World*, p.416.
26. Searing, *Westminster's World*, p.416.
27. A. Adonis, *Parliament Today* (Manchester: Manchester University Press, 1990), pp.113–14.

# Intra- and Extra-Parliamentary Role Attitudes and Behaviour of Belgian MPs

## LIEVEN DE WINTER

In terms of outputs and activities situated inside and outside parliament, Belgian MPs display a wide variety of behavioural patterns, between but also within parliamentary groups. Belgian MPs spend nearly 30 hours a week on activities situated inside parliament, while the other half is mostly allocated to constituency activities (party and pressure group work, local office, individual and collective constituency service, participation in social life and private occupation). The multivariate analyses of determinants of 26 dimensions of behaviour indicate that variables ensuing from past and current positions MPs occupy in different (non-)political networks, from demands made upon them as position holders and resources ensuing from these positions, explain overwhelmingly more variance in behaviour than less 'fixed' determinants like role attitudes, psychological incentives and office goals.

### ANALYSES OF ROLE ATTITUDES AND BEHAVIOUR OF BELGIAN MPS

Few empirical analyses of role attitudes and role behaviour of Belgian MPs have been carried out, due to the predominance of the legalistic approach (focusing on the formal aspects of the functioning of the legislature and of its relations with other institutions) as well as the historical approach (focusing on factors determining specific outputs of parliamentary decision making) to the study of parliament.

The first branch of genuine social science approach to parliament and parliamentarians to develop was highly descriptive and exploratory and focused on the socio-demographic and political background characteristics of Belgian MPs.[1] Debuyst[2] expanded this focus on backgrounds by studying recruitment patterns and some general role orientations, but without linking these variables to actual behaviour. Several authors have studied the ideological attitudes of national legislators.[3] However, only the surveys conducted by Debuyst and the members of the Loewenberg team have produced more than descriptive-exploratory analysis of the Belgian MP.[4]

Lieven De Winter is Lecturer in the Départment de Sciences Politiques et Sociales at the Université Catholique de Louvain and in the Faculteit Sociale Wetenschappen at the Katholieke Universiteit, Brussels.

All these studies were based on surveys among MPs and focus on attitudes rather than behaviour. Other authors that did focus on behaviour only rarely went beyond univariate description either. Those who did try to explain patterns of behaviour usually only considered the impact of background variables. Research on intra-parliamentary behaviour includes MPs' attendance[5] and specialisation,[6] their interventions in plenary meetings,[7] their use and the success of private member bills and amendments[8] and the content of their political discourse.[9] Voting behaviour only attracted the attention of a few authors.[10] With regard to extra-parliamentary behaviour, several researchers analysed MPs' constituency case work,[11] while two authors made an inventory of the positions parliamentarians hold inside and outside parliament.[12]

Yet, despite more than 35 years of empirical legislative research, there has been little accumulation of scientific knowledge with regard to the attitudinal, background and situational determinants of differences in legislative behaviour of Belgian MPs.[13] Up until my doctoral research,[14] empirical research on role attitudes and behaviour was dispersed, fragmented, primarily derived from descriptive-exploratory studies, methodologically unsophisticated and theoretically underdeveloped.

## STRUCTURAL CONSTRAINTS OF BACKBENCH BEHAVIOUR

The few analyses of voting, debate, legislative and control activities of Belgian MPs indicate that the use of these crucial tools of parliamentary decision making is largely determined by party, and especially by its governmental status and ideological profile. The strong constraints parties put on the voting behaviour of individual MPs follow primarily from the nature of parliamentary government in Belgium, labelled a *particratie*, which reduces the main function of parliament to the maintenance of the coalition government, whereby government control and lawmaking are only secondary functions.[15] Extreme fragmentation of the party system (number of effective parties = 8.2 in 1995) has complicated the forming of coalition governments, that since the 1970s require the inclusion of four or more parties.[16] Therefore, a workable degree of cabinet cohesion and stability can only be achieved by strongly reducing the impact of other decision makers: MPs, individual ministers (and even the PM), the civil service, the judiciary and intra-party bodies, all this to the benefit of the majority party executives and more in particular of the party presidents.[17]

This severely restricted role of parliament and its members is reinforced by several other factors. First there is an electoral system in which the voters decide only on the number of seats a party gets, the parties themselves decide who will receive them. Second, there is the oligarchisation of the selection process of parliamentary candidates,[18] the locus of decision having shifted away from the regular rank-and-file member to the constituency party board or congresses. Finally, parties have at their disposal a large battery of statutory rules, material resources and informal means of influence which further strengthens their control over intra-parliamentary behaviour of MPs.[19]

Thus the analysis of voting and policy contents of parliamentary activities at the individual level makes little sense, as little variation occurs within parliamentary groups. However, Belgian MPs do behave in very different ways with regard to other components of behaviour inside and outside parliament. The analysis in this article is therefore restricted to those components of role behaviour that are less collectively determined by the party factor, for which large variation also occurs between MPs of the same party.

VARIANCE IN INTRA- AND EXTRA-PARLIAMENTARY ROLE BEHAVIOUR

Table 1 presents the number of parliamentary outputs (bill initiation, parliamentary questions, interpellations, debating, committee and plenary attendance, as registered in parliamentary records) the members of the House of Representatives produced in the research period (1979–81) as well as the number of hours they devoted to specific intra-parliamentary activities (budget data collected through our survey). For each type of behaviour, the overall average for the research population is presented, as well as the extreme scores (minimum and maximum), the score for the least active quartile of the population (that is, the score of the first *quartile*, the highest score found amongst the 25 per cent of the least active MPs) and the bottom score of the most active quarter of MPs (that is, the score of the third quartile) and the number of cases on which the figures have been calculated.

Table 1 indicates that individual MPs differ strongly in the ways they allocate their time to different components of 'genuine parliamentary work'.[20] Some MPs focus on committee work, others on activities which take place within the general assembly, others devote most of their time to preparing thoroughly their activities in parliament, whilst others are generally inactive in parliament. Table 2 suggests equally large variations in extra-parliamentary activities: national and subnational party work, pressure group work and contacts, local office holding, case work, attendance of constituency local life, private occupation, speeches and debates, and media coverage.

The data presented above already suggest that 'the average Belgian MP' does not exist, and we have to think in terms of distinct types of MPs,

TABLE 1

VARIANCE OF PARTICIPATION IN INTRA-PARLIAMENTARY ACTIVITIES
IN THE 1979–1981 LEGISLATIVE TERM

| Type of activities and outputs | Average number | 1st quar- tile | 3rd quar- tile | Min- imum | % MPs score =0 | Max- imum | Eta$^2$ | N of cases |
|---|---|---|---|---|---|---|---|---|
| *Hours devoted weekly to genuine parliamentary work* | | | | | | | | |
| Attendance at plenary session | 8.3 | 5.0 | 10.0 | 0 | 0.8 | 25 | 0.11 | 129 |
| Attendance at committee meetings | 6.9 | 4.0 | 9.0 | 0 | 0.8 | 18 | 0.14 | 130 |
| Attendance at group meetings | 2.3 | 2.0 | 3.0 | 0 | 0.8 | 6 | 0.25 | 128 |
| Work in party research centre | 2.5 | 1.0 | 3.0 | 0 | 11.7 | 12 | 0.25 | 128 |
| Individual preparation of genuine parl.work | 6.9 | 3.5 | 10.0 | 0 | 8.5 | 22 | 0.07 | 129 |
| *Private member bills* | 3.1 | 0.0 | 8.4 | 0 | 29.7 | 16 | 0.18 | 155 |
| *Questions* | | | | | | | | |
| – written answer | 66.3 | 0.0 | 62.0 | 0 | 6.5 | 1033 | 0.35 | 155 |
| – oral answer | 2.3 | 0.0 | 3.0 | 0 | 41.9 | 21 | 0.11 | 155 |
| – urgent question | 1.4 | 0.0 | 2.0 | 0 | 46.5 | 15 | 0.19 | 155 |
| *Interpellations* | 2.0 | 0.0 | 3.0 | 0 | 41.3 | 21 | 0.27 | 155 |
| *Interventions in* plenary debate | 25.3 | 6.0 | 29.0 | 0 | 2.6 | 227 | 0.40 | 155 |
| *Committee reporting* | 1.7 | 0.0 | 3.0 | 0 | 52.3 | 12 | 0.26 | 155 |
| *Average attendance (in %)* | | | | | | | | |
| – House during plenary sessions | 61.1 | 50.4 | 74.2 | 23.8 | 0.0 | 92.3 | 0.29 | 155 |
| – committee meetings | 72.8 | 61.6 | 86.8 | 21.8 | 2.0 | 100.0 | 0.41 | 149 |

TABLE 2

VARIANCE OF PARTICIPATION IN EXTRA-PARLIAMENTARY ACTIVITIES

| Type of activities | Average number hours | 1st quar-tile | 3rd quar-tile | Mini-mum | Max-imum | Eta$^2$ | No of cases |
|---|---|---|---|---|---|---|---|
| *Party work (in hours)* | | | | | | | |
| Work in national party | 3.2 | 0.0 | 4.0 | 0 | 50 | 0.23 | 128 |
| Work in local and constituency party | 4.1 | 2.0 | 5.0 | 0 | 20 | 0.19 | 128 |
| *Pressure group work* | | | | | | | |
| Leadership office held | 3.4 | 2.0 | 4.0 | 1 | 15 | 0.12 | 50 |
| Contacts with (hours) | 1.2 | 0.0 | 2.0 | 0 | 10 | 0.15 | 128 |
| *Local office (hours)* | | | | | | | |
| Only local office holders | 7.5 | 2.0 | 12.0 | 0 | 30 | 0.09 | 106 |
| *Case work* | | | | | | | |
| Number of hours | 5.2 | 2.0 | 8.0 | 0 | 20 | 0.18 | 128 |
| Number of cases | 2134 | 625 | 2250 | 50 | 12500 | 0.19 | 134 |
| *Attendance constituency social life (hours)* | 8.1 | 4.0 | 10.0 | 0 | 50 | 0.14 | 127 |
| *Speeches, debates rallies (hours)* | 2.9 | 1.0 | 4.0 | 0 | 16 | 0.15 | 126 |
| *Private occupation* | | | | | | | |
| Only part-timers (hours) | 8.9 | 3.0 | 15.0 | 1 | 50 | 0.15 | 61 |

displaying different patterns of intra- and extra-parliamentary behaviour, depending on the time and effort they invest into the different components of their 'job kit'. In addition, these variations between individuals are not entirely due to the impact of party. In fact, also within parliamentary groups, the variation between individuals is considerable. The values of the *eta squared* in Tables 1 and 2 indicate that there is a large amount of variation in behaviour of individual MPs which cannot be simply accounted for by party, and which must be due to the impact of other factors, like role orientations, personality characteristics, goals, multiple position holding, and individual resources.

## INTRA- AND EXTRA-PARLIAMENTARY ROLES AND BEHAVIOUR

### Intra-Parliamentary Role Attitudes

The different patterns of behaviour presented in Table 1 are also reflected in the general role attitudes of MPs towards the different components of work inside parliament. When asked which task inside parliament MPs considered as most important the question was answered along two patterns (see Table 3).[21]

TABLE 3

LEGISLATORS' OPINIONS ON THE MOST IMPORTANT TASK OF AN
MP INSIDE PARLIAMENT

| Task | % of responses | % of MPs | N of resp. |
|------|------|------|------|
| *Functional definitions* | | | |
| – (non-legislative) government control | 22.7 | 67.1 | 100 |
| – legislation | 22.0 | 65.1 | 97 |
| – specialisation | 9.8 | 28.9 | 43 |
| – individual research, study | 5.7 | 16.8 | 25 |
| – policy orientation and innovation | 5.2 | 15.4 | 23 |
| – representation of groups and categories | 3.6 | 10.7 | 16 |
| *Spatial definitions* | | | |
| – committee work | 19.1 | 56.4 | 84 |
| – work in plenary sessions | 4.3 | 12.8 | 19 |
| – work in parliamentary group | 3.6 | 10.7 | 16 |
| *Other* | 3.9 | 11.4 | 17 |

In most cases references were made to activities related to the classical functions of parliament (government control, legislation, policy orientation and innovation, and representation) and the ways in which to perform these well, by specialisation and individual research and preparation. The first two functions were mentioned by about two-thirds of the respondents, while few mentioned the latter two institutional functions.

The other group of answers relates to the physical environment in which parliamentary activities take place. While a majority mentioned committees (where they spend on average seven hours a week), only a small minority mentioned parliamentary group meetings and plenary sessions, in spite of the fact that in the latter environment MPs spend more than eight hours a week (see above).

### Representational Roles

In the written questionnaire of our survey, MPs were asked to indicate up to three foci of representation out of 12 alternatives. Table 4 shows that the representational focus of Belgian representatives is multi-faceted. For nearly half of the respondents, 'constituents' represent one of the three most important representational foci. This category refers to all inhabitants in the electoral circumscription. The second most important focus is composed of socio-economic categories, with workers as the most important sub-category, followed by farmers, self-employed and entrepreneurs. The third most important focus is another constituency-located category, that is, the party's electorate in the MP's circumscription. The national party electorate scores at the same level. Next comes the inhabitants of specific linguistic communities (the Flemish, followed by the French-speaking and the German-speaking parts of the population).

TABLE 4

REPRESENTATIONAL FOCUS OF BELGIAN MPS

| FOCUS | N of resp. | % of resp. | % of MPs |
|---|---|---|---|
| Clients | 22 | 5.5 | 16.1 |
| Preferential voters | 25 | 6.2 | 18.2 |
| Constituency party voters | 47 | 11.7 | 34.3 |
| Constituents | 65 | 16.1 | 47.4 |
| National party voters | 47 | 11.7 | 34.3 |
| Denominational categories | 25 | 6.2 | 18.2 |
| – Catholics | 20 | 5.0 | 14.6 |
| – freethinkers | 4 | 1.0 | 2.9 |
| – socialist pillar | 1 | 0.2 | 0.7 |
| Socio-economic categories | 58 | 14.4 | 42.3 |
| – workers | 38 | 9.4 | 27.7 |
| – farmers | 4 | 1.0 | 2.9 |
| – independents, entrepreneurs | 10 | 2.5 | 7.3 |
| – farmers+independents+entrepreneurs | 3 | 0.7 | 2.2 |
| – general | 3 | 0.7 | 2.2 |
| Socio-demographic categories | 17 | 4.0 | 12.4 |
| – women | 5 | 1.2 | 3.6 |
| – youth | 3 | 0.7 | 2.2 |
| – underprivileged, disabled, migrants | 6 | 1.4 | 4.4 |
| – other | 3 | 0.7 | 2.2 |
| Citizens of specific province or sub-region | 8 | 2.0 | 5.8 |
| Citizens of specific linguistic community | 38 | 9.5 | 27.8 |
| – Flemish | 24 | 6.0 | 17.5 |
| – French-speaking | 12 | 3.0 | 8.8 |
| – German | 2 | 0.5 | 1.5 |
| Citizens of specific region | 21 | 5.2 | 15.4 |
| – Walloons | 12 | 3.0 | 8.8 |
| – Brussels | | | |
| – general | 4 | 1.0 | 2.9 |
| – French-speaking | 3 | 0.7 | 2.2 |
| – Flemish | 2 | 0.5 | 1.5 |
| All Belgian citizens | 30 | 7.4 | 21.9 |

The constitutional norm which prescribes that MPs should be representatives of the nation and not of their constituency is adhered to by only one out of five respondents. Denominational categories are mentioned by nearly a fifth of the respondents. This category basically refers to representation of Catholics, although a few mention freethinkers. Then comes the more personal following of the MP: his preferential voters and his clients, that is, those who were served by the MP's case work.

These three Belgian region are mentioned by 15.3 per cent. This time, the Wallonia and Brussels are mentioned most. Only 12.4 per cent mention socio-demographic categories: women, youth, underprivileged, disabled, migrants, the aged, and so on. Finally, some MPs referred to geographic entities which are situated between the three national regions and communities on the one hand, and the electoral circumscription on the other, such as a province, a sub-region within a province, or a city.

These data show that Belgian MPs define their representational focus in terms of the population of different types of territorial entities (ranging from the entire nation, over regions, linguistic communities, provinces and constituencies), and/or in terms of different types of segments of the population within these entities (defined in terms of party, socio-economic, socio-demographic and denominational characteristics). Hence, 'the' representational focus of 'the' Belgian MP does not exist. In practice, this focus is composed of very different foci, and the number of MPs with exactly the same set of representational foci is very small.[22]

These foci of representation clearly reflect the cleavage structure of the political system. The territorial foci reflect the centre–periphery cleavage, which also lies at the heart of the communautarian conflict, the socio-economic focus represents the traditional cleavage between working and other classes, while the denominational focus reflects the old conflict between church and state. The distribution of the foci between MPs of different parties confirms that as far as the socio-economically, denominationally and regionally/linguistically defined foci of representation are concerned, MPs tend to represent primarily those categories which their parties appeal to at large.

REPRESENTATIONAL STYLE AND ROLE CONFLICTS

Concerning policy representational style, 63.0 per cent displayed a trustee attitude, and 29.9 per cent the delegate one.[23] Given the complexity of his representational foci, the Belgian MP is likely occasionally to experience voting role conflicts between the policy demands made by different foci. We explored four major conflicting foci of representation: the national party and parliamentary group, the constituency party and activists, pressure groups and the voters. The demands of these foci can conflict amongst each other, but also with an MP's personal opinion. The responses indicate that MPs tend to follow their national party opinion in the case of conflict with the pressure group they represent,[24] and do so even more strongly in the case of a conflict between the national and the constituency party.[25] In the case of conflicts between an MP's own opinion and that of his parliamentary group or his voters, most MPs give in to the will of the parliamentary party.[26] Yet towards their voters most MPs follow their own opinion.[27] Hence, Belgian MPs may act as trustees towards their voters, but towards their national party they act like delegates, as the party statutes and political culture prescribe.

EXTRA-PARLIAMENTARY ROLE ATTITUDES AND BEHAVIOUR

Time budget data presented in Table 1 and 2 indicate that activities situated outside Parliament constitute an important part of the Belgian MP's time budget. In fact, if we group the activities which are basically situated within a legislator's constituency and those mainly situated at the capital, we notice that the average MP spends about as many hours on activities situated in Brussels as on constituency-based activities. Belgian MPs have ample opportunities to participate in constituency-based activities, as the distance between the capital and the constituency is for most MPs less than an hour of driving and most MPs tend to go to their constituency home every evening.

TABLE 5

LEGISLATORS' OPINIONS ON THE MOST IMPORTANT TASK OF AN
MP OUTSIDE PARLIAMENT

| Task | % of resp. | % of MPs | N of resp. |
|------|-----------|----------|-----------|
| – constituency case work | 18.6 | 73.9 | 113 |
| – constituency and local party work | 17.1 | 66.0 | 104 |
| – participation in local life of constituency | 13.1 | 52.3 | 80 |
| – listen to represented | 12.3 | 49.0 | 75 |
| – inform represented | 11.2 | 44.4 | 68 |
| – representation of constituency at national level | 6.6 | 26.1 | 40 |
| – national party work | 4.4 | 17.6 | 27 |
| – general party work | 4.1 | 16.3 | 25 |
| – pressure group work | 3.8 | 15.0 | 23 |
| – collective constituency work | 3.1 | 12.4 | 19 |
| – research, innovation | 2.0 | 7.8 | 12 |
| – public relations and campaigning | 1.6 | 6.5 | 10 |
| – international responsibilities | 1.1 | 4.6 | 7 |
| – local mandate | 1.0 | 3.9 | 6 |

This localist blend of the job of the Belgian legislator also emerges from the ways in which MPs define their role outside parliament (see Table 5). The first six most important extra-parliamentary role activities all refer to the constituency. About three out of four MPs mention individual case work, two out of three mention work in the constituency and local party organisation, and over half mention participation in the constituency's social life. Next come activities related to policy communication with the constituency: listening to what the represented have to say and informing them about a wide variety of political matters. About one out of four mentions pork barrel activities, that is, the representation of the constituency's collective interests at the level of national government. About one out of six mentioned party work at the national level and less mentioned pressure group work. Involvement in the field in the solution of collective constituency problems is mentioned by one out of eight.[28]

Let us now examine in detail a number of specific extra-parliamentary activities.[29]

*Party Work*

Belgian MPs are quite active within their party organisation, at different levels. They occupy on average 1.3 party leadership positions (which consume on average seven hours a week of their time).[30] Four out of five hold leadership positions at the national level (party presidency, secretariat, executive, research centre, administrative commission, the organisation of federations and of public officials, youth and women's organisation, and so on). About one out of four holds party leadership positions at the level of the constituency and local party organisation. Finally, one out of ten holds a party leadership position at the international level, usually in the International or European Federation of the party.

MPs occupy party leadership offices at the national level for obvious reasons of acquisition of influence. As the parliamentary party as such does not constitute the most important decision-making body in Belgian parties, MPs try to combine their mandate with an office in the party which yields more power. In addition, national party office can provide for secretarial staff and equipment, better access to information, the party research centre, campaign resources, and so on.

An MP will try to become an office holder in the constituency or local party in order to extend his support amongst the rank-and-file members and party officers, who often decide on his candidacy and chances for re-election. Local party officers demand their MP's involvement for bolstering the membership, funds and activity of the local organisation. In addition, their delegates at the party congress decide on important issues like governmental participation, in which MPs have an interest at stake as well.

Also, being the outspoken leader of a strong constituency party will raise one's standing within the national party organisation. Finally, involvement in constituency and local parties can be warranted in the case of strong internal conflicts, calling MPs to serve as conciliators between warring factions.

## Involvement in Pressure Groups and Other Organisations

Table 2 indicated that the average MP spends two and a half hours a week in dealing with pressure groups. Contact with pressure groups consumes on average 1.2 hours a week. The holding of a leadership office in a pressure group consumes on average about three and a half hours (if we exclude those who do not hold such an office). Table 6 represents the different types of pressure groups, organisations and institutions situated in the socio-economic, cultural and other sectors of society in which MPs occupy leadership positions.[31] The degree of participation in or the influence on political decision making varies strongly between these groups and institutions, as well as the levels at which they operate. These levels vary from the national (and even international) levels, to sub-national levels like regions and linguistic communities, constituencies, and sometimes even include the local level.

TABLE 6

AVERAGE NUMBER OF LEADERSHIP POSITIONS IN SECTORS PER MP

| Type of organisation | Average number of positions |
| --- | --- |
| – cultural-leisure | 1.5 |
| – social & health | 1.4 |
| – mixed economy | 0.8 |
| – education & science | 0.8 |
| – socio-economic pressure group | 0.7 |
| – finance, commerce, industry | 0.5 |
| – linguistic & nationalist | 0.2 |
| – action groups | 0.1 |
| – women's organisations | 0.1 |
| – denominational | 0.1 |
| *TOTAL* | *6.2* |

The sector which counts most MPs in leadership positions is the sector of culture and leisure. It includes cultural organisations and institutions, the tourism sector, the media and cultural formation organisations, foundations and trusts. The social and health sector draws nearly as much attention. It includes all types of health care institutions like the politically prominent *mutualités*, health centres, the co-operatives, social services and social security *caisses*, organisations and institutions for the elderly, juveniles, disabled and family organisations. Then comes the mixed economy sector, which includes institutions active in the sector of regional expansion and development, urbanisation and housing, and the sector's advisory committees. Also in the education and science sector and sector of socio-economic pressure groups (trade unions, and organisations of employers, farmers, middle classes and liberal professions) we find a relatively large presence of MPs. Next we find the sector of finance, commerce and industry, which includes financial institutions (holdings, banks, insurance companies), industrial and commercial enterprises, and the financial institutions of the pillar organisations. Finally, four sectors are relatively neglected: linguistic and nationalist groups, action groups (ecology, human rights, peace and anti-apartheid), women's organisations and denominational institutions (church and freemasonry). As far as differences between parties are concerned, the involvement of MPs in leadership functions in different pressure groups, organisations and institutions is strongly related to the representational focus of their parties, and the structural relation between the party and organisations active in some of these sectors.

Belgian MPs hold pressure group leadership offices for a variety of reasons. First, pressure group office holding is one of the prominent career paths which leads to a seat in parliament, especially for MPs with socio-demographically less advantageous backgrounds. It serves as an apprenticeship and a power base for the further political career. In addition, in some parties intra-party pressure groups exercise an important and sometimes exclusive control over the candidate selection and deselection process.[32] These intra-party pressure groups also support the actual election of their candidates. First, they contribute to the MP's campaign costs. Second, they promote the candidate in their membership periodicals, as well as in the newspapers they control or are affiliated with. Third, they organise meetings in which the candidate can present himself personally to the members and activists of the organisation. Finally, in case of non-election, they can lobby within the party for having their candidate 'fished up' as co-opted senator or member of a ministerial cabinet, or provide for a fall-back cushion within their organisation, like a position in the group's research centre.

Intra- and extra-party pressure groups can also provide important resources relevant to intra-parliamentary work. Our research revealed that pressure groups are important sources of assistance with regard to the drafting of bills and amendments, interpellations and parliamentary questions. The holding of a pressure group office also provides for secretarial staff and equipment, an office not far from the Parliament, covering parliamentary expenses and serving as an additional income. Being a leader of an important pressure group will also boost a backbencher's status within the party and towards governmental actors (cabinet, civil service). Finally,

Table 5 suggested that many MPs define their role as one of representative of specific groups or social categories. Hence, through office holding they may want to keep in close touch with, and to some extent even control, the demands made by the groups that constitute their focus of the representation.

## Local Office

The tradition of cumulation of a local mandate with a seat in parliament represents an element of a wider tendency toward localism within the Belgian political culture. More than three out of four representatives combined their parliamentary mandate with a local office (devoting 7.5 hours a week to their local duties). Of these *cumulards*, a majority were only members of the local council. Yet, about one out of three MPs held offices at the executive level, as mayor or alderman. As a consequence, Belgian MPs tend to spend a considerable proportion of their time on their local office (on average 7.5 hours weekly, see Table 2).

There are many reasons why Belgian MPs combine their parliamentary mandate with a local office. First, many MPs already held local office before getting elected to parliament, and this was often one of the reasons why they were recruited and got elected. The local office in fact offers visibility and notoriety within the constituency, often more than the seat in parliament, unless one belongs to the elite of the party. In addition, the exercise of important local offices (like that of mayor of a big city) can serve as an effective preparation for ministerial office.[33]

The combination of the salaries of local and national office can allow an MP to become a full-time professional politician, dropping any outside job. The local mandate also offers good facilities for serving the constituency, and can be a way of keeping in touch with one's constituency and its problems. The dual mandate often gives a legislator control over the constituency party with regard to the recruitment of activists, the grooming of candidates for office and fund raising. It also blocks an avenue of advancement which might otherwise be used by a potential rival.

Given the fact that the role of the Belgian MP in decision making is limited, local office is often a more creative job than that of backbencher. It includes executive as well as legislative aspects, with relatively high prestige and large personal resources (office, staff, car, budget, patronage). It gives one the power to allocate substantive material and non-material public resources. Furthermore, at the level of local politics, less political compromises have to be made.[34] In addition, the public standing of mayors is often higher than that of legislators.[35] Consequently, the local mandate is often psychologically more rewarding than the parliamentary one. In fact, our analysis of career ambitions indicates that the position to which Belgian MPs aspire most is that of mayor, more than the one of minister!

CONSTITUENCY SERVICE

*Case Work*

The average MP spends five hours a week on constituency case work and takes care of 2,134 cases per year. The major channel of contacts with MPs with regard to case work demands is the surgery. Belgian MPs hold regular (at least once a month) surgeries in the different communes of their constituencies. These surgeries are usually announced in the local papers and in the local publications of the party and pressure group. He usually holds his surgeries in the back room of a bar, in the local offices of the party or pressure group, and in offices in the town hall if a mayor or alderman. In addition, when MPs participate in local social life, they return home with their pockets full of beercards on which they have noted down the requests of people they met at these social gatherings. Contacts by phone or letter are only frequently used by better educated clients.[36]

Demands for assistance vary enormously in content. The most prominent demands are for employment, which includes general demands for a job as well as for political support for recruitment and promotion in the civil service. Nearly seven out of ten MPs reported this sector as the most important. The second most important sector relates to income problems, generally to obtaining a (higher) social security transfer (like pensions, child allowances, and so on). The third sector is housing, which includes social housing, as well as obtaining building permissions. Problems related to the army constitute a sector of average importance, and include problems of professional army men as well as draftees. Then we find four sectors of about equal importance: education, culture, and leisure (which basically concern problems of obtaining scholarships), taxes (problems of tax declaration, evasions and overtaxing), transport and communication (rapid telephone connections, road works and security), and family problems (divorce, juvenile delinquency, adoption). The least important sector is related to problems with the police and justice (immigration, legal support, prisoners). As this sector primarily includes the annulment of traffic fines, it comes as no surprise that respondents report this sector to be the least important one, since it is most likely to be also regarded by public opinion as the most illegitimate one.

Once the MP has collected the demands from his constituents, the real work of problem solving starts. MPs will write to national or local government departments with competence in the areas in which the problems are raised. A case supported by an MP usually gets faster or better treatment. In addition, as most civil servants obtained their position thanks to the intervention of a politician, an MP of a traditional party can usually count in each administrative unit on 'men of confidence' which he can contact personally. If he has no personal access to civil servants, he will address the ministerial cabinet of the responsible minister of the department, especially if this minister belongs to his party.

Case studies revealed that on average an MP needs two months to bring a case to a successful conclusion. The rate of success varies between 50 and 90 per cent. The relatively high rate of achievement explains the success of case work in Belgium in terms of the number of people making use of this system of redress of grievances. On the other hand, it strengthens the public's opinion that in Belgium citizens cannot obtain their rights through regular administrative channels without the support of a politician, which enforces the illegitimacy connotation of case work.

While the individual constituent clearly profits from this system, case work has also many positive sides for the MP. First of all, there is the electoral payoff.[37] In order to cash in electorally on their services, most MPs maintain voluminous and detailed files of every performed favour, files which are activated during every electoral campaign, with letters sent out to every beneficiary reminding him of the past services and soliciting his vote in the current election. Second, persons who received valuable services (like an important job or promotion in the civil service) are asked to contribute to the MP's campaign fund and to become a party member.

Yet given the fact that in Belgium MPs are hardly ever elected by virtue of their preferences votes, but rather by virtue of their place on the list, boosting one's preferences votes score by case work does not directly reinforce electoral security. Yet, as legislators engaging in extensive constituency service are better known and more favourably evaluated than those who are less solicitous of their constituents, selectors will tend to promote marginal candidates to the safe seats if they have good constituency records. In addition, as many clients are or become party members, they represent loyal troops which can be mobilised during the intra-party primary (poll) or constituency party conferences which decide on the selection of candidates.

For many legislators, case work represents one of the most psychologically rewarding parts of the job. Public service and concern for the welfare of their fellow citizens are often genuine and serve as strong motivations of MPs. It also gives them a sense of competence and effectiveness, which they often do not get through their activities in parliament. Finally, through constituency service the MP becomes a VIP in the constituency while as a backbencher in the legislature he is only one amongst several hundreds of other backbenchers.

Contacts with constituents during case work secures some insight into the political thinking and attitudes of an MP's constituents. On the other hand, a very attentive constituency style can decrease linkage between constituents' opinions and the representatives' standpoints in parliament. Nursing individual constituents well can create some freedom of manoeuvre with regard to more general policy issues on the legislature's agenda. Well-nursed constituents are less likely to rebel against their representative if he takes up policy positions different from their own. Also, our analysis of specialisation indicated that four out of ten of our respondents mentioned case work as the origin of (one of) their subject specialisations. Finally, Belgian MPs evoke the spin-offs of constituency service for legislative oversight as a legitimisation of their investments into case work. Problems raised as case work supposedly reveal which governmental services do not perform well, and give MPs their own sense of how policies adopted in parliament work out in practice and of how well or badly government is working.

*Collective Service*

Satisfying collective constituency needs, 'in the field' as well as in the national government, is viewed as an important role of Belgian MPs. Given the strong impact of Belgian parties on executive decision making, MPs can through contacts with ministers, their cabinets, party nominated civil servants, and so on pull a lot of strings at the executive decision-making process, satisfying demands of individual constituents as well as of the collective constituency.[38]

When asked what MPs managed to do for their constituency as a whole, a large majority of MPs mentioned attracting governmental subsidies for communication and transport infrastructure works (like roads, ports, rail, and telephone connections) and governmental and private investments stimulating the economic development and employment in their constituency (Table 7). About one out of three was able to provide collective infrastructure relating to the educational, health, cultural and sports sector. Fewer managed to solve urbanisation and housing problems and problems regarding the environment and physical security. Typically, Belgian MPs also intervene for problems related to the linguistic status of communes on the linguistic frontier). Finally, we find helping local governments (with regard to mergers and financial resources).

*Communicating with Constituents and Participation in Local Life*

Constituency party and pressure group work, local office and case work contribute to strengthening an MP's visibility and notoriety amongst the constituency inhabitants. Constituents want to be represented by somebody they trust as a person, who they see often, who is 'one of them', who is always open to their concerns, someone whose assurances they can trust. The generation of trust usually necessitates face-to-face contacts. Personal

TABLE 7
COLLECTIVE SERVICES PROVIDED BY LEGISLATORS TO THEIR CONSTITUENCY

| Task | % of responses | % of MPs | N of responses |
|---|---|---|---|
| – communication and transport infrastructure | 29.1 | 82.9 | 121 |
| – economic investments and employment | 25.2 | 71.9 | 105 |
| – service infrastructure | 11.5 | 32.9 | 48 |
| – housing, urbanisation | 7.0 | 19.9 | 29 |
| – general infrastructure | 6.5 | 18.5 | 27 |
| – environmental and security measures | 6.3 | 17.8 | 26 |
| – solution of community problems | 4.6 | 13.0 | 19 |
| – institutional problems of local government | 4.1 | 11.6 | 17 |
| – agricultural problems | 2.9 | 8.2 | 12 |
| – social security problems | 1.4 | 4.1 | 6 |
| – other | 1.4 | 4.1 | 6 |
| *Total* | *100.0* | *284.9* | *416* |

contact with constituents increases their chances of recalling the legislator, liking him, and eventually voting for him. With regard to the context of these contacts, an MP does not only act as a one-way channel of representation and information, from the constituents to the government and the party policy makers on what the nation thinks and will tolerate. MPs also serve as a channel to the electorate on how government or party policies are to be understood and justified. In fact, Belgian MPs believe that their constituents are also interested in the work they do in Parliament. Yet, in many cases the policy content of these contacts is quite limited.

Table 8 presents the kind of channels MPs use in order to communicate with their 'base'. Amongst the four most used channels, three refer to the party, at the constituency, local and national or general level. This confirms that MPs see their 'base' first in party terms and second in terms of general constituency, which is reached through the second most frequent channel of communication, that is, participation in local community life.

Belgian MPs attend a wide variety of meetings and social gatherings organised by a wide variety of local and constituency organisations, groups and institutions (like chambers of commerce and trade unions, pensioners, cultural, sports, youth or women organisations within and outside the pillar, local government boards, and so on). On average, the Belgian MP spends about eight hours a week on this type of activity. Yet, one should not forget that pressure group and constituency party work probably includes time spent on attending similar events organised by these political institutions and their dependent organisations. Thus the number of hours MPs serve as a 'local notable' or even as a 'flower pot' most probably exceeds the hours presented in Table 2. This role includes inaugurating buildings, festivities,

TABLE 8

COMMUNICATION CHANNELS BETWEEN MPS AND THE REPRESENTED

| Channel | % of responses | % of MPs | N of responses |
|---|---|---|---|
| – constituency party | 16.8 | 46.0 | 69 |
| – local presence activities | 16.1 | 44.0 | 66 |
| – local party | 15.4 | 42.0 | 63 |
| – national party or party in general | 13.7 | 37.3 | 56 |
| – pressure group | 10.7 | 29.3 | 44 |
| – case work | 8.3 | 22.7 | 34 |
| – speeches, hearings, etc. | 7.6 | 20.7 | 31 |
| – mail, phone calls, documentation | 3.4 | 9.3 | 14 |
| – addressing through media | 1.7 | 4.7 | 7 |
| – local office | 1.7 | 4.7 | 7 |
| – opinion polls | 1.5 | 4.0 | 6 |
| – occupational contacts | 1.2 | 3.3 | 5 |
| – other | 1.9 | 5.3 | 8 |
| *Total* | *100.0* | *273.0* | *410* |

distributing prizes at schools, dedications, *vernissages*, balls, receptions, openings of commercial and cultural initiatives, sports manifestations, fancy fairs, even funerals and weddings.

Apart from pressure groups, the other communication channels are directed to an audience wider than the party of the pressure group: case work, giving speeches, holding hearings and attending conferences, answering mail and phone calls, writing articles in the press, nursing contacts generated by occupational involvement, and local office. Hence, using different channels of communication, Belgian MPs reach a wide variety of constituents, whom it would be impossible to reach if they remained within the confines of the party, pressure group or pillar.

*Private Occupation*

Nearly half (46.6 per cent) of the Belgian MPs hold a (part-time) job as well as their legislative mandate. For those 'part-time MPs', it consumes nearly nine hours a week. The combination of a private occupation with a parliamentary mandate depends on the type of profession previously held. Part-time continuation is easier for some professions (like liberal professions, academics and entrepreneurs) than for others (like workers and civil servants).

MPs hold on to their prior occupation or even engage in a new one while being a Member of Parliament for several reasons. The private occupation constitutes an additional income, and often offers additional resources like office, staff and information. It can facilitate contacts with constituents. It can give a sense of competence and influence which the mandate does not always offer. Finally, it offers a cushion in case of non-election or voluntary withdrawal from politics.

### Determinants of Role Behaviour

We examined in detail through bivariate and multivariate methods all the factors that potentially could determine the differences in behaviour patterns presented in Tables 1 and 2. We can only present in general terms the explanatory power of different sets of variables referring to different theoretical approaches.

Our general hypothesis was that personal orientations towards the role of the MP in Belgium will determine to some extent what was confirmed by the bivariate analysis, revealing that Belgian MPs devote their time and energy to intra- and extra-parliamentary activities which they believe normatively are an essential part of the role of MP inside and outside parliament. Hence, one of the main criticisms on legislative role theory, stating that role attitudes are not related to observable behaviour, proves to be unjustified in our case.[39] The lack of association in previous research is basically due to the fact that the relation between roles and behaviour has predominantly been tested as far as representational style orientations – one of the most ambiguous concepts of legislative role theory – are concerned. However, role attitudes which refer to more clearly identifiable types of activities do seem to correspond to a higher level of involvement in these components of legislative behaviour.

Apart from hypotheses drawn from role theory, we also formulated and tested the relationships between, on the one hand, intra- and extra-parliamentary behaviour and, on the other hand, factors like political socialisation (basic and transitional political socialisation, and factors related to specific legislative specialisation, like age of first entry to parliament, seniority, governmental experience), and recruitment, in terms of selection methods used and role expectations of the MPs' selectorates. From the psychological approaches, we retained as determinants an MP's willingness to continue his career and the personal satisfaction he obtains from participating in different components of behaviour in and outside parliament. Drawing on the rational choice and goal-oriented approaches, we considered the effect of MPs' ambitions for higher office in and outside parliament, for re-election, and for policy influence. Finally, organisation theory underlines the effect of MPs' institutional and non-institutional resources, in terms of personnel and instances that assist him in his activities, of electoral safety, and personal resources which stem from an MP's socio-demographic background characteristics, like age, education, occupation, language skills and gender.

The question that interests us in the framework of this volume on roles of MPs is the genuine impact of each of the determinants found in bivariate analyses, that is, the impact of each determinant, independent of all others. For this we used stepwise multiple regression analysis, allowing us to identify the independent variables which contribute most to the explanation of the variation in the behavioural component under consideration and establish how much all independent variables retained in the regression equation taken together explain variation of the dependent variable.

It is impossible to present in this article all the results of the multiple regression analyses of the determinants hypothetically associated with variation in the 26 dependent variables. In nearly all cases they produced very plausible results, confirming the relations formulated in our hypotheses, explaining in most cases a quite satisfactory amount of the total variation of the dependent variable (especially with regard to intra-parliamentary behaviour), usually with only three to four independent variables.

When considered together, the regression analyses allow us to evaluate the overall explanatory power of not only each independent variable with regard to types of behaviour considered, but also of 'sets' of determinants related to different theoretical approaches. We will do this by calculating the success rate (in per cent) of a set of determinants by comparing the number of times a determinant was retained in the 26 regression analyses with the number of times this determinant was considered theoretically relevant in our bivariate starting hypotheses.[40] The higher the success rate of a specific set of explanatory variables, the more this set determines variance in intra- and extra-legislative behaviour of Belgian MPs, in comparison with other sets of explanatory variables.

The set of determinants that contributes most to the variation of intra-parliamentary activities is related to party, in terms of its degree of governmental participation (relevant to all control and law-making activities and retained in the regression equation for seven components of behaviour out of 26 for which their were assumed to be theoretically relevant, that is an overall 'success rate' of 27 per cent), its status as traditional party (relevant to some extra-parliamentary activities (15 per cent)), and finally party size (12 per cent). Hence, membership of a specific type of party not only completely determines Belgian legislators' voting behaviour and policy positions, it also determines considerably the levels of activity inside and outside parliament.

With regard to positions in and outside the legislature, leadership position holding has an independent impact, especially the positions of leadership of the parliamentary group (for some intra-legislative activities (overall success rate of 15 per cent)), leadership of the national party (15 per cent) and membership of the national party executive (for extra-parliamentary activities) (19 per cent), leadership of pressure groups (12 per cent), and local office holding (12 per cent).

Where individual role attitudes are concerned, in spite of the promising results of the bivariate analysis, this type of determinant is only picked up once in the multiple regression analysis (five per cent). This suggests that MPs' role definition do not exercise an impact sufficiently independent from the other determinants considered, like party characteristics, position holding or selectors' role expectations. Hence, this suggests that roles labelled by Searing as 'preference roles' are also structurally constrained for instance by the status of the party and selectors' demands.[41]

However, even when the behavioural impact of preference roles is the result of their association with more important determinants, the study of preference roles does not necessarily become obsolete in legislative research. Often, reliable data with regard to these other determinants is difficult to obtain, due to constraints on the length of survey questionnaire, their less public character (like extra-parliamentary positions) or taboo character (office ambitions). Collecting data with regard to the components of behaviour related to preference roles is often time consuming. Hence, collecting information about MPs' role attitudes towards work inside and outside parliament can present a short-cut solution for legislative researchers aiming at establishing the kinds of behaviour MPs of a given legislative system display inside and outside the legislature, without having to go into the demanding task of collecting and analysing a wide variety of data concerning behaviour and attitudes related to the main roles of the MP.

Of the four political socialisation factors, early interest in politics has been picked up three times (12 per cent), early participation in politics once (four per cent), basically for forms of behaviour in which party attachment can be expressed. The other indicators of basic and transitional socialisation were not included in any equation. Hence, the general contribution of our four indicators of political socialisation is quite weak.[42]

Selectors' expectations have been retained in the regression equation three times (15 per cent), and the modes of selection twice (33 per cent). Hence, factors related to the candidate selection process remain also in the multivariate analysis relevant for subsequent behaviour inside and outside parliament. Hence, candidate selection is not only 'the secret garden of politics',[43] but also a place which determines how its visitors will flourish outside the garden.

As far as psychological factors are concerned, personal satisfaction with a specific activity occurs several times as a determinant of the level of involvement in this activity (success rate of 11 per cent), while the general level of satisfaction with one's life as an MP also is relevant to some forms of extra-parliamentary activity (eight per cent). Office goals emerge three times as a significant determinant of involvement in activities relevant for attaining the office aspired to (five per cent). Perception of the electoral, policy or career effectiveness of an activity is retained only five times (five per cent). As argued above, these perceptions do not constitute a sufficient condition for high levels of participation. Hence, to some extent, general and specific personal satisfaction with life as an MP and the activities it involves serve as an incentive for participation.

With regard to resources and background factors, particular help received from one of the numerous sources of assistance only emerges three times as significant (twice involving persons of activist groups)(five per cent). Electoral marginality was only retained once (four per cent). Age affected five types of behaviour in a negative way (19 per cent), while level of education emerged three times (12 per cent). Of the numerous relations considered concerning occupational backgrounds, nine are relevant to intra-parliamentary components of behaviour, and five for extra-parliamentary behaviour (most concerning time invested in private occupation)(four per cent). Finally, gender emerges only twice as a relevant factor (eight per cent). Hence, of the resources considered, only those related to age, education and gender exert to some extent an effect independent from other factors.

Finally, if one makes a distinction between the determinants which are 'fixed', that is, those which are structurally defined by an MP's present positions or his past (positions, socialisation, recruitment and career, resources and backgrounds), and those which are less fixed (preference roles, personal satisfaction, goals), we find that the fixed determinants were retained in the regression equations 82 times against only 15 times for the non-fixed once.[44] This means that in Belgium behaviour of MPs is predominantly determined by structural factors ensuing from the past and current positions they occupy in different political and non-political networks, by the behavioural demands made upon them as position holders and by resources ensuing from these positions. On the whole, personal preferences with regard to the role an MP can play inside and outside parliament, personal satisfaction with the job as a whole and with its specific components, ambitions for higher office and policy influence and electoral goals do not emerge as important independent determinants of legislative behaviour in Belgium. Hence, the purposive models based on individual preferences and choice which have dominated American legislative research since the mid-1970s, do not seem to be productive in the case of a highly structured institution and its wider political environment. As argued by neo-institutionalist scholars like Searing,[45] in order to understand the behaviour of individual legislators, one has in the first instance to identify the constraints and opportunities which come with MPs' positions inside their institution as well as in other institutions and social networks (political and non-political), and the associated formal and informal rules and roles which constrain behaviour. Rational legislators, calculating their self-interests, do not act upon them in a vacuum. The strength of these constraints will define the extent to which individual preferences and choices are allowed to affect behaviour.

CONCLUSION

In this chapter, we presented the main results of our research on the determinants of behaviour of Belgian MPs, as far as role behaviour and role-related attitudes are concerned. We have examined 12 types of behaviour inside parliament, and 14 outside parliament. The analysis first shows that a wide variety of patterns of behaviour exists, also between MPs of the same parliamentary groups.

Belgian MPs spend nearly 30 hours a week in activities (usually meetings) situated inside parliament. Their personal role attitudes point to the importance of government control, legislation, committee work and specialisation. The representational focus of Belgian MPs is very complex, as it includes a wide variety of foci, often in unique combinations. Most MPs adopt a trustee representational style towards the represented, but act as delegates towards their parties.

As far as MPs' jobs outside parliament are concerned, about half of their entire time budget is allocated to activities situated inside the constituency, which is also reflected in MPs' role attitudes towards their work outside parliament. Most Belgian MPs hold one or more leadership positions within their party organisation. In addition, they occupy a wide variety of leadership positions in different types of pressure groups, organisations and institutions. Traditionally, Belgian MPs cumulate their parliamentary mandate with an office in local government, which constitutes an electoral asset and source of influence and personal satisfaction. Holding these types of offices is supportive to the political career and provides influence and resources which the mandate does not provide. MPs are also active and successful case workers and promoters of local and constituency interests. In addition Belgian MPs engage in many activities which allow for face-to-face contacts with their constituents, such as social functions and gatherings organised by a variety of groups and institutions at the local and constituency level. Finally, nearly half of the Belgian MPs exercise a private occupation aside with the mandate.

The wide range of types of behaviour considered and the large number of potential determinants withheld in our study allows us to evaluate the overall explanatory power of not only each independent variable with regard to types of behaviour considered, but also of 'sets' of determinants related to different theoretical approaches. We found that determinants which are structurally 'fixed' (ensuing from past and current positions MPs occupy in different political and non-political networks, the behavioural demands made upon them as position holders and the resources ensuing from these positions) explain overwhelmingly more variance in behaviour that less fixed determinants like role attitudes, psychological incentives and office goals.

## NOTES

1. J. Beaufays, 'Tentative d'analyse sociologique du député catholique belge', *Courrier Hebdomadaire du CRISP*, No.573 (1972); D. Schmidt, *Die Beteiligung der Nationalitäten in der Politischen Elite in Belgien 1944–1968. Ein Beitrag zum Verständnis der belgischen Nationalitätenfrage* (Kiel: Christian-Albrechts-Universität, diss., 1970); H. Van Hassel, *Sociografische aspecten van de Belgische Senaat, 1919–1958* (Leuven: KUL Departement Politieke Wetenschappen, diss., 1959).

2. F. Debuyst, *La fonction parlementaire en belgique. Mécanismes d'accès et images* (Bruxelles: CRISP, 1967).

3. B. De Bakker, *Bijdrage tot een sociografie van de Belgische politieke tegenstellingen* (Leuven: Departement Politieke Wetenschappen, diss., 1969); M. Deridder, R.L. Peterson and R. Wirth, 'Images of Belgian Politics: The Effects of Changes on the Political System', *Legislative Studies Quarterly*, Vol.3, No.1 (1978), pp.83–108; G. Dierickx, *De ideologische factor en de Belgische politieke besluitvorming* (Leuven: KUL Departement Politieke Wetenschappen, Ph.D., 1978); G. Dierickx, 'Ideological Oppositions and Consociational Attitudes in the Belgian Parliament', *Legislative Studies Quarterly*, Vol.3, No.1 (1978), pp.133–60; G. Dierickx, 'Politieke conflictbeheersing in België, Italië en Zwitserland', *Tijdschrift voor Sociologie*, Vol.5, No.4 (1984), pp.451–72; A.-P. Frognier, 'Parties and Cleavages in the Belgian Parliament', *Legislative Studies Quarterly*, Vol.3, No.1 (1978), pp.109–32; A.-P. Frognier and G. Dierickx, 'L'espace idéologique au Parlement belge. Une approche comparative', *Res Publica*, Vol.22, Nos.1–2 (1980), pp.151–7; R.S. Wirth, *Cleavage, Conflict and Parliament: Patterns of Legislative Coping in Belgium* (Knoxville: University of Tennessee, Ph.D., 1977).

4. The following authors used the Belgian data collected by the Loewenberg team: Deridder, Dierickx, Frognier, Kim, Loewenberg, Peterson and Wirth.

5. F. Drion, 'L'absentéisme parlementaire. Diagnostic et remèdes', *Res Publica*, Vol.22, No.1 (1980), pp.79–100; J. Janssens, *Het absenteïsme in het Belgisch Parlement tijdens de sessies 1968–1969 en 1969–1970* (Leuven, KUL Departement Politieke Wetenschappen, diss., 1972).

6. G. Goossens, *De parlementaire activiteiten van de leden van de Kamer van Volksvertegenwoordigers. Onderzoek betreffende de zitting 1974–1975* (Leuven, KUL Departement Politieke Wetenschappen, diss., 1976).

7. M. Deweerdt, 'De parlementaire werkzaamheden van de Belgische parlementsleden tijdens de zitting 1977–1978', *Res Publica*, Vol.20, No.4 (1978), pp.647–83; C. Hocepied, 'De activiteitsgraad van de Belgische senatoren tijdens de zitting 1982–1983', *Res Publica*, Vol.26, No.4 (1984), pp.645–61.

8. E. Clijsters, W. Van Schoor and V. Meeusen, 'De effectiviteit van wetsvoorstellen en amendementen als parlementair wetgevend initiatief', *Res Publica*, Vol.22, Nos.1–2 (1980), pp.189–212.

9. G. Dierickx, 'Ideological Oppositions and Consociational Attitudes'; G. Dierickx,

## 152    MEMBERS OF PARLIAMENT IN WESTERN EUROPE

'Parlementaire debatten en politieke taal', *Res Publica*, Vol.22, Nos.1–2 (1980), pp.259–88; L. Vrijdaghs, 'Het eurorakettendossier in het Belgische en Nederlandse parlement', *Namens*, Vol.3, No.3 (1988), pp.4–9, 52–7.

10. L. Holvoet, 'De stemmingen over het investituurdebat in Kamer en Senaat', *Res Publica*, Vol.22, Nos.1–2 (1980), pp.35–76; E. Langerwerf, 'Het stemgedrag in het parlement. Onderzoek in de Kamer van Volksvertegenwoordigers voor de periode 1954–1965', *Res Publica*, Vol.22, Nos.1–2 (1980), pp.177–88; M. Verminck, 'Concensus en oppositie in het Belgisch parlement tijdens een verkiezingsjaar', *Res Publica*, Vol.28, No.3 (1986), pp.475–87.

11. E. De Becker, *Het parlementslid als makelaar in dienstbetoon* (Leuven: Departement Politieke Wetenschappen, diss., 1984); S. De Pauw, 'Rational choice, sociaal dienstbetoon en de mythe van de collectieve probleemoplossing', *Res Publica*, Vol.38, No.1 (1996), pp.135–58; M. Deweerdt, *Funkties en disfukcties van het dienstbetoon door parlementsleden. Een onderzoek bij de Vlaamse Volksvertegenwoordigers* (Leuven: Departement Politieke Wetenschappen, diss., 1975); L. De Winter, 'Het sociaal dienstbetoon van politici als niet-juridische vorm van probleemoplossing', *Kultuurleven*, Vol.50, No.3 (1983), pp.232–42; L. De Winter, 'De socialistische partij en politiek dienstbetoon', in J. Brepoels, L. Huyse, M. Schaevers and F. Vandenbroucke (eds.), *Eeuwige dilemma's. Honderd jaar socialistische partij* (Leuven: Kritak, 1985), pp.127–39; L. De Winter and P. Janssens, *De stemmotivaties van de Belgische kiezer* (Brussel: Dimarso-Gallup Belgium, 1988); L. De Winter, 'Politiek dienstbetoon', in R. Dillemans (ed.), *Wegwijs Politiek* (Leuven: Davidsfonds, 1994), pp.425–31; L. De Winter, 'Le service aux électeurs en tant que forme de l'échange politique', in P.-H. Claeys and A.-P. Frognier, *L'échange politique* (Bruxelles: Editions de l'Université de Bruxelles, 1995), pp.209–25; D. Magdelijns, *Politiek dienstbetoon van de S.P. bij regeringsdeelname en bij oppositie (1977–1985)* (Leuven: Departement Politieke Wetenschappen, diss., 1987).

12. H. De Bondt, *Stratificatie van de Belgische Parlementsleden bij middel van hun extraparlementaire bindingen* (Leuven: Departement Politieke Wetenschappen, diss., 1971); M. Ronsmans, *De cumulatie van mandaten door de Belgische parlementsleden* (Leuven: KUL Departement Politieke Wetenschappen, diss., 1985).

13. In most cases research populations were restricted to MPs of one specific legislative term. Therefore data sets available on different aspects of individual legislative behaviour gathered separately by each researcher could usually not be merged. Hence, variables operationalised in one research project could not be used to explain differences in behaviour and attitudes found in another project. For a first attempt to integrate data sets, see L. De Winter, 'Parlementaire en buiten-parlementaire activiteiten van Vlaamse volksvertegenwoordigers', *Res Publica*, Vol.22, Nos.1–2 (1980), pp.223–57.

14. L. De Winter, *The Belgian Legislator* (Florence: European University Institute, Ph.D., 1992).

15. L. De Winter, 'De partijpolitisering als instrument van de particratie. Een overzicht van de ontwikkeling sinds de Tweede Wereldoorlog', *Res Publica*, Vol.23, No.1 (1981), pp.53–107; L. De Winter, 'Party Encroachment on the executive and legislative branch in the Belgian polity', *Res Publica*, Vol.48, No.2 (1996), pp.325–52.

16. L. De Winter and P. Dumont, 'The Belgian Party System(s) on the Eve of Disintegration', in D. Broughton and M. Donovan (eds.), *Changing Party Systems in Western Europe* (London: Cassell, 1997, forthcoming); L. De Winter, A. Timmermans and P. Dumont, 'Coalition Formation and Governance in Belgium: Of Government Gospels, Evangelists, Followers and Traitors', in W. Müller and K. Strøm (eds.), *Coalition Government in Western Europe* (forthcoming).

17. L. De Winter, 'Parties and Policy in Belgium', *European Journal for Political Research*, Vol.17, No.4 (1989), pp.707–30; De Winter, 'Party Encroachment'; L. De Winter, A.-P. Frognier and B. Rihoux, 'Belgium', in J. Blondel and M. Cotta (eds.), *Party and Government. An Inquiry into the Relationship between Governments and Supporting Parties in Liberal Democracies* (London: Macmillan, 1996), pp.153–79.

18. L. De Winter, 'Twintig jaar polls, of de teloorgang van een vorm van interne partijdemocratie', *Res Publica*, Vol.22, No.4 (1980), pp.563–85; L. De Winter, 'Belgium: Democracy or Oligarchy?', in M. Gallagher and M. Marsh (eds.), *Candidate Selection in Comparative Perspective. The Secret Garden of Politics* (London: Sage, 1988), pp.20–46.

19. L. De Winter, 'The Belgian Parliament', in G. Kurian (ed.), *World Encyclopedia of Parliaments and Legislatures* (New York: Congressional Quarterly, forthcoming); K. Deschouwer, 'Belgium', in R. Katz and P. Mair (eds.), *Party Organisations. A Data Handbook* (London: Sage, 1992), pp.121–98.

20. Only meetings of parliamentary groups and with the party's research centre take up a fairly homogeneous part of the time budget.

21. As is the case with many questions to be treated below, multiple answers were allowed and coded. Hence, the last column of Table 3 presents the number of times a specific answer was given, the first column represents the percentage of a particular answer with regard to the total number of answers registered, and finally, the middle column presents the percentage of MPs who gave this answer compared to the total number of respondents. Hence, the percentages of the middle column are necessarily higher than that of the first column, as MPs often gave two or more answers to open-ended questions.

22. Eighty five per cent of the respondents had a set of main foci which was unique in the sense that no other MP included the same foci in the same order of importance.

23. Some MPs could not make a choice: most of them stated that they would follow the national party line, some said that one should live in close contact with the voters.

24. In nearly six out of ten cases of conflict, the pressure group representative decided to follow his party's position. Less than one out of ten stuck to the position of the pressure group.

25. In 63.7 per cent of the conflicts, the demands of the national party prevailed over the demands of the constituency party. Still, in more than one out of five conflicts, MPs sided with their constituency party.

26. The most common reaction is to yield to the majority opinion of the parliamentary group (in about half of the conflicts). In 15 per cent of the conflicts, they voted against party line, while in an equal number of conflicts they abstained. Another common way of facing this type of conflict is avoiding the vote, which is mostly done by leaving the Chamber.

27. In nearly nine out of ten of the conflicts, MPs decided to follow their own opinion. Only in one out of ten, they decided to yield to their voters' opinion.

28. Four types of activities were mentioned by less than ten per cent of MPs: research, learning and innovation, public relations and campaigning, involvement in international politics, and surprisingly – given the prominence of the local cumul – the local mandate.

29. With regard to position holding, wherever possible, data is presented for all 212 members of the House, and not only for survey respondents. This gives a fuller and more reliable picture of party differences.

30. Only those offices held at the end of 1980 were taken into consideration. Figures represent party office holding of all 212 House Representatives, and not only the survey respondents.

31. Only positions which involve responsibilities, like leadership or executive functions, are included. Mere membership positions are not included.

32. See De Winter, 'De partijpolitisering'; De Winter, 'Party and Policy'.

33. L. De Winter, 'Parlement et parti politique comme trajectoire de la carrière ministérielle en Belgique', *Les Cahiers du CRAPS* (Université de Lille II), No.12, pp.40–54.

34. While at the national level, majority MPs have to arrive at compromises with competitors of at least three parties, as mayor they often command absolute majorities. In the 1982–88 period, a majority of the Belgian communes were led by a single party majority (J. Ackaert, 'Nationale schaduwen over de gemeentepolitiek', *Kultuurleven*, Vol.55, No.7 (1988), pp.629–35.

35. IMADI, *Studie naar het vertrouwen dat de Belgische bevolking heeft in de eerlijkheid en bekwaamheid van een aantal (overheids–)organisaties en maatschappelijke sleutelfiguren* (Antwerpen: IMADI, 1989).

36. De Becker, *Het parlementslid als makelaar*, p.66.

37. The importance of the political exchange between services for preference votes can be illustrated in several ways. First, as shown above, Belgian MPs believe that case work is the most effective activity in order to attract preference votes. Second, this opinion is also shared by the public at large. Third, electoral research revealed that at least four out of ten clients vote for the service rendering MP (De Winter and Janssens, *De Stemmotivaties*).

38. The prominence of pork barrel activities of the Belgian MP is also related to the 'non-

rational' way in which public expenditures are allocated in Belgium. Given the on-going conflicts between the different regions and cultural communities, departmental spending is carefully distributed over the regions and communities, so that each unit receives public investments according to its size. Hence, many projects are allocated to constituencies which normally, in terms of socio-economic cost/benefit calculations, would not be able to attract such investments. As the decisions on the allocation of public investments are largely based on political criteria, rather than on socio-economic cost/benefit calculations, politicians in Belgium have a larger pork barrel market to manipulate than in many other countries.

39. For a critique of legislative role analysis, see R. Hedlund, 'Organisational Attributes of Legislatures: Structure, Rules, Norms, Resources', in G. Loewenberg, S.C. Patterson and M.E. Jewell (eds.), *Handbook of Legislative Research* (Cambridge: Harvard University Press, 1985), pp.321–94.

40. This number does not always equal 26 (that is the 12 intra- and 14 extra-parliamentary components of behaviour examined in our research), as some determinants were considered hypothetically relevant only to a limited number of components.

41. Preference roles are 'associated with positions that require the performance of few specific duties and responsibilities. They are comparatively unconstrained by the institution and are therefore more easily shaped by the preferences of role players' (D.D. Searing, 'Roles, Rules, and Rationality in the New Institutionalism', *American Political Science Review*, 85 (1991), p.1249. Yet, in the seven regression analyses in which role orientations were initially included, only once role orientation was retained in the final equation (involvement in local life). In three of them, a variable relating to personal satisfaction was withheld. This suggests that role orientations are not only surrogate determinants but most likely also more inaccurate predictors of behaviour than psychological incentives. Maybe some respondents verbally adopt a specific role as they believe it is the most legitimate, while in reality they engage in activities which correspond more to their incentives.

42. Age of entry to parliament is only relevant to TV and radio coverage (four per cent), seniority is important basically for some types on intra-legislative behaviour (15 per cent), while governmental experience is important for some extra-parliamentary forms of behaviour (11 per cent). Yet, socialisation factors situated in a legislator's adulthood, that is MPs' political career characteristics, seem to perform better than factors related to basic socialisation experiences occurring usually in one's adolescence and early adulthood. Hence, legislators' behaviour is more affected by events and experiences situated in the more recent past.

43. Gallagher and Marsh, *Candidate Selection in Comparative Perspective*.

44. There is hardly any difference between intra- and extra-parliamentary components (41 fixed against seven non-fixed for the former type, 41 fixed and eight non-fixed for the latter type).

45. D.D. Searing, *Westminster's World. Understanding Political Roles* (Cambridge: Harvard University Press, 1994).

# Rules, Reasons and Routines: Legislative Roles in Parliamentary Democracies

## KAARE STRØM

Parliamentary roles, the behavioural patterns or routines that legislators adopt, can be viewed as strategies for the employment of scarce resources toward specific goals. This article argues that parliamentary behaviour can be understood against the background of four typical and largely hierarchically ordered objectives that parliamentarians have: reselection, re-election, party office, and legislative office. Legislative roles describe the ways in which parliamentarians harness their scarce resources in order to reach their goals. These strategies are in turn affected by the institutional rules under which parliamentarians operate. The article examines the specific legislator objectives under parliamentary government and discusses the roles that describe the various ways in which they pursue these goals.

In representative democracies, voters have to live with what elected politicians do. Therefore, the study of elite behaviour has a venerable tradition in political science. Much of this scholarship has examined the regular patterns of behaviour of Members of Parliament. The object of such studies has been defined in terms of the roles of parliamentarians. 'The noun "role"', Donald Searing claims in his magisterial study *Westminster's World*, 'is a word that we cannot do without'.[1] And yet the scholarly focus on legislative roles has for some time been in decline. 'Articles continue to be produced on the topic, but they aren't much discussed. There aren't any major research projects under way on political roles. Nor are there signs of significant innovation in theory and method.'[2] The causes of this predicament lie partly in the role theory literature itself, particularly in the conceptual confusion that many forms of role analysis have engendered. Among the three traditional approaches to the study of political roles, the structural and interactional approaches have suffered from this problem in particular. Role theory has not provided us with a theory – more commonly what has been on offer has been a conceptual framework.

Searing attributes responsibility for this decline in the prominence of legislative role analyses to the ascendancy of the rational choice tradition in

Kaare Strom is Professor of Political Science at the University of California, San Diego. He would like to thank Kelly L. Mann and Stephen M. Swindle for valuable assistance, and Rebecca Morton, Wolfgang C. Müller and Stephen S. Smith for helpful comments.

legislative studies, particularly within American academe. The impressive growth of this research tradition, with its emphasis on individual preferences and incentives rather than group norms and socialisation, has shifted the emphasis of this field of study away from the traditional conceptions of roles. Though Searing sees merit in the rise of *homo oeconomicus*, he wishes to supplement this image of political behaviour with *homo sociologicus*, in particular with a motivational role theory based on the marriage of the economic and sociological traditions.

Searing's project builds in particular on the new institutionalism as conceived by March and Olsen, on their 'genuine synthesis of rules and reasons that recognises the importance of understanding the interactions between them'.[3] Searing distinguishes between *position roles* and *preferences roles*, between roles driven primarily by rules and reasons, respectively. In identifying the latter roles in particular, he operates inductively on the basis of a wealth of interviews with British parliamentarians themselves.

The scope, ambition and innovative character of Searing's work will make it a natural starting point for much empirical work on the roles of parliamentarians, as several of the articles in this volume demonstrate. The purpose of this contribution is somewhat different. Building on a number of Searing's valuable insights, I shall suggest that parliamentary roles can be fruitfully understood within the neo-institutional rational choice tradition in political science.[4] Although I agree with Searing's efforts to embed role analysis in motivations and institutional analysis, I disagree with his dismissal of the rational choice tradition as a form of tunnel vision that distorts our understanding of parliamentary politics.[5] Indeed, this research tradition is perfectly conducive to a marriage of 'rules' and 'reasons', and its parsimony and deductive rigour make it the most plausible vehicle for such a theoretical project. Institutions are the 'rules' that constrain 'reason', and they do so to a greater or lesser extent. Position roles (fully institutionally determined strategies) and preference roles (institutionally unconstrained strategies) are the polar points on a continuum of constraint. Most real-world legislative roles lie somewhere in between.

What are legislative, or parliamentary, roles?[6] How do they shape political behaviour? In what ways are parliamentary roles themselves a function of the institutional rules that govern parliamentary life? How can a simple conception of legislators' goals and parliamentary institutions help us understand and predict differences in legislative behaviour across parliamentary democracies? These are the questions to which this essay is devoted. In addressing them, I shall draw on evidence primarily from European parliamentary democracies, but also from the United States Congress and other legislative settings whenever that will be illuminating.

The analysis that follows is divided into seven parts plus the conclusion.

First, I discuss the concept of parliamentary roles and suggest that roles can be thought of as *strategies for the commitment of scarce resources.* I then relate this discussion of parliamentary strategies to a conception of parliamentarians' objectives. The latter framework is derived in substantial part from the study of the United States Congress but, I argue, much more broadly applicable. Thirdly, I discuss parliamentary resources and organisation and the ways in which these features help or hinder parliamentarians in their pursuit of their objectives. I discuss the relationships between these objectives as well as their dependence on particular legislative rules or institutions. The next four sections discuss how legislative strategies (goals) are shaped by the rules under which parliamentarians have to compete for four political 'goods' they typically pursue: reselection, re-election, party office and legislative office. Finally, I show how this perspective may possibly help us understand the origins of different legislative roles and conclude the analysis.

## PARLIAMENTARY ROLES: RULES, REASONS AND ROUTINES

The study of legislative roles in parliamentary democracies has proceeded from a number of different perspectives.[7] The scholarly literature thus associates roles with tasks or with functions, with behaviours, or with motivations. Norms associated with different roles are in turn described in positive or normative ways. Searing defines roles as 'particular patterns of interrelated *goals, attitudes,* and *behaviors* that are characteristic of people in particular positions'.[8] Surveying the literature, he distinguishes between structural, interactional and motivational approaches. The first of these three focuses on norms related to institutional functions, the second on individual negotiation and learning in specific settings, and the third on the purposes, goals, and incentives of the politicians themselves. Searing favours the third of these, the motivational approach, in large part because it seeks to reconstruct the conceptions parliamentarians have of their own activities.

The motivational approach sets great store by the relationship between the behaviours that define roles and the motivations that underlie them. In fact, Searing defines these motivations, or preferences, as part of the roles in which he is interested. I agree with Searing that the motivational approach is the most promising approach to the roles of parliamentarians. However, I wish to draw a distinction between preferences and roles which is somewhat different from Searing's. This article argues that legislative roles can be viewed as *behavioural strategies* conditioned by the institutional framework in which parliamentarians operate. By invoking the concept of strategy, I wish to suggest that parliamentary role analysis can fruitfully be conducted under the broad umbrella of the most suggestive and parsimonious of motivational approaches: the rational choice tradition. Roles are routines, regular patterns of behaviour. But although such routines may be shaped by cultural expectations as well as by personal idiosyncrasies, they are most likely of all to flow from reasoned and deliberate pursuits in which parliamentarians engage. Besides all their other charming idiosyncrasies, legislators are goal-seeking men or women who chose their behaviour to fit the destinations they have in mind. In doing so they have to pay close attention to the institutions in which they operate. The institutional features that most matter are partly those of the legislature itself, but also those of their national and local parties, as well as the rules of the electoral process. *Parliamentary roles, therefore, are routines, driven by reasons (preferences), and constrained by rules.*

The choice-theoretic approach distinguishes clearly between preferences and strategies. Preferences are the exogenously given 'tastes' that actors such as parliamentarians have over the outcomes that affect their political fortunes, such as nominations, elections and appointments in parliament. But while the goals of politicians surely influence the patterned behaviour that we may call roles, they do not in themselves constitute such roles. Instead, it is more meaningful to tie the concept of roles to that of strategies, which we may loosely think of as game plans.[9] Strategies are endogenous prescriptions as to how actors (here: parliamentarians) may most successfully and efficiently act to maximise the likelihood of whatever outcomes they favour. Thus conceived, strategies are akin to the common definition of roles: they are likely to take the form of consistently patterned political behaviour.

Strategies have to prescribe specific forms of behaviour under the control of the actors in question. For parliamentarians, strategic choices will typically have to do with their commitment of scarce resources such as their time, media access and other organisational assets. We can thus conceive of role distinctions as differences in the allocation of scarce resources. These different patterns of resource allocation are in turn driven by differences in the efforts parliamentarians put into the pursuit of their different goals. Some members spend a lot of their time trying to get renominated, others engage mainly in activities designed to boost their general election prospects, and yet others put their efforts into work that is likely to pay in terms of party or legislative distinctions within parliament. In the next section, I outline a conceptual scheme with which we can capture this range of legislator objectives.

## LEGISLATOR PREFERENCES

The motivations of legislators have been a focal point of a rapidly growing literature on legislative organisation and behaviour in the United States.

This literature has transformed scholarship on the United States Congress and essentially contributed to the shift that Searing observes, from sociological role analysis to rational choice incentive-based explanations of legislative behaviour. The single work most responsible for this revolution is David Mayhew's book, *Congress: The Electoral Connection*.[10] Although Mayhew did not formalise his argument or put it in game-theoretic terms, it had a profound impact on scholars in the rational choice tradition, which was only beginning to get into its stride in the 1970s. Mayhew's argument is that much can be understood about the behaviour of United States Congressmen if one assumes that they are 'single-minded seekers of reelection'.[11] The pursuit of re-election, he argues, 'underlies everything else, as indeed it should if we are to expect that the relations between politicians and public will be one of accountability'.[12]

Mayhew's stark stylisation proved both catchy and enormously influential. Nonetheless, other scholars have added to it and abandoned some of its simplicity. Joseph Schlesinger adds some nuance to the electoral motivation.[13] Much in the vein of Mayhew, he argues that political ambition is the key to understanding candidate behaviour and even to political parties as organisations. Political ambition, however, can take several different forms: discrete, static and progressive. *Discrete* ambition is the desire for a particular office for a single term. Politicians with discrete ambition thus do not subscribe to Mayhew's conception of the single-minded seeker of re-election. *Static* ambition consists in the pursuit of the same office for multiple terms. Finally, *progressive* ambition is where an individual aspires to some office more powerful or important than the one that he or she now holds.[14] This is where one political office becomes a stepping stone for another and more desirable one. Thus, Mayhew's archetypical congressmen holds only one of three possible forms of political ambition, as Schlesinger portrays it. If indeed most congressmen harbour static, rather than discrete or progressive, ambitions, it may be because their terms are short and because for many of them (especially those from populous states), the risks of running for higher office are prohibitive.

A seminal work in Mayhew's own generation was Richard Fenno's *Congressmen in Committees*.[15] Unlike Mayhew, Fenno argues that members of Congress (and by implication other legislators) have multiple objectives, which may often conflict. Some of these goals, however, are more basic than others: 'Of all the goals espoused by members of the House, three are basic. They are re-election, influence within the House, and good public policy.'[16] Fenno adds to these external career considerations and private gain, which he treats peripherally or not at all. In a more recent book, Gary Cox and Mathew McCubbins build on the insights of both Mayhew and Fenno and expand on Fenno's second motivation in particular.[17] And although Cox and McCubbins explicitly reject the assumption that members of Congress are single-minded in their quest for re-election, they 'do believe that it is an important component of their motivation'.[18] The authors go on to formulate a formal model of party leadership in which the Speaker of the House (the effective leader of the majority party) cares not only about personal re-election, but also about his party winning a majority, as well as about being re-elected as Speaker by the new Congress. In on-going research, Stephen Swindle formulates a more general model of candidate preferences.[19] He assumes that candidates are driven by re-election, but also prior to that by the need to secure renomination, and subsequently by what he calls 'office', which is to say, any discretionary appointment (such as party leadership posts or committee assignments) within the legislature.[20]

Building on this analysis, I shall assume that parliamentarians have four distinct types of goals related to their legislative service. In addition, they may of course have other goals that pertain to their lives outside parliament, as Fenno suggests. The four parliamentary goals, or the components of the parliamentary utility function, are: (1) reselection (renomination), (2) re-election, (3) party office, and (4) legislative office. By *party office*, I mean such positions as party leader, whip, member of the parliamentary party leadership or some steering committee, or front-bench status, in other words such forms of privilege that are entirely under the control of the party itself. By *legislative office*, I mean positions to which a member must be elected by parliament as a whole, or by some cross-partisan sub-set of the legislature, such as speaker/president, committee chair, and so on. In one sense, legislative office represents a generalisation of the speaker's desire to be re-elected as speaker, that is, to control the principal legislative office in the United States system. In pure two-party systems, the distinction between party and legislative office may in practice be of no consequence, if the majority party controls access to all important legislative offices. In multi-party parliamentary democracies, on the other hand, the allocation of such offices is often at the hands of some decisive coalition of parties.

Clearly, success or failure in the pursuit of each of these goals bears on the attainment of the rest. That is to say that the typical legislative objectives are interrelated and indeed often hierarchically ordered. For example, in most legislatures, party renomination is critical to the attainment of any of the other goals. If you do not receive your party's nod for the ballot, you cannot in most cases be elected, and if not elected, you obviously cannot enjoy any of the benefits of parliamentary membership. That is to say that election is necessary for any further goal in parliament. The iron-clad necessity of election in democratic legislatures makes the 'single-minded pursuit of reelection' the primary instrumental goal of legislators. Typically, party office is also a prerequisite for legislative office, although the necessity here is less strict. Some members become legislative leaders (for example, presiding officers) without achieving any high position in their respective parties.

We can therefore identify a fairly clear hierarchy of member objectives. The first goal, which is often necessary for any further ambition, is to gain ballot access, most commonly by receiving one's party's nomination. Once nomination has been secured, election is the next higher goal. Both of these are critical for any further goal achievement. Once elected, parliamentarians may to some extent be able to choose between party and legislative career objectives. To the extent that these are interrelated, partisan office is probably more likely to be a precondition for advancement in legislative office, rather than *vice versa*. Yet the hierarchy between these objectives may be much less strict than in the Westminster model.

Let us now consider the hypothetical cases of maximum and minimum institutional constraint on legislative strategies. The former case, maximum constraint, would seem to follow from three jointly sufficient conditions: (1) strict hierarchy of goals, (2) perfectly competitive elections and (3) legislators that are fully informed about their competitive circumstances. If these conditions would hold, if politics were perfectly competitive and parliamentarians had full information about the opponents and all their various constituencies (the party leadership, parliamentary caucuses, nominating committees, voters), then we would expect their preferences to be lexicographic. The goal of renomination would be paramount, and once members had chosen the action that maximised their probabilities of nomination, they would then maximise general election prospects, then party office, and only lastly legislative office goals. Minimum constraint would occur where none of the above conditions is present, that is, where (1) nomination is inconsequential for electoral success, (2) elections are non-competitive or impossible to predict and (3) partisan and legislative office are fully decoupled.

Reality is hardly ever that clear-cut. Yet, if members have some uncertainty about their prospects of reaching any one of their objectives and these are not fully hierarchically ordered, they may think of their strategic choices as trade-offs under risk.[21] This is the situation of partial constraint that I believe characterises most real-world parliamentary life. Under these circumstances, members have some freedom to choose preference roles, yet their strategies are shaped by the demands of the goals that they pursue.

## RESOURCES AND INSTITUTIONS

The strategies of parliamentarians are prescriptions, or game plans, that help them align their employment of resources with their objectives. Strategies thus cannot be directly observable, but we should be able to infer them from actual behaviour. What sorts of behaviour, then, can we use to identify different parliamentary strategies? I have suggested above that parliamentarians' strategies have to prescribe the commitment of scarce resources such as their time, media access and other organisational assets. But where can these resources be put to use and for what purposes? To answer these questions, we need to think systematically about the scarce resources that parliamentarians have at their disposal. We also need to take institutions seriously.

Empirical role analysis has indeed often focused on legislators' use of their scarce and consequential political resources, such as their voting power, time, attention, media access or money under their control. The ultimate such resource, of course, is their voting power, which they can use to promote causes that favour their constituency, their party, some social group to which they have ties, or perhaps their personal vision of the common good. Parliamentarians can also influence the parliamentary decision-making process in other ways, by sponsoring, amending or filibustering bills, by participating in legislative investigations or audits, by asking questions of ministers, and so on. All such activities take time, and some may also require the legislator to make the effort to develop policy expertise. There are plenty of competing demands on a legislator's time and attention. One set of such demands emanates from his electoral constituency, in which there will often be virtually insatiable demands for attention to individual case work and district projects. Local or national interest groups will present yet another set of demands. Last, but certainly not least, the parliamentary and extra-parliamentary party leadership will expect the member's loyalty and diligent service in a variety of arenas, including perhaps campaign efforts for other candidates, service on committees or in offices that have little or negative electoral payoff, and the like. The choices that parliamentarians make between these competing demands on their resources constitute their political strategies.

These strategies will be institutionally conditioned. Institutions have indeed made a comeback in our understanding of political phenomena through various neo-institutional approaches. According to the new institutionalists, institutions affect roles in several ways. All of them would agree that institutions affect the range of behaviours available to social actors (players) such as members of parliament. Institutions do so by *enabling* and *constraining* behaviour, that is to say, by making some such forms of behaviour feasible and others not feasible.[22] The neo-institutional rational choice literature would in turn tell us to look for institutionally induced incentives that different legislators face under different circumstances. Parliamentary roles, I would suggest, can best be understood as consistent strategies induced by the members' pursuit of the different objectives we have discussed, constrained by the institutional environment in which they operate. When a parliamentarian chooses to focus his energies on constituent case work, for example, we first seek an explanation of that behaviour in his goals and in the constraints that political institutions place on his behaviour and opportunities.

The political institutions that most powerfully enable and constrain parliamentarians are those that regulate their attainment of ballot access, re-election, party office and legislative office. The first two of these objectives will be conditioned in large part by the electoral system (but also by party organisation). The third and fourth objectives are most directly affected by *party* and *legislative organisation* and *procedure*.

Electoral systems have several critical implications for the political lives of parliamentarians. They control access to the election ballot and place that power in the hands of local activists, central party leaders or the voters themselves. Electoral systems also determine the effects of ballot placement on electoral prospects, and they have implications for the incentives for competition or co-ordination between parliamentary candidates.

Legislative organisation is, according to Krehbiel, 'the allocation of resources and assignment of parliamentary rights to individual legislators or groups of legislators'.[23] In the great majority of modern legislatures, members are elected equal. All members, regardless of, say, the pluralities by which they gained election, have the same parliamentary rights and privileges. With rare exceptions, voting rules in legislatures are egalitarian and 'undifferentiated', and each legislator's vote counts as much as that of any other. One person, one vote. Yet, in reality there are all kinds of differences between members. Such differences take two general forms: *hierarchy* (vertical differentiation) and *specialisation* (functional or horizontal differentiation). These forms of differentiation define *legislative organisation*. Parliamentary organisation (the distribution of rights and powers assigned to parliamentarians individually and collectively) and procedures (decision-making rules within parliament) define a large part of the repertoire of member strategies. For example, parliamentary standing committees may or may not be an important arena for strategies aimed at re-election or partisan advancement in parliament. Whether or not they do, will depend on the specific composition, powers and procedures of the committees. For example, if committees engage in highly visible and well-publicised hearings or investigations, they may be important arenas in which re-election and perhaps renomination goals can be pursued. If committees meet behind closed doors, but have substantial powers to initiate or amend bills before parliament, then they may be important arenas for the pursuit of party or legislative office. If neither of the above is true (as with standing committees in the British House of Commons), then committees are unlikely to be of much significance for legislative strategies.

The critical challenge is therefore to identify the institutions that most significantly impinge on the ability of legislators to achieve their various objectives. It is to that task that I now turn, assuming (1) that legislators focus their resources and activities on objectives for which their own efforts are most likely to be pivotal, and (2) that members need to be fairly secure about their ability to realise lower-order goals before they will give serious attention to higher order ones.

## CANDIDATE SELECTION

Candidate selection (or nomination) is the first official step on the way to parliament, and the first hurdle that incumbent members have to face. There is typically a large number of regulations on the selection of legislative candidates by the relevant political parties. Some such regulations are embedded in national legislation, although relatively few countries (including, however, the United States and Germany) go very far in regulating the candidate selection process through ordinary legislation. More commonly, regulations are imposed by the parties themselves, which means that they may differ between different parties in the same political system, or even between different electoral districts in the same party. Our understanding of the candidate selection process is still incomplete, and the subject has not given rise to many ambitious theoretical studies.[24]

The candidate selection process may be more or less centralised. In some parties, such as the Liberal Democratic Party in Japan or the conservative parties in France, the national executive committee seems to be a decisive player,[25] but more commonly the process is decentralised to the individual constituencies. Some parties, especially those with a civil-libertarian bent, practise intra-party democracy in the form of party primary elections, but in far more parties local party officers and/or officials are effectively in charge. Under multi-tier electoral systems, different procedures may be in place at different tiers. Finally, some corporative parties allow selected interest groups (for example, labour unions, farmers' groups) an institutionalised role in the candidate selection process.

The importance of the selection process varies according to the electoral system under which general elections are held. In single-member district systems, of course, candidate selection is critical to electoral success. The same is by and large true in closed-list proportional representation (PR) systems, in which nomination at the top of a major party list can virtually guarantee election and thus remove practically all risk from the general election. Under open-list proportional representation, and under the single transferable or non-transferable vote, on the other hand, candidate selection is far less likely to guarantee success. Under these systems, parties nominate multiple candidates in each district, and the success of each candidate depends on the preferences of the ordinary voters. Thus, party nomination is typically necessary for electoral success, but often by no means sufficient. In political systems that allow independents or write-in candidates easy access to the ballot, however, party selection may not even be necessary. Yet, nomination by a major party is probably everywhere helpful.

Nonetheless, reselection efforts may not be a very salient concern for the legislator to begin with. First of all, we expect the motivation to be particularly salient in cases where the party's endorsement is scarce or contested. In some systems and parties, the deck is heavily stacked in favour of incumbents interested in re-election. This used to be the case for British parties, though mandatory reselection has made life a little less secure for incumbents in the Labour Party. In such parties, strategies focused on reselection are unlikely to dominate legislator behaviour. And, indeed, none of the many parliamentary roles described by Searing seem to describe a parliamentarian whose main goal is reselection. In systems where ballot access is easy, we would expect a similar lack of concern. Closed-list PR systems with competitive selection processes would tend to place themselves at the other end of the continuum. Here, selection is critical and the specific placement a candidate gets on the list is likely to be decisive.

How is the pursuit of reselection likely to influence legislative strategies or roles? The motivation can find expression in a variety of behaviours, depending on the locus and rules of the candidate selection process. If the national executive committee is decisive, then we would expect behaviour designed to please the central party leadership (such as legislative obedience and diligence). If the more common pattern of local control obtains, then reselection-minded legislators should aim to please their local constituents and specifically the often narrow set of party selectors more than the ordinary constituency voter. Local activists would tend to be the decisive constituency, and issue-oriented local efforts (rather than, for example, random case work for constituents) the most plausible key.

## ELECTION

As noted in an earlier section, the electoral motivation forms the basis of the most famous and powerful explanations of the behaviour of politicians. The fact that democratic societies fill most important political offices directly or indirectly through elections obviously supports such understandings of the political process. Getting elected is crucial, indeed strictly necessary, for members of almost all significant legislative chambers. Yet, there may be scenarios under which parliamentarians' behaviour is not at all or not significantly constrained by the electoral connection. That is where (1) legislators cannot realistically aspire to be re-elected or (2) candidate selection is virtually tantamount to election. In the former case, re-election is impossible. In the latter, it is more or less assured once the member has been reselected. In neither case would we expect the re-election motive to dominate legislative behaviour.

Both situations could occur for a number of reasons having to do with the electoral system. If legislators cannot hope to be re-elected, it is most commonly because the constitution or other binding regulations prohibit their re-election. Although formal term limits are uncommon in parliamentary democracies, they do exist in many presidential regimes, especially in Latin America. Costa Rica, Mexico, Ecuador and the Philippines are examples.[26] In American state legislatures, rather strict term limits have become much more common over the past decade. In a number of Latin American countries, they are even more strict. The Costa Rican and Mexican constitutions, for example, permit no re-election for any member of the national legislature. Where such restrictions apply, it is obviously senseless for members to worry about re-election (at least in the short term), and we expect their behaviour to be driven by all sorts of other considerations. Where re-election is restricted in parliamentary democracies, it is typically due to informal party rules rather than constitutional prohibitions.

The opposite situation is where politicians, once selected, have little or no reason to worry about the general election. This is most likely to be the case for high-ranking candidates of major parties in closed-list PR systems. In Norway, for example, the first-ranking candidates (or even number two or three) of either the Labour Party or the Conservatives in large districts like Oslo do not have to give a lot of attention to their personal re-election prospects. Naturally, these are list positions that party leaders such as prime ministerial candidates often occupy. For those who wish to escape electoral competition, the next best thing is to be the candidate of the favoured party in uncompetitive single-member districts. Once selected, Democratic candidates for inner-city congressional districts in the United States typically have little to worry about in the general election. The same could be said for British Labour candidates in major industrial cities, as well as for Conservative candidates in the south-eastern English countryside. As a consequence, such candidates should be free to devise legislative strategies not significantly constrained by the electoral connection.

Most parliamentarians, however, are not so lucky. Competitive single-member districts and systems that permit intra-party preference voting are likely to exhibit particularly high levels of electoral constraint. In such systems, the fate of each legislator depends not only on the general support of his (or her) party (which he may be able to affect only marginally), but also on his own personal standing with the voters. The effects of the popularity of co-partisans vary widely between such systems. Under the single, non-transferable vote, long used in Japanese elections, members are in no way helped by votes for other candidates from their own party. In fact, if one's own vote is held constant, increased support for a fellow partisan is as likely to hurt as to help. Under the same conditions in a single transferable vote system (such as Ireland), on the other hand, increased support for co-partisans is more likely to help than hurt, as long as candidate preferences are positively constrained by party.

But electoral formula is not the only factor that determines the constraining power of elections on legislative strategies. Members' concern for re-election is also likely to show cyclical fluctuations, which may be dramatic. Legislators elected for long and fixed terms (such as US senators) can have the luxury of a respite from the pressures of campaigning in the first part of their terms. Members of legislatures where the power of parliamentary dissolution is restricted can at least feel a little more insulated than where a prime minister or president (perhaps from an unfriendly party) may freely choose to dissolve parliament at any time.

In their perennial (or nearly so) struggle for re-election, members develop a number of strategies designed to improve the popular standings of their parties and, in particular, themselves. The literature on political campaigns is replete with descriptions of the former and more general phenomenon. The latter topic has been examined mainly in the growing literature on the *personal vote*. In their analysis of personal voting in Britain and the United States, Cain, Ferejohn and Fiorina distinguish between personal contacts, casework, project assistance, mail solicitations and 'surgeries'.[27] The more electorally constrained the member, and the more his or her fortunes depend on a personal vote, the more diligently we should expect that person's resource commitments to conform to these patterns. Searing identifies two types of 'constituency members' among the backbenchers in House of Commons: 'welfare officers' and 'local promoters'. It is roles such as these that we should expect to see among members with particularly competitive electoral constituencies.

PARTY OFFICE

Most members of parliaments have to give serious attention to their prospects for reselection and re-election. For many, or at least for good parts of the tenure of many, the pursuit of these objectives stretches their time and resources toward their limits. Although most might in principle wish to rise above the ranks of backbenchers, few in practice have the opportunities to do so without jeopardising their political survival. But although few are actually chosen, many may condition their parliamentary behaviour on the aspiration to rise above the rank of backbencher, either through party or parliamentary office.

The degree to which such aspirations affect legislative strategies and thus roles depends upon opportunities as well as on constraints. And the institutions that in turn shape the opportunity structures are themselves in part parliamentary ones and in part those that pertain to other political offices, particularly those likely to be valued above a backbench position in parliament. Whereas candidate selection and election processes are not necessarily any different in parliamentary systems than in presidential ones, the incentive structure defined by the structure of party and legislative office opportunities clearly diverge from those of non-parliamentary regimes.

A defining characteristic of parliamentarism is that the cabinet 'emerges from' parliament itself. In the classical Westminster tradition, this implies not only cabinet accountability to parliament, but also that members of the cabinet are drawn from the membership of the legislature (and continue to serve there). In this sense, the cabinet is a true sub-set of the legislative branch of government and the relationship between the two branches one of *internal delegation*. This constitutional arrangement has obvious incentive effects for parliamentarians with progressive ambition. In presidential regimes, such ambition is by definition incompatible with continued legislative service. In order to serve in higher political office, members have to look beyond the confines of the legislature and ultimately to give up their seats here. In parliamentary systems, on the other hand, higher (particularly cabinet) office is achieved through a career in parliament, and there is no sense in which politicians have to choose between two discrete career paths.

Party office, such as one's party parliamentary leader, deputy leader, whip or a member of its parliamentary executive (steering) committee, is one of the two types of ambition that members of parliament might harbour beyond re-election. As mentioned above, we can at least analytically distinguish this kind of ambition from legislative office ambition, although in practice the separation of the two ambitions and the attendant behavioural strategies may be more or less sharp. Party office objectives are most likely to be associated with progressive ambition in Schlesinger's classical sense. Parliamentarians who aspire to party leadership positions in parliament are also likely to harbour explicit or implicit ambitions of becoming cabinet-level leaders within their respective parties. This is particularly likely in systems where cabinet members are either required or permitted to hold simultaneous membership in parliament, and where a large share of cabinet members are in fact recruited directly from parliament. The United Kingdom, Ireland, Belgium and Italy are examples.[28]

Party office in parliament is normally filled by election among the party's members in parliament. Often, however, these selections are subject to formal or informal approval by the party leadership, particularly perhaps in governing parties. For cabinet office, of course, the approval of the party leadership is even more crucial and in fact usually decisive. Parliamentarians who aspire to party office therefore have two constituencies they have to please: their peers and the party leadership. Ways to please the party leadership would seem to include loyalty, diligence, versatility and a willingness to take on arduous and unrewarding tasks for the good of the party. The same behaviours may in general also be good ways to build favours among one's fellow partisans, although unswerving loyalty to the party hierarchy may find more favour among the party's leaders than among the backbenchers.

A successful aspirant to party office must therefore be willing to devote time and energy to party objectives, even if that means neglecting one's local constituency or supporting causes that have little local support. The strategy may or may not involve the acquisition of policy expertise, which can at least be useful for credit-claiming purposes.[29] A politician who has such ambitions and who can afford to take such risks *vis-à-vis* his or her constituency, is likely to fall into the category of backbenchers that Searing calls *ministerial aspirants*, or perhaps *policy advocates*. Clearly, this is a potentially treacherous pursuit for MPs who face stiff competition for reselection or re-election.

## LEGISLATIVE OFFICE

Legislative office is the final source of the benefits that drive parliamentary behaviour. Legislative office refers to all those positions in parliament that are involved in the execution of important legislative responsibilities and which are predominantly non-partisan or cross-partisan in nature. Of course, most parliamentary offices are directly or indirectly filled through partisan selection processes. Yet, the 'inter-party mode' is not the only aspect of parliamentary politics. Building on King, Andeweg and Nijzink identify both the 'non-party mode' and the 'cross-party mode' as important facets of legislative politics in European parliamentary democracies.[30] These facets of parliamentary politics are reflected in such symbolic issues as seating arrangements, where in Norway and Sweden members are seated by district, regardless of partisan affiliations. More importantly, specialised parliamentary committees sometimes constitute fora in which members may advance relatively independently of their fortunes within their own party hierarchies. Indeed, for some politicians, a parliamentary committee career may be an alternative to cabinet aspirations. Andeweg and Nijzink also point out the plethora of intra-parliamentary caucuses, such as for regional, gender or language groups, that exist within many parliaments.

Even more importantly, internal affairs committees and boards of presiding officers sometimes offer opportunities for legislative office that may compete with more partisan career paths. According to Jenny and Müller's informative survey of presiding officers in European parliaments, such offices vary considerably both in partisanship and in power. Powerful and partisan presiding officers, such as the Speaker of the United States House of Representatives, are by no means the only or even the most common type of presiding officer in Europe. In fact, only Greece has a president who is both very powerful and highly partisan. In many other parliamentary democracies, MPs may become speaker (presiding officer) without having achieved any high position in their respective parties. This pattern is most typical of Westminster-style parliaments, but similar cases can be found in Belgium, Iceland and Switzerland as well.[31]

The institutions that most decisively affect members' pursuit of such legislative office are those that regulate the selection, powers and accountabilities of presiding officers and other relevant internal officers of parliament. Since these rules are manifold and complex,[32] it is difficult to generalise about their specific effects. In the most general terms, we would expect to see parliamentarians increase their efforts toward legislative office as (1) their reselection opportunities improve, (2) their re-election opportunities improve, (3) the availability and attractiveness of legislative, versus partisan, office increase and (4) their opportunities for partisan office decrease. In other words, strategies aimed at legislative office should be particularly common among MPs with relatively secure seats and limited frontbench prospects and in parliaments where legislative offices are plentiful and desirable.

The strategies of those who seek legislative office are most akin to the roles Searing lumps into his category of 'parliament men'. Of all his backbench roles, this is the most diverse category, with the largest set of subtypes. The general role of parliament man is also a fair description of frontbencher Charles Seymour's ultimate career choice in Jeffrey Archer's novel *First Among Equals*.[33] As Searing puts it, the parliament man is 'a role that is neither widely recognised nor well defined'.[34] This is primarily because there are so few parliament men. To Searing, this scarcity 'seems strange, for this role was common and indeed dominant during earlier eras'.[35]

But should this paucity be such a surprise? Applying the argument I have developed above, the incidence of parliament men should decline as reselection and re-election get more competitive, and as the supply of legislative office declines relative to that of partisan office. Putting the issue in such comparative statics terms, we may in fact recognise a plausible description of the evolution of the British House of Commons over the past century. What has happened is precisely that the conditions that favour parliament men (or strategies aimed at the pursuit of legislative office) have become less and less prevalent. Indeed, today's British House of Commons, with its high levels of partisanship and the relative insignificance of its non-party and cross-party modes, is one that we would expect not to be very conducive to legislative office pursuits.

## CONCLUSION

In order to understand representative democracy, we need to develop analytical tools by which we can make sense of the behaviour of the elected representatives of the people. The concept of roles is one such tool that has been prominently employed in studies of legislative institutions. Role analysis promised to give us simple and applicable tools with which we could describe and explain legislative behaviour. Yet, in contemporary political science role analysis has fallen somewhat out of favour. This is, I believe, at least in part because role analysis has not always been quite clear about what it can do and, perhaps even more importantly, about its own limitations. The concept itself has seemed to subsume individual beliefs, common expectations, actual behaviours and even institutional functions without clear demarcations or causal stipulations between these different components.

Recent parliamentary role analysis, most notably represented by Searing, has attempted to clarify these issues and to privilege conceptions of motivation rather than system functions. I applaud such efforts, and in this article I have tried to go one step further by suggesting how parliamentary role analysis can in fact be cast as a study of the *strategies* of legislators. I have suggested that we think of roles as strategies for the commitment of scarce resources. These strategies are likely to be conditioned by the relative scarcity of various institutionally generated 'goods' that parliamentarians seek. Such goods include reselection, re-election, party office and legislative office. Ultimately, then, the incidence of different parliamentary roles should bear a powerful and predictable relationship to the supply of such political benefits.

The argument I have developed suggests that much of the diversity of parliamentary lives is subject to relatively simple explanations. We can gain important insights by portraying legislators as if they were purely instrumental in their pursuits of different benefits that legislative institutions afford them. Yet the diversity of institutions means that the simplest of models of legislative behaviour may be inadequate for cross-national purposes. For example, there are many institutional circumstances in which we would definitely not expect members of parliament to be single-minded in their pursuit of re-election.

I have emphasised the personal instrumentality of legislative roles. To some, this may seem both cynical and restrictive. However, I do not want to argue that altruism and other non-self-interested motivations play no role in determining the behaviour of parliamentarians. Clearly, my aim has been to simplify reality, and the motivations of legislators are much more complex than any simple scheme can capture. The point that I wish to emphasise, however, is that many legislators cannot afford to indulge their less self-interested motivations. Doing so might lead to a shorter political career than they might otherwise enjoy. And the powerful ways in which political institutions thus constrain the strategies of elected representatives may be one of the more general and comprehensible features of democratic politics.

## NOTES

1. Donald Searing, *Westminster's World* (Cambridge, MA: Harvard University Press, 1994), p.1.
2. Searing, *Westminster's World*.
3. James March and Johan P. Olsen, *Rediscovering Institutions* (New York: Free Press, 1989). See Searing, p.28.
4. Roughly speaking, the new institutionalism can be divided into at least three clearly identifiable camps, each of which sometimes noisily lays claim to the label: (1) a sociological approach, identified with organisation theorists such as March and Olsen, (2) a structural approach, identified with statist literature on public policy and regime change (for example, Peter Evans, Dietrich Rueschemayer and Theda Skocpol (eds.), *Bringing the State Back In* (Cambridge: Cambridge University Press, 1985)), and a rational choice literature which in political science largely originated in the study of American national institutions and in some fundamental puzzles in the social choice literature (for example, Kenneth A. Shepsle, 'Studying Institutions: Some Lessons from the Rational Choice Approach', *Journal of Theoretical Politics,* Vol.1, No.2 (April 1989), pp.131–47). Kathleen Thelen and Sven Steinmo, 'Historical Institutionalism in Comparative Politics', in Sven Steinmo, Kathleen Thelen and Frank Longstreth (eds.), *Structuring Politics: Historical Institutionalism in Comparative Analysis* (Cambridge: Cambridge University Press, 1992)) subsume the first two of these traditions under the label 'historical institutionalism'.
5. Searing, *Westminster's World*, p.28.
6. In this analysis, I shall use the terms 'parliament' and 'legislature' (and 'parliamentary' and 'legislative') interchangeably. It is true that the two terms have different origins, and that there has been a tendency to apply the latter term mainly to national assemblies in presidential systems. In this context, however, I shall make no systematic references to presidential regimes, and my objective is simply to avoid monotony of usage.
7. Though the terms parliamentary democracy and parliamentary government are often used interchangeably, it may be useful to distinguish between them. By *parliamentary democracy*, I mean a system in which the popular majority, through its elected representatives in the legislative branch, effectively controls public policy. I shall use *parliamentary government* more narrowly to refer to the institutional arrangement by which the executive is accountable, through a confidence relationship, to the parliamentary majority. This conception is more parsimonious than the conventional definition of parliamentary government, in which this form

of government is defined in terms of the parliament's power to *select and dismiss* the executive branch of government. See Arend Lijphart (ed.), *Parliamentary versus Presidential Government* (Oxford: Oxford University Press, 1992); Matthew S. Shugart and John M. Carey, *Presidents and Assemblies* (Cambridge: Cambridge University Press, 1992). In fact, many regimes conventionally classified as parliamentary have no formal mechanism by which parliament selects the executive, which suggests that the critical constitutional property is rather the cabinet's *ex post* accountability to parliament.

8. Searing, *Westminster's World*, p.18; emphases in the original.
9. See, for example, James D. Morrow, *Game Theory for Political Scientists* (Princeton: Princeton University Press, 1994).
10. David Mayhew, *Congress: The Electoral Connection* (New Haven, CT: Yale University Press, 1974).
11. Mayhew, *Congress*, p.5.
12. Mayhew, *Congress*, pp.16–17.
13. Joseph A. Schlesinger, *Political Parties and the Winning of Office* (Ann Arbor, MI: University of Michigan Press, 1991).
14. Schlesinger, *Political Parties*, pp.39–40.
15. Richard Fenno, *Congressmen in Committees* (Boston: Little, Brown, 1973).
16. Fenno, *Congressmen*, p. 1.
17. Gary C. Cox and Mathew D. McCubbins, *Legislative Leviathan: Party Government in the House* (Berkeley: University of California Press, 1993).
18. Cox and McCubbins, *Legislative Leviathan*, p.109.
19. Stephen M. Swindle, 'The Structural and Electoral Determinants of Party Versus Candidate Voting', Ph.D. dissertation in progress, University of California, San Diego, 1996.
20. See also Kaare Strøm, 'A Behavioral Theory of Competitive Political Parties', *American Journal of Political Science* 34 (May 1990), pp.565–98; and George Tsebelis, *Nested Games: Rational Choice in Comparative Politics* (Berkeley: University of California Press, 1990).
21. This would imply that each possible action could lead to any one of a number of different consequences, and that the members could have some well-founded estimate of the probabilities associated with each of these possible outcomes.
22. In addition, Thelen and Steinmo tell us, historical institutionalists believe that institutions shape preferences themselves, as well as behaviour. Rational choice neo-institutionalists would not have to deny this, since preferences in their models are exogenous and the models therefore agnostic. Yet theorists in this tradition typically analyse institutions and preferences as if they were mutually independent. Where structural neo-institutionalists part company with the school I have called sociological is in the extent to which institutions themselves are seen as endogenous. To the sociological organisation theorists, institutions themselves are fundamentally autonomous and subject to myriads forms of unintended consequences. To explain institutions is therefore at best a thankless job, at worst an undesirable scientific project. To structuralist institutionalists, on the other hand, institutions such as parliaments are themselves enabled and constrained by more fundamental social forces that may be called structures. Social class relations and the way a society is inserted into the global (or at least transnational) economy are examples of such deeper social structures that bound, even if they do not fully determine, the characteristics of political institutions.
23. Keith Krehbiel, *Information and Legislative Organization* (Ann Arbor, MI: University of Michigan Press, 1991), p.2.
24. For helpful surveys, see Michael Gallagher and Michael Marsh (eds.), *Candidate Selection in Comparative Perspective* (London: Sage, 1988); Richard S. Katz and Peter Mair (eds.), *Party Organization* (London: Sage, 1992); and Austin Ranney, 'Candidate Selection', in David Butler, Howard R. Penniman, and Austin Ranney (eds.), *Democracy at the Polls* (Washington, DC: American Enterprise Institute, 1981).
25. Gallagher and Marsh, *Candidate Selection*, pp.242–4.
26. See John M. Carey, *Term Limits and Legislative Representation* (Cambridge: Cambridge University Press, 1996).
27. Bruce Cain, John Ferejohn and Morris Fiorina, *The Personal Vote: Constituency Service and Electoral Independence* (Cambridge, MA: Harvard University Press, 1987).

28. See Rudy B. Andeweg and Lia Nijzink, 'Beyond the Two-Body Image: Relations between Ministers and MPs', in Herbert Döring (ed.), *Parliaments and Majority Rule in Western Europe* (New York: St. Martin's Press, 1995).
29. See Mayhew, *Congress*, pp.52–61.
30. See Anthony King, 'Modes of Executive–Legislative Relations: Great Britain, France and West Germany', *Legislative Studies Quarterly* 1 (Feb. 1976), pp.11–36; and Andeweg and Nijzink, 'Beyond the Two-Body Image'.
31. Marcelo Jenny and Wolfgang C. Müller, 'Presidents of Parliament: Neutral Chairmen or Assets of the Majority', in Döring (ed.), *Parliaments and Majority Rule in Western Europe*.
32. See, for example, Jenny and Müller, 'Presidents of Parliament'.
33. Jeffrey Archer, *First Among Equals* (London: Hodder & Stoughton, 1984).
34. Searing, *Westminster's World*, p.161.
35. Searing, *Westminster's World*, p.162.

# Index